'A Life of Extremes
THE BRITISH DISCOVER MODERN FINLAND 1917–1941

Tony Lurcock grew up in Kent, and studied English at University College, Oxford. He became lecturer in English at Helsinki University, and subsequently at Åbo Akademi. Returning to Oxford, he completed a D.Phil. thesis, and taught there, and in America, until his recent retirement. His two previous compilations of accounts of Finland by British travellers are *Not So Barren or Uncultivated: British Travellers in Finland 1760–1830* (CBe, 2010) and *No Particular Hurry: British Travellers in Finland 1830–1917* (CBe, 2013). He has published numerous review articles, mainly on eighteenth-century literature and on biography.

Poster for the 1940 Olympic Games featuring a statue by Waino
Aaltonen of the middle- and long-distance runner Paavo Nurmi, who
won nine Olympic gold medals and three silver medals between 1920
and 1928. The 1940 Games were suspended indefinitely following
the outbreak of World War Two.

'A Life of Extremes'

THE BRITISH DISCOVER MODERN FINLAND
1917–1941

Tony Lurcock

'Everything progresses well. It's a life of extremes.'
Lady Diana Cooper,
Helsinki, 1938

First published in 2015
by CB editions
146 Percy Road London W12 9QL
www.cbeditions.com

Front cover:
Paimio Sanatorium, designed by Alvar Aalto and completed in 1932.
Photograph: Sami Heikinheimo © Archtours

Printed in England by Imprint Digital, Exeter EX5 5HY

ISBN 978-1-909585-15-7

Contents

Acknowledgements

Once again I am indebted to many people who have given help, made suggestions, and curbed occasional excesses. The two stalwarts, Silvester Mazzarella and Pontus Lurcock, have stayed the course, and will perhaps be relieved to have seen it to the end. Jonathan Clark has again taken great trouble to produce the maps, as well as enduring regular updates at the Rose and Crown.

For other help I thank Magnus Cederlöf, Terry Curran, Tim Davison, Harry Ferguson, Alex Martin, Andrew Newby Simon Offard (Imperial War Museum), David Ripley, and David Wilson.

During the time that I have been working on this volume two good friends of the project have died. Bill Mead read an early draft many years ago, and encouraged me to keep writing. I regret not having gone back to him soon enough for information about several of the writers appearing here who were his personal acquaintances. I have sorely missed the company of Tim Griggs, in person, by phone, and by email; the book too has missed his bold editing. Writing is not as much fun without him.

The publisher and author are grateful to Karl Grotenfelt, whose generosity has made the publication of this book possible.

It has been a tedious business attempting to locate the copyright holders of many of the books cited; some of the publishers, departed, have left no addresses. Several, I discovered, lost their archives in the Blitz, and others have long since been absorbed in a bewildering chain of international takeovers. Every effort has been made to trace or contact copyright holders. The publisher will rectify at the earliest opportunity any omissions or errors brought to his notice.

Extracts from Noël Coward, *Future Indefinite*, © NC Aventales AG 1954, reprinted by permission of Alan Brodie Representation Ltd (www.alanbrodie.com); extracts from Harold Macmillan, *The Blast of War*, © Harold Macmillan 1967, reprinted by permission of Pan Macmillan; extracts from *Direction North* by John Sykes, published by Hutchinson, reproduced by permission of The Random House Group Ltd.

Place Names in Swedish and Finnish

In the previous volume, *No Particular Hurry*, British writers still used the Swedish place names but Finnish had started to creep in. The change is now quite decisive, as one would expect, but far from complete. In this volume travellers explore every part of the country, visiting many places which have never had a Swedish name. In the Åland Islands and the archipelagos there are very few Finnish versions of the Swedish names. Once again, many writers name places which I have not located. In a book of this size it has not proved possible to provide a map which shows every small village and settlement, but most places can be found on the website http://kansalaisen.karttapaikka.fi/kartanhaku/osoitehaku.html?lang=en. The site recognises only Finnish names.

Borgå	Porvoo
Ekenäs	Tammisaari
Enare	Inari
Enontekis	Enontekiö
Fölisön	Seurasaari
Gamla Karleby	Kokkola
Hangö	Hanko
Helsingfors	Helsinki
Nykarleby	Uusikaarlepyy
Nyslott	Savonlinna
Nystad	Uusikaupunki
Raumo	Rauma
Sordavala	Sortavala
Sveaborg	Suomenlinna
Tammerfors	Tampere

Tavastehus	Hämeenlinna
Tourneå	Tornio
Uleåborg	Oulu
Vasa	Vaasa
Vyborg	Viipuri
Åbo	Turku

Beyond Finland

Nargö	Naissaar
Reval	Tallinn

In 1914 Saint Petersburg became Petrograd, in 1924 Leningrad, and in 1991 Saint Petersburg again.

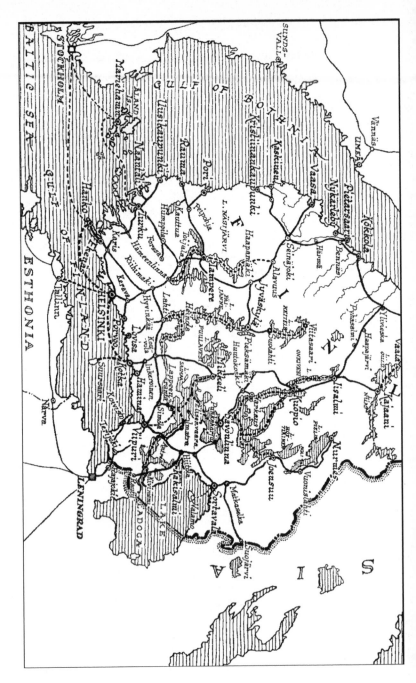

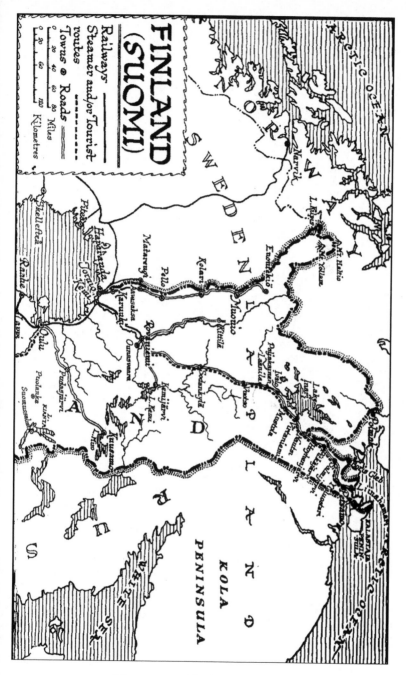

Map *c*.1930 with place names in Finnish

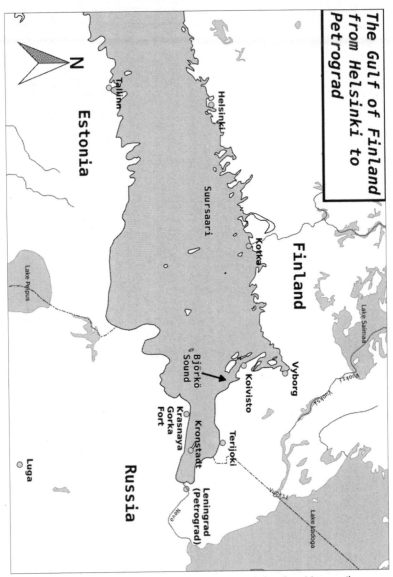

The Gulf of Finland from Helsinki to Petrograd

N

Estonia

Tallinn

Helsinki

Suursaari

Kotka

Finland

Vyborg

Lake Peipus

Björkö Sound

Koivisto

Krasnaya Gorka Fort

Kronstadt

Terijoki

Lake Saimaa

Vuoksi

Vuoksi

Vuoksi

Russia

Neva

Leningrad (Petrograd)

Lake Ladoga

Luga

© OpenStreetMap contributors

Prologue

On 6 May 1919, the British Consul General in Finland, Henry McGrady Bell, received from the British Prime Minister, Arthur Balfour, the following telegram:

PLEASE CONVEY FOLLOWING STOP HIS BRITANNIC MAJESTY'S GOVERNMENT ACKNOWLEDGE THE INDEPENDENCE OF FINLAND AND ITS GOVERNMENT

'I got out my colourful consular uniform,' wrote Bell, 'and, replete with sword and medals, presented myself at the Ministry of Foreign Affairs.' There he was received by the acting Foreign Minister, Leo Ehrnrooth, who conducted him to the Palace, where he delivered the news to General Carl Gustaf Emil Mannerheim, the Regent of Finland. The same evening Bell attended the meeting of the Diet, where he heard the Premier announce the news: 'Recognition by the mighty British Empire is of the greatest importance, and meets with our deepest satisfaction.'

> Helsingfors was beflagged. A banquet was given at General Mannerheim's residence at which I was the guest of honour, and, as such, privileged to escort his beautiful daughter Sophy to the dinner-table. During the evening the General decorated me with the White Rose of Finland; and so ended a very satisfying episode in my humble diplomatic career.

The end of one episode for Bell, quoted from his memoir *Land of Lakes* (1950), was the beginning of a new era for Finland, and for those who travelled there.

Preface

The Epilogue to No *Particular Hurry: British Travellers in Finland 1830–1917* (2013) concluded with a hint of anticipation:

> De Windt wrote of his hotel in Tampere that 'there was a quaint mixture of modernism and the primitive, peculiar to this country, and not without its charms'. In the next phase of the British discovery of Finland the quaint and the primitive more or less cease to be attractions. The independent Finland after 1917 was 'the new nation', and ushered in a new era for travel writing; foremost among the interests of British visitors would be the advanced social institutions, the architecture, the music, and the Winter War.

The present book is, unashamedly, a sequel, and completes a trilogy tracing the journeys and experiences of British folk in Finland, from the earliest recorded explorers to the volunteers and observers who found themselves there during the Second World War.

The format has seemed satisfactory enough for me not to want to change it. The first book, *Not So Barren or Uncultivated*, described Finland as an outpost of Sweden; the Swedish-speaking inhabitants of the coastal areas were, confusingly, often described as 'Swedes'. The second, *No Particular Hurry*, presented British experiences in the Grand Duchy of Finland, part of the Russian empire. Finally, and very satisfyingly, in this third volume Finland is independent.

Several readers of *No Particular Hurry* have indicated to me that I was going beyond what they understood by 'travellers', citing particularly the naval officers who were with the British

Fleet in the Baltic 1854–5. The definition was stretched also by the inclusion of two travellers, Annie Margaret Clive-Bayley and Rosalind Travers, who each stayed the greater part of a year in Finland. This, I considered, made the accounts of their travels – some to quite distant parts of Finland – especially valuable, since their knowledge and experience of the country left their writings relative free of the facile generalisations and reflections which often form impressionistic accounts of short visits. As for the naval officers, I felt, and still feel, that their Finland experiences were well worth retelling; where else might they have appeared?

In this third volume I have continued to use the term 'traveller' flexibly, but have withdrawn it from the title. The authors who are my source material are, after all, chosen primarily to display their discovery of Finland, and many of their books are not 'travel books' as the term is generally understood. The first two volumes covered more than 150 years, yet the twenty-four years presented here contain more and more varied material than either of the earlier periods. The dates of this third volume are exact: from 6 December 1917, when Finnish independence was declared, to the same date in 1941, when the changing alliances of the war led to Britain declaring war on Finland. These bookend dates give a neat compactness to a book whose pattern is almost classical: a beginning, a middle and an end. It opens with the perilous activities of British spies, agents and mariners crossing the border with Bolshevik Russia, and closes with accounts of the heroism and the destruction of the Winter War and its aftermath. The intervening twenty years contain an amazing variety of experiences and reflections as visitors record their responses to a Finland which was rapidly establishing its place in the world. The variety of authors, and their very different forms of narrative, make this volume a literary kaleidoscope as well.

During this period much of the travel is away from the

coastal areas, and is therefore in Finnish-speaking Finland; one tourist who had hired a Swedish guide had a lot of trouble. The travellers in the earlier volumes rarely had any knowledge of Finnish; here quite a few of them seem to get by. In the tourist areas now summer guides – usually university students – spoke English, among several other languages.

Most towns in Finland were still known by their Swedish names, though; 'Helsingfors' was still the preferred form in England during the Second World War. The map in the sixteenth edition of Cook's *Traveller's Handbook to Norway, Sweden, Denmark and Finland* (1936) gives the place names in both languages, with Swedish first. In the next edition (1939) Finnish comes first. As in my earlier volumes, I have kept the Swedish names when they are used in the quoted texts, and the Finnish names in my own text. In the few places where this could be confusing I have made use of parentheses, and have again provided a list of place names in each language. Several of the writers describe places such as Vyborg and Sortavala, which were lost to Russia in the 1944 armistice, as were Terijoki and the island of Valamo with its monastery.

Introduction

For Lady Diana Cooper 'a life of extremes' comprised 'ghastly moments and enchanting ones'; for other British writers it reflects a much wider variety of experiences. Most obvious is the British discovery – or rediscovery, rather – that Finland is a land for all seasons. Before about 1820 the British travellers seemed indifferent to the weather, and took Finnish winters in their stride. Then, for the next century, Finland became a destination for summer holidays, even the few travellers who ventured as far north as Lapland preferring to brave the mosquitoes than to hazard the cold. Now, although summer holidays remain as attractive as ever – '[t]he geniality of the climate in these northern regions is surprising,' wrote F. J. North – they become overlaid with a variety of other interests and attractions. Only about a third of the summer visitors represented in the following pages could be described as vacationists.

'All seasons' includes exuberant descriptions of spring: in Turku James Bramwell was assured by one of his students that 'in the North the spring does roar. You'll hear for yourself.' He did, and he describes it vividly. The Finnish autumn, too, was a new discovery for the British. 'Those early days of October,' wrote Constance Malleson, 'were the most brilliant I could ever remember living through.' In November, though, John Gibbons found the climate anything but genial:

> I believe it's pleasant enough in the summer, but there under that wintry sky it's a dour country and a frightening one. The earth is so hard, and as it rings under your boots you feel that never again in all creation can a flower or a bud or so much as a blade of grass force its feeble way through that frozen hardness.

I

The 'life of extremes' can be seen in the many contrasting images of Finland. On one hand we can still read fascinated descriptions of a peasant culture with unchanging traditions, even remnants of *runo* singing, as well as hay-making and gold-panning. On the other hand travellers' accounts describe and extol the social advances of the 'new nation', with the word 'modern' applied to almost everything.

The variety of visitors had now become very wide. Two of the ladies were aristocrats, several of the more accomplished tourists stayed in the best hotels, others were professionals (journalist, geologist, tubercular specialist, politician), a few were on secret service missions, and some were simply young and adventurous. The writing is as varied as the writers: some is elegant and literary, some very practical and down-to-earth, some scholarly, some thrilling and some scenic. There are plenty of set pieces: epic lunches with Sibelius; getting a drink during prohibition; evading the armed sentries at the Russian border; a lake steamer picking up passengers; travelling in a troop train in the Winter War.

During the years described in this book the name of Nokia would have suggested to visitors nothing much more than rubber boots and toilet paper, yet, led by the Nokia revolution, Finland became in 2010 the first country in the world to make internet access a legal right. More than a century before this the telephone had, it seems, already become such a right; here already Finland was a pioneer country. Helsinki had a telephone exchange in 1882, and in the 1930s, North records, from Suurisaari, an island far out in the Baltic, 'there is a wireless telephone service, that costs only about threepence for an ordinary conversation'. Sydney A. Clark describes with awe how the 'Session Hall' in the new parliament building has 'the most modern of voting devices' with voting buttons on every desk: 'the vote on any bill or motion is recorded by this intelligent machine within ninety seconds.'

Many of the earliest travellers were well-to-do, and even titled, but it was the exclusivity of wealth rather than of rank that permitted them to travel, usually with servants, to such a distant country. The Victorian and Edwardian period saw middle-class travellers discovering Finland, the journey made easy with the advent of steamer and railway travel, but still requiring a substantial outlay of time and money. By the 1930s, though, Finland was open to anyone who had £10 in his pocket, or indeed in her pocket. Bill Mead would perhaps never have set foot in Finland at all had he not been allured by 'the £10 return journey to Helsinki'.

'A Life of Extremes' is, of course, an anthology as well as an account. The books which provide the material are no longer in print, so the collection is, if nothing else, a useful piece of dredging. The period from 1917 to 1941 was crowded with political and military incident. I have assumed that many British readers of this book will be largely unfamiliar with the Finnish aspects of these incidents, so have included background which will, inevitably, be superfluous for some and perhaps inadequate for others. It is a delicate balance, but, as I wrote in an earlier Preface, it is by no means necessary to read the Introduction.

The background of independence

This third volume opens in 1917, with Finland finally independent of both its Swedish and its Russian neighbours. By the Treaty of Hamina (1809) Finland had been ceded by Sweden to Russia; it was not incorporated, but became an autonomous Grand Duchy, keeping its former constitution and legal system, and retaining the Lutheran faith. Alexander I both confirmed and extended 'the framework of laws and institutions' inherited from Sweden. Well before the accession of Nicholas II in 1894 this benign arrangement had begun to unravel. The development and decay of the relationship with Russia are clearly reflected in the writings of British travellers from the end of the century. Annie Margaret Clive-Bayley noticed immediately on landing in Turku in 1893 that 'the names of the streets were indicated in Russian, Swedish and Finnish, a precaution quite necessary, as there are Russians who scorn to know the languages of the conquered country'. By the 1890s Finland was being systematically reined in, with traditional rights, such as its own postal service, removed.

The appointment of General Bobrikov as Governor-General in 1898 and the 'February Manifesto' delivered by Nicholas II in 1899 were clear indications of 'a new policy towards Finland'. The nationalist movement was known outside Finland partly because of the popularity of Sibelius's music, which, wrote Rosa Newmarch, 'seemed more and more to sum up and express the spirit of an ancient race lately reborn among the natives'. A recent Finnish historian, Eino Lyytinen, has explored this subject:

> The 1905 Revolution in Russia brought the first demands for Finnish independence, but it was only after the March Revolution of 1917 and the announcement of the Russian Provisional Government concerning the 'right of nations to decide their own destinies' that the idea of national independence was voiced with more affirmation.

The break could finally be effected when Russia was too preoccupied for Finland to be any sort of priority. So it was that the Finnish Diet proclaimed Finland an independent sovereign state on 6 December 1917; formal full recognition by the Russian government was conveyed by Trotsky a month later. Britain did not follow suit for another seventeen months.

There were complex reasons for this long delay. The proclamation of 6 December was very far from marking the magical transformation of a repressed province into a united nation enjoying blossoming independence. Finland was in the midst of a power struggle which in late January 1918 broke into a civil war between the Social Democrats (the 'Reds') and the non-socialist Senate (the 'Whites'). The fighting was bitter and violent, and when it ended, after four months, there were 36,000 dead. Mannerheim, a Finnish aristocrat who had served thirty years as an officer in the Imperial Russian Army, led the 'Whites' to victory with the aid of the German Baltic Division.

The new Finnish government began forging strong military links with Germany, seeing this as the likeliest way of securing the new nation against future Russian influence or aggression. On 9 October the Finnish crown was officially offered to Prince Fredrick Charles of Hesse, brother-in-law of the Kaiser. Wishing to distance himself from all this, Mannerheim resigned as Commander-in-Chief, left the country, and 'embarked on a grand tour that established him in the eyes of many foreigners as a Finnish statesman and leader'. In December, with Germany defeated and the monarchy scheme hastily abandoned, the government elected him Regent.

The reality of Finland's independence had been given *de facto* acknowledgement by Britain and America in January 1918; the reluctance to recognize it *de jure* was a result of the obvious concern of both countries about the stability of a state which had marked its independence with a civil war, and which had moved decisively into the German sphere of influence: 'the political and commercial treaties concluded with Germany in March 1918 virtually reduced Finland to the status of a vassal,' writes D. G. Kirby; they 'offered scope for German economic penetration which would have turned Finland into a virtual German colony'. The choice of a German-born king had deepened these worries. It was only when 'all hopes of a reconstituted Russia had faded away' that the barrier could be overcome and *de jure* recognition of Finnish independence granted.

The reluctance of Britain to act against Russia's interests had been evident since the turn of the century. Pro-Finland pressure groups in Europe, and especially in Britain, had had no effect;

H. W. Nevinson, a campaigning journalist, had actually taken the Finnish cause to King Edward VII at Buckingham Palace, asking him 'to write a personal letter to the Tsar' to dissuade him from a military invasion of Finland, but was informed by the King's equerry of the royal response: 'it would be interfering with the affairs of a friendly Power, but he thanks you for your information.'

Bell's description of his 'humble diplomatic career' rather underplays his actual achievements during his year as Consul General; Augustus Agar (in Finland on a secret service assignment) had a high regard for him: 'his handling of British and allied interests in Finland,' he wrote, 'was a masterpiece of common sense and tact, which produced invaluable practical results'. Among Bell's many responsibilities was the large number of British refugees from Russia who had come over the border to Finland early in 1919, and were 'quarantined' by the Finns at border camps. He cleverly sidelined their complaints about poor treatment; he 'was already having trouble enough with the Finnish authorities about the Germans', and he considered that the refugees were very fortunate not to be in Russian prisons. He realistically describes himself as a 'war diplomat'; he was, briefly, succeeded by Sir Coleridge Kennard, a chargé d'affaires whose intimate knowledge of Russia and of its people was of great use when Finnish concerns had moved from Germany back to Russia.

An independent Finland required the appointment of a British minister. There was some agitation in the Finnish press for Bell to be appointed, but he took the realistic decision to resign from his consular post, just over a year after his appointment. The first Ambassador to Finland was Lord Acton, formerly British Consul General in Zurich; appointed on 2 September, he left after only eight months. Bell relates an incident when his Lordship had hired a car in Helsinki, not knowing it to have been stolen; the police spotted it and fired in the air to stop it, not knowing who the occupant was. 'Acton promptly sent a dispatch to London proclaiming that the Finns had tried to assassinate him!' Bell wrote diplomatically that 'there were tears on neither side when [his] departure was announced'.

The British discover modern Finland

There is very little in the earliest British accounts of Finland which anticipates the Finland we know today, whereas the later Victorian and the Edwardian travellers, represented in *No Particular Hurry,* show modern Finland in the making. The present volume records British impressions of the Republic of Finland, a modern state, no longer ruled by either of her neighbours, and anxious in all sorts of ways to emphasise her political, cultural and linguistic independence. What might be regarded as the manifesto for the new republic was a work published in three volumes in 1923–5, and in an abridged 600-page English translation in 1926. The Preface, by Edward Hjelt, Rector of Helsinki University, sets a bright tone from the first page:

> The Finnish poets had prophesied of a time when the spring flood should rise and burst the barriers which constrained the Finnish people, when the fetters should fall from its hands and liberty blossom forth, and the song of patriotism should ring out high and free.

This was the Finland visited and described by the new wave of British travellers. As Anssi Halmesvirta has written:

> The British were delighted to see how the 'Whites' had stopped the spread of the 'Bolshevik menace' westward, but, in the 1920s–30s, they preferred to see a democratic Finland that also provided milk for the workers' children and stood aloof from German influence.

It is surprising to notice how much the interests and impressions of the British had developed in only a few years. In the

7

decades before independence they had written with surprise, and usually with admiration, about female emancipation. Now it was no longer a novelty – after all, it was even reaching Britain; Kay Gilmour remarks on 'the number of women engrossed on work that in most countries is reserved exclusively for men', but adds 'all this is only to be expected in the pioneer land which ceded universal and equal votes to men and women as far back as October 1st 1906'. The remarkable educational system is still admired, but is now seen and understood in a wider context, as part of a developing social democratic society. It is more or less assumed that visitors will take a sauna, and the 'tar-boat experience', described in such terrifying detail in several earlier accounts, is now mentioned, if at all, matter-of-factly – just another way of getting around. 'The boats,' writes Gilmour, 'redundant with the advent of the railway have been preserved for travellers.' North explains that the pressure of tourism had 'resulted in a change of procedure', so that the 'calm waters' areas are bypassed by rail, and the busy tourist can can experience just the thrills, without a lot of tedious scenery.

At the end of *No Particular Hurry* I wrote:

> By about 1912 published accounts of summer tours in Finland were becoming repetitive; the format of the books is easily recognisable: embossed covers, thick paper, and many photographs, often supplied by the Finnish Tourist Association. The growing list of popular destinations had become predictable; there were half-a-dozen accounts of Kangasala, Imatra, and the tar-boats, for example, to choose from for this selection.

By the 1920s this pattern had changed. To some extent there is a reversion to the eighteenth-century pattern of travel books which provided principally an account of a country, rather than details of the author's journey. In some of the volumes cited below the writers do not readily concede that they have actually travelled in Finland themselves, even when they evidently have. They produce not so much travel books as processed accounts of their experiences. Readers who are interested in travel writing find books like these frustrating. Most of these authors, do, though, allow occasional personal experiences to survive, and many of these I have managed to extract. Almost every book included in the present volume contains a great deal of detailed historical and geographical information about Finland, sometimes skilfully incorporated, sometimes not.

The difference which a generation can make is striking. Sylvia MacDougall had written in *A Summer Tour in Finland* (1908): 'socialism is bad enough anywhere, but in this land where every lake and forest is impregnated with old traditions, it is a sin.' She would hardly have recognised, or have wished to recognise, the Finland admiringly described by Frank Fox less that twenty years later: 'it is,' he wrote,

> a country where, on the whole, a good balance has been struck between freedom and licence; where the respective interests of Capital and of Labour in the production of national wealth are being considered in a fair spirit; where there are no very rich and few very poor; where the standards of education are high and education is not interpreted in the narrow sense of solely 'book-learning', where there is an excellent system of co-operation and a careful study is made of the preservation of the national physique.

This, from *Finland Today* (1926), gives what might be regarded as a résumé of the new British interest.

Halliday Sutherland records an anecdote told him by Yrjö Hirn, Professor of Aesthetics at Helsinki University, concerning Edward Westermarck, Professor of Sociology at London University:

During his first years of study in England he was invited to dinner by a family who had not met him personally, and knew nothing about him except that he came from Finland. When in his full height he made his entry among them he saw that his hostess gave some order to the servant; he thought he heard some furniture being moved in the dining-room, and through an indiscretion he afterwards learnt that in pure tactfulness a child's high chair had been provided so that the guest from Finland should not feel uncomfortable by not reaching up to the table.

Westermarck had evidently been assumed to be Sami. '[T]he very common confusion amongst English people between the Finns and the Lapps,' wrote L. Dudley Stamp, 'is responsible for the prevalence of extraordinarily erroneous ideas about the country.' Hirn mentioned that as late as the 1930s the *Encyclopædia Britannica* pictured 'A Finn with his native conveyance of reindeer and sledge'. Ignorance about Finland abounded: visiting England in 1899, Professor Werner Söderhjelm had been asked, 'Has Finland many *colonies*?' In the 1960s, on a trip back to England, I was asked by a friend – a graduate – 'if they had houses in Finland.'

British visitors often wrote as if to correct such misapprehensions. Cecil Gray, especially, was indignant at the assumption that Finland was primitive or backward is especially striking:

One's first impression, indeed, on arriving at Helsingfors – or Helsinki as it is called in the vernacular – is that one has been magically transported not so much to a new country as to a new age . . . So far from being a mere collection of log-cabins and ice-huts, as most people probably suppose, Helsingfors is, on the contrary, one of the most modern and up-to-date cities in Europe, in comparison with which London and Paris seem – and are – in many respects backward and old-fashioned.

There was no shortage of information available for anyone who was genuinely interested in learning about Finland: the bibliography of this present volume is evidence of this.

A new breed of traveller

The books written during this period reveal the new class of traveller. After the high-octane adventures of spies, agents and speedboat crews over the newly created border with Bolshevik Russia we meet men and women on summer holidays, adventurers, sailors, cyclists, writers, journalists, and, as the storm clouds break in 1939, politicians and war correspondents. There is a very different flavour now: little suggestion of the Grand Tour, even on a reduced scale, fewer accounts of cities and beauty spots, and much more a discovery of Finnish people in their ordinary occupations, often in unspectacular parts of the country. The writers rely less on the Finnish Tourist Association for their photographs: 'I have endeavoured to illustrate the commonplace rather than the spectacular,' wrote North. By taking their own pictures they can further distance themselves from the most popular tourist sights, though few can resist including a shot of Helsinki Railway Station.

While Finland continued to appeal to travellers who wanted to get off the beaten track, especially in Lapland, it was quickly dubbed 'the new nation', and started to attract also a new sort of visitor, drawn by ideological interest and cultural curiosity. 'Between the two world wars,' wrote Sir Paul Dukes in his Foreword to Bell's *Land of Lakes*, 'it was recognised almost as a truism that Finland was "a model democracy".' Finland had, as early as 1906, extended parliamentary suffrage to all adult men and women; now it became recognised as a pioneer in social policy as well. 'One could write a useful book,' wrote Fox, 'on any one of the chief social questions as they are answered in Finland: on the position of women in society; on the co-operative movement; on the education, mental and physical, of the race.' British travellers in earlier periods had often recorded their surprise at discovering civilised institutions and enlightened attitudes in such a remote and unknown country; now books were written by travellers who had gone to Finland with the express intention of learning about those very institutions, and seeing them at close quarters. Even a little pocket book for tourists, Kay Gilmour's *Finland* (1931), has a long chapter on 'Finland, the Pioneer Republic', which describes aspects as diverse as Agricultural Co-operation and the Ebenezer Kindergarten. 'For only in a young country,' she writes, 'unhampered by traditional prejudices are such experiments possible.' Another pocket book, Sydney A. Clark's *Finland on £10* (1938), goes much further:

> The world is aware of Finland as a sturdy, self-reliant nation which has shown extraordinary capacity in several lines. It looks to Finland as a proving ground for experiments in living which are of immense importance to the whole future course of our hard-pressed civilisation.

Mrs Tweedie had written in 1897 of her astonishment 'that so remote a country, one so little known and so unappreciated, should thus suddenly burst forth and hold the most advanced ideas for both men and women'. Between the wars there was considerable British curiosity about this distant socialist democracy, bordering the much grander socialist experiment in the Soviet Union. 'Crossing the bridge,' wrote Arthur Ransome as he entered Bolshevik Russia, 'we passed from one philosophy to another.' Some of the visitors of this period were on their way to or from Russia, going to admire the Socialist Utopia. The admirers of Finnish social democracy were, by contrast, more curious than idealistic, and were convinced rather than credulous.

The dust jacket of Clark's little handbook assumes that the interests of even low-budget travellers included social policy:

A great curiosity has been awakened concerning the post-war republic of Finland. How does Finland do it? What is her formula for success? With a population half that of London in an area three times that of England, with a language of mysterious origin and great difficulty, she has quickly set her mark on civilisation. Her co-operative movement has aroused the keen interest of economists. Her athletes have startled the world. Led by Sibelius and Saarinen she has blazed her own great path in music and architecture.

Clark displays so much enthusiasm for Finland that he feels obliged to conclude, 'I hope sincerely that my praise of Finland has not exalted her to a pedestal of tedious perfection.' Finland was getting known, as always, not only by books but also by book reviews: the *Spectator*, reviewing Gibbons's *Keepers of the Baltic Gates*, quotes: 'I was surprised at the youth and development of these countries . . . In all Helsinki they don't seem to have a slum or a shabbily-dressed man or woman.' The reviewer adds: 'It is a mixed pleasure for us who live further south to read this book.'

On 23 September 1830 Captain Charles Colville Frankland had woken up early in Helsinki and, he wrote, 'sallied out to look at the city. It indeed surpasses any expectation I had previously formed; it is the most beautiful and the most interesting new city I ever beheld.' In 1856 Selina Bunbury, returning to the Baltic after the war, had remarked on the contrast between 'antique Reval [Tallinn] and active modern Helsingfors'. Well before 1917 it had become clear that Helsinki was announcing itself as a modern city, distinctly different from all other capitals on the Baltic. Now its buildings came to be seen by visitors as an embodiment of the nation's independence.

The excitement which belongs to new and hard-won independence can be seen especially in responses to the architecture. From the 1890s Finnish architects had made 'an uncompromising break with tradition; 'there were to be no more of Engel's classical columns,' wrote T. W. Atchley. Saarinen's railway station and Sonck's Kallio church were especially admired, as was Sirén's Parliament House, completed in 1931. 'Modern Finnish architecture,' wrote L. Dudley Stamp, 'like Finnish art, has the vigour of a youthful nation.' For Gilmour

> The modern buildings in Helsinki are its most exhilarating feature. One feels that in architecture for the first time the force and vitality of the nation, untrammelled by old tradition, unfettered by considerations of environment, unlimited by space or time, have found full expression.

Fox energetically endorses this; for him Finland is the exciting exception to 'the astonishing sterility of modern art in architecture'. 'Their architects,' he writes, 'have studied old traditions to learn, and not merely to imitate.' Alexander MacCallum Scott's response is even more enthusiastic:

> The streets are like galleries in a museum of architectural exhibits. The citizens talk about these buildings as they talk about pictures, plays and politics. Here the architectural styles of the future are being tried out.

Helsinki promotes itself in brochures today as 'one of the finest Art Nouveau cities in Europe', where tourists are invited to 'take a stroll to view the pearls of Jugend style', often described as the Finnish National Romantic Style. Recording his arrival from Estonia in the early 1920s, Scott was surprised to find in Helsinki 'a universal disparagement of Reval [Tallinn]. It was old-fashioned, I was told, dirty, insanitary . . . it was a dismal place.' The contrast was unmissable: Helsinki, he wrote, was 'intensely modern, spacious, well built, [and] clean'. Independence had, it seemed, quite literally involved a clean break.

'Never have I been struck by the quality of cleanliness so forcibly as in Finland,' wrote S. Jones in *Blackies Girls' Annual* in 1928. 'Houses, streets, hotels, even railway stations, trains, and steamers appear to be cleaner there than it is the nature of such places to be anywhere else.' Adeline Hill Tickell agreed: 'For its surpassing cleanliness,' she wrote(1930), 'Finland is comparable to Holland.' On the evidence of their descriptions of Finland one might believe that for the British cleanliness is a curious phenomenon, to be found only in strange foreign locations. Tickell continues, 'I heard a man say as he was bidding farewell to a friend on the quay, "I shall be really glad to get home to see a little honest English dirt."' To this day British visitors to Finland note its cleanliness, in rather the same way that Finns arriving in England remark how dirty it looks. 'It is no exaggeration,' wrote Sutherland, 'that by comparison with the streets of London you could eat food off the pavements of Helsinki.'

The 'clean break' had, of course, been from Russia. Since the eighteenth century British travellers had been describing the sudden change they perceived when crossing the Russian border. One of the most vivid expressions, perhaps, was by Edward Daniel Clarke in 1800: 'A few miles, nay, even a few yards conduct you from a land of hospitality and virtue, to a den of thieves.' Noël Coward made the same distinction, and breathed an almost audible breath of relief crossing the border from Russia in 1939 into a Finland which was 'most beautiful and gay and clean'.

The National Romantic Style was, and still is, widely admired, but visitors commended also more ordinary housing, in the country as well as in town. Sir Walter Citrine, an eminent trade unionist, made a point of choosing for himself the workers' houses which he inspected, and compared them very favourably to British equivalents. 'Even the dock quarters,' wrote Gibbons, 'might have been the park promenade of some London upper-middle-class suburbia.'

During the 1930s British writers were beginning to notice

Alvar Aalto; 'almost single-handed,' wrote the *Times* obituary in 1976, 'he made his country a place of pilgrimage for all who sought enlightenment as to the aesthetic possibilities of the new architecture.' His Paimio Sanatorium (1932) was the Mecca of these pilgrimages; John Langdon-Davies explained why:

> In other countries hospitals have been built to resemble Gothic cathedrals, Empire saloons, Victorian drawing-rooms, or even just warehouses, in the mistaken belief that a building like a warehouse will prove the cheapest kind of hospital. But at Paimio we have something which at first does not appeal to the ordinary man, who has never seen a building constructed solely for the purpose it is to serve, who because monasteries in the Middle Ages were seats of learning, imagines that Gothic arches are essential to culture even in the steel and concrete age.

The British architects and journalists who began to visit Finland to view the work of Saarinen, Sonck, and Sirén as well as the young Aalto were part of another development in the inter-war years: the arrival of British travellers with specialised interests, which extended far beyond social institutions. Fishermen and yachtsmen came to find the space, silence and solitude which they needed for their pursuits; writers on athletics came to see what had produced world champions like Kolehmainen and Nurmi; and musicians and others came to meet Sibelius.

*

In 1924–5 there was an important British Military Mission to Finland, led by General Walter Kirke. He was accompanied by Lieutenant Colonel P. L. W. Powell, whose son Anthony, then at Oxford, spent two vacations in Helsinki, where he experienced what he called 'a new entirely unfamiliar mode of life'. In his autobiography he writes that *Venusberg* (1932), the second of his many novels, 'recalls some of these Finnish interludes, though much of the novel's background, especially the political circumstances, are altogether imaginary'. The town he describes in the novel as 'an obscurely northern capital' was, he writes, 'a mixture' of Helsinki and Tallinn. Even a diligent reading of the novel gives few suggestions of Helsinki: it mentions the civil war; a German military presence; the House of Knights; a nightclub 'with a telephone on every table'; a lady called Frau Koski; cross-country skiing; and refers to a meteorite which 'fell near this town in the middle years of the last century'. Powell's autobiography describes 'a social world, familiar in Russian novels':

> Dinner-parties took place at the mid-Victorian hour of five-thirty in the afternoon – sometimes advanced to six-thirty as a concession to foreigners' taste for dinner at a late hour – and, if the occasion did not merit a white tie, the older generation of men would wear (rather than the modern dinner-jacket) a black tie and a black waistcoat with a tail coat. The considerable colony of White Russian refugees augmented the sense of living in a 19th century Russian novel or Scandinavian play.

The world of dinner parties did not feature on most travellers' itineraries in this period. Cook's *Handbook* advises that 'evening dress is seldom worn in summer even in leading hotels of the capital'; in this volume only Lady Diana Cooper writes of dressing formally for dinner, and that was with Mannerheim.

It takes both time and unaccustomed humility for the English to recognise, let alone to admit, that things may be ordered better in another country. Nonetheless, during these inter-war years Finland made strong impressions on a long succession of visitors from Britain. Even Noël Coward, a noted epicurean, 'found nothing to criticise in Finland and much to admire'. Atchley, an English lecturer at Helsinki University, explained:

the Englishman in Finland cannot help being struck by the widespread respect for the things of the mind. He notices the love for education among all classes and the general concern about 'culture.' There is no large monied middle class which is indifferent to such things.

This homogeneity of society was widely noted and admired. North remarks on the 'comparatively slight differences to be seen between the standards of living attained by various sections of the community'. Sutherland agrees, adding that 'Class distinctions are further reduced by the children of all classes meeting in secondary schools and at the universities'. Malleson, travelling in 1941 in a train crowded with officers, remarked:

> No observant traveller can fail to remark how rarely, in Finland, you see officers with 'silly ass' faces or with haughty, overbearing, bullying faces. You might be inclined to think that it is because Finland has no class institutions of the Eton and Harrow kind; and because a large number of officers must be drawn direct from the people.

Two generations later Finnish society is still regarded in Britain as a pattern for social mobility: a speech in 2012 by a Labour politician, Ed Miliband, then Leader of the Opposition, included the claim that 'If you want the American dream – go to Finland. This isn't surprising. It's harder to climb the ladder when the rungs are further apart.'

The Finns' fervent belief in education, which had already been singled out for admiration by Mrs Tweedie, among others, in the 1890s, continued to be noted by one English visitor after another, and becomes a recurrent theme in this volume. Sir Walter Citrine, in Finland during the Winter War, visited the Alexis Kivi School in Helsinki, where he found everything 'as good in quality as ever I have seen in the schools of any country'. Langdon-Davies agreed: 'the school buildings are palaces compared to the school buildings almost anywhere in Europe'.

Atchley described how 'an Oxford graduate in Helsingfors was amazed to see students going to lectures at eight o'clock in the morning and nine o'clock at night'. 'This belief in education,' he continues, 'is general in Finland, but the Finnish-speaking section of the population has a blind passion for it'. Agnes Rothery was overawed:

> School buildings are conspicuous in every hamlet, town, and city: public schools, private schools, co-educational schools, normal schools, domestic and agricultural schools, schools for adults, vacation schools, Finnish-speaking, Swedish-speaking.

Nursery schools became peepshows for British visitors, while particular praise was reserved for the People's High Schools (*högskolan*; *kansanfolkopisto*). Their object, wrote Gilmour,

> is to awaken a new spiritual life in the young people, sons and daughters of peasants, between the ages of sixteen and twenty-five who have had an elementary education. To do this, quite as much stress is laid on on the intellectual as on the practical courses.

'In Finland,' adds Atchley, 'there has for a long time been a belief that education is as desirable for women as for men.'

Universal literacy had been noted in Finland way back in the nineteenth century; a century and a half later it is still not taken for granted in England. Perhaps because of this, wherever they go in Finland travellers are amazed by the proliferation and size of the bookshops. 'The Finns,' writes Rothery, 'are passionate, omnivorous, and incessant readers.' Like many others, she marvels at Stockmann's Academic Book Shop; Sutherland claims that 'with its twelve miles of shelves [it] is the largest in Europe'. No writer is more impressed than Gilmour:

> One of the most surprising things in Finland is the prevalence of good bookshops and libraries in places where

any bookshop at all is a matter of surprise to the stranger. You may find them in the smallest villages far into the Arctic zone and apparently beyond the reach of all ordinary intellectual life. They are not the sort of bookshop one expects in a rural area. Here are no light, cheap novels to while away a dull hour, but good, solid, philosophical, historical, literary and religious works necessitating serious study for their digestion.

This was, she wrote, 'a direct result of the Folk High School and kindred organisations'.

Finland on £10

While the institutions of the new republic brought wave after wave of curious visitors, Finland's more established and traditional attractions had not disappeared. It had never been easier or more comfortable to take a holiday in Finland, and never again would it cost so little. 'In no other country covered by the £10 Series,' wrote Clark, 'will money stretch quite so far.' Above all it was the low cost of travel which made Finland so cheap. 'It is a fact,' continues Clark, 'that when I first examined these tariffs I exclaimed to my family, "I'll have to call the book *Finland Twice* on £10."' The travellers' repeated exclamations become almost tedious: Carleton Smith, who contributed the chapter on Finland to Clara E. Laughlin's *So You're Going to Scandinavia* (1938), found living in Finland so cheap that, he wrote, 'whenever my travel budget is depleted I hasten up to Finland and stay there until I've caught up'. To the modern visitor this is both incredible and dispiriting.

Finland no longer provided the type of experience which the more famous travellers of these years were seeking – summed up in the title of Graham Greene's *Journey Without Maps* (1936) – and now we catch only occasional glimpses of the sort of 'time warp' journey which was still possible in southern Europe. Such glimpses are given even in the late 1930s by

Bernard Newman, who heard *runo* singers, and who saw the congregation leaving a Sunday service in the traditional village church boats.

The Finnish Tourist Association, founded in 1887, had made travelling within the country increasingly comfortable. It was one of the attractions of Finland that travellers could enjoy the illusion of exploring uncharted territory and yet always be within easy reach of a telephone and a reassuring voice instructing them in English how to find the nearest hotel. Sutherland, for example, wanting to get to Utsjoki and knowing no Finnish, was stranded in a forest cottage in Lapland when the telephone rang: it was the manageress of the Inari hotel, who 'told me that I was at the inn and post office of Onnela, where I must stay until Friday morning, when the post boat left at 10 a.m.' Real exploration did linger on here and there. In the pages which follow Jim Ingram is the last of the genuine adventurers to have published a record; the Karelia he discovered was genuinely primitive. 'Imagine any country in Europe as it must have looked a thousand years ago,' he wrote, 'and you will have a fair idea of what present-day Finland looks like.' Most of the British travellers now neither sought nor found anything primitive. After 'a quarter-century of roaming in out-of-the-way places near the equator,' wrote Harry A. Franck in *A Scandinavian Summer* (1930), travelling in Scandinavia seemed tame and disappointing:

> To say that I was tired of roughing it for the benefit of my friends of between-the-covers would imply that one can rough it in Scandinavia, which is only in the mildest sense true. There are no slums in the Scandinavian lands, no easily approachable poor, almost no roadsters, none of those picaresque types whose name is legion in, for instance, Spain or Greece.

'Roughing it' certainly had no place in the vocabulary of the

Tourist Association. The holidays described in their brochures promoted comfort above all. Gilmour offered safe advice:

> When travelling off the beaten track it is wisest to frequent *only* the hotels of the Finnish Tourist Association, or those recommended by them. Once only was it my experience to deviate from this rule, and I learned my lesson. The food provided at this hostelry was excellent, the linen spotless; but the rooms, hermetically sealed for the winter, rose to a temperature of 28 Centigrade, and with this intense heat came an invasion of red bugs. Such a thing would not be met with in one of the Finnish Tourist Association's buildings.

The Tourist Association's booklet *Tourist Inns and Communications 1939* lists magnificent hotels in Aulanko, Punkaharju, as well as Savonlinna and Koli; there is a surprisingly large number in Lapland. Even there all the hotels are advertised as being open twelve months a year.

Such holidays are for those who wish to observe rather than to explore; Finland encouraged what might be termed spectatorial attitudes, from hotels, trains and steamers, as Mrs MacDougall had written in 1908: 'Delightful lake steamers are found all over Finland, furnished usually with comfortable wicker deckchairs in which one can laze and revel in the scenery.' In various little ways some of the realities of Finland were being softened for tourists; V. C. Buckley was disappointed that he did not find the real Finland in at out-of-the-way café at Lapua:

> The parlour was clean, but a hideous wall-paper, artificial flowers, and antimacassars were poor substitutes for the log walls and wooden utensils of the old Finnish cottages I had seen at the folk-museum in Helsinki.

The implication here, that the place to see an authentic Finnish cottage is a museum, is another sign of the times.

Hardly anyone now regarded Finland as a place for adventure, either imagined or actual: you could simply have a tour leader take the strain. A brochure lists forty-two tours, of which twenty-two were available in 1939. They vary in length from five to fifteen days; most of them are in eastern and central Finland, but Lapland tours go as far as Liinahamari, Finland's only ocean port, at the far end of the Arctic Highway (now part of Russia). The prospectus for these tours, which all begin from Helsinki, reads very like the preamble of a modern package tour:

> Payment in Finnish currency according to the following tariff.
>
> The prices quoted in sterling are approximate and are only intended to facilitate the work of our clients abroad.
>
> The prices include: all fares (II class train, I class steamer with berth, if the journey is by night, motor bus, motorboat, rapids boat), sleeping berths and reserved seats on trains; hotel rooms (single or double), breakfast, lunch, dinner and service; services of guides and forwarding of passengers and hand luggage by car according to plan of journey; sightseeing by car with guide in the principal places visited by tourists according to plan of journey; entrance fees to museums and sights.

Something should be said about guides. Since the tourist months coincided with the school and university vacations, visitors often found themselves being guided by students. 'On no account,' writes North, 'should they be confused with the "guides" of many southern tourist centres – . . . mere mercenary touts.' You are likely to find 'a University student chosen for the job during the tourist season because he can speak four or five languages in addition to his own, and speak them in such a way that he can discuss matters intelligently with you'.

The concern for the comfort of tourists went beyond hotels:

parks had been laid out in the popular towns, and places such as Punkaharju offered, writes North, 'an ideal retreat for those who find pleasure in unspoilt nature'. Punkaharju was both a national park and a nature reserve; Finland was well ahead of Britain in establishing Areas of Outstanding Natural Beauty. Despite the evident attractiveness of these guided tours no British holidaymaker seems to have recorded taking one.

When you compare the writing of this era to that of the earliest British travellers there are many striking differences. Then the literary models had been the formal letter, the essay, classic travel books such as Samuel Johnson's *Journey to the Western Isles*, the scientific treatise and, perhaps, the military report; individual experiences stand out as rarities. This changed with the Victorian and Edwardian writers; the women travellers, especially, included more accounts of their own experiences, making the genre less documentary and more direct. The interwar travellers extend these developments, sometimes expropriating the techniques of the novelist. Some of the accounts contain a great deal of naturalistic dialogue which, combined with a general lack of pretension, gives a distinctive voice to the writing of this era. Although travellers now rarely seemed to find themselves out of reach of an English speaker, they were not frustrated when they did, but saw it even as welcome confirmation that they were really off the tourist trail, and having 'an adventure'. If all else failed there was always what North calls 'the comprehensive smile that serves when speech is not possible'. The mystifying tradition of travellers recording conversations with Finnish people without having a word in common with them goes back to the eighteenth century. Since none of the writers in the current volume knew much Finnish, one must suppose that the conversations they record are usually imaginative reconstructions rather than literal transcripts. This creative dimension makes writers like Ingram and Newman vivid and readable, while others, such as Malleson and

Bramwell, offer descriptive writing which is both literary and elegant.

On the pages that follow there is often more emphasis on character than on scenery. The Finnish people who are described are usually credible characters, unlike the caricatures or national stereotypes sometimes presented in earlier times. Some of the works covered in this section are by professional writers, who are simply turning their hand to Finland for one book; their skills are evident in the use of episode and anecdote as well as of dialogue. As a result the Finnish scenes described in the following pages come alive as they had rarely done in earlier writing.

Prohibition

One of the first acts of the Finnish government was the prohibition of alcohol in 1919; earlier attempts had been vetoed by the Tsar, but he was now history, and there were now women in parliament. The first reaction of British visitors was usually consternation: Agar and his companions, embarking at Hull on his secret service mission to Finland in 1919,

> heard to their horror that the Fennia was a dry ship . . . Hampsheir was sent hastily into town to secure as much alcohol as he could find. He returned with a rather odd collection: four dozen bottles of stout and a dozen bottles of port.

Finland was anxious to encourage tourists, and partly for this reason enforcement of prohibition was not very rigorous; visitors could nearly always find a drink, as Fox explained:

> the government allows the supply of wine and spirits on doctors' certificates through the chemists' shops. A doctor's certificate is not difficult to obtain, and it permits the holder to purchase wine or whisky in reasonable quantities and at a reasonable price.

It was possible – at a price – to get liquor at almost any restaurant or hotel; there are several amusing accounts of the ingenious ways in which travellers were able to circumvent the laws. On the islands smuggling was rife; Fox records his own experience:

> As a visitor to the country, though ignorant of the language, I was able, within a half-hour's visit to a particular island, to learn the whereabouts of a 'shop.' This was a neat little villa, surrounded by a good garden. Having learnt the procedure, I did not go to the front door, but passed through the back garden, where there was a fairly extensive poultry run. All the fowls, I noted, wore the white feathers of a blameless life. Knocking at the door of a shed in the poultry yard, admission was at once granted. No questions were asked; the kerosene can of spirit was produced, the litre can was filled, carefully corked, and handed over for 35 marks (the equivalent of about four shillings). For this sum I obtained enough white spirit to poison half a dozen ordinary men.

Prohibition was ended in early 1932; although it affected few of the travellers featured here, it provides several entertaining accounts of the puzzled British responses to an unfamiliar restriction.

Transport

From the middle of the nineteenth century there had been a regular steamer service from Stockholm to St Petersburg (Kronstadt) by way of Turku, Helsinki and Tallinn. By the twentieth century the service from Stockholm was much as it is today, though not as rapid: the journey time to Turku was ten and a half hours, and this was by far the most popular way of arriving in Finland. There were weekly steamer services from Hull to Helsinki, taking four and a half days on the luxurious *Aallotar*, and to Turku on the less-than-luxurious *Arcturus*. In the 1930s air travel became possible, and some more adventurous British travellers flew out from London (Croydon Airport). Franck has a whole chapter 'Flying to Finland'. Writing in 1930, he describes flying by seaplane from Stockholm to Helsinki in a well-appointed saloon, seating nine, and featuring an opening window for every seat, and a flushing toilet. The regular flight to Helsinki, though, was from Stockholm via Turku. Clark, who wrote that air travel was 'a subject dear to my heart', described this journey, though he certainly could not have accommodated it within his £10 budget.

> Particularly do I love the flight from Stockholm above the inner and outer skerries, above the blue Baltic, which becomes a mere ribbon crossed in fifteen minutes, above Mariehamn, chief port of the Ålands, and so above endless Finnish isles and crinkled channels to the landing at Turku, whence a further hop of three-quarters of an hour carries one to Helsinki. A gorgeous flight this is and gorgeously varied in aspect, the last lap over forest, waterway and country town, giving one a fair cross-section of all Finland. From Helsinki's airport, with its brand-new buildings, the company takes passengers by bus in a half-hour's beautiful ride to its central office on the Esplanade, a pebble's toss from the capital's chief hotels.

In the eighteenth and early nineteenth centuries this journey often took many weeks: from Stockholm it could take three days to get to Grisslehamn, where ice in winter or lack of wind in summer could cause long delays. On the Finnish mainland, near Kustavi, it was another two days' journey to Turku.

Within Finland travel was still nearly always by land and water. During these years the railway network was expanding, and rail travel became ever more popular with tourists. Almost all those who used the trains remarked how unbelievably cheap they were: Ingram wrote that 'for the sum of one English pound I was able to travel nine hundred miles third-class'. Travellers were impressed also by their cleanliness: 'It is possible to travel several days continuously in Finnish trains with no sign of grime or travel stain,' wrote Gilmour. 'Should anything be upset, the conductor will send a boy along with a dustpan and brush to sweep the carriage.' The ease of rail travel even for those who understood no Finnish is described by North:

> The guard comes through the train announcing the name of each successive stop, and tells you if it will be a restaurant station and how long you will stay. Since, naturally, he tells you in Finnish, it is most unlikely that you will understand him, although you will probably admire the musical rhythm of his words, but that is by no means a cause for alarm, for, if you are as fortunate as we often were, your guard will keep you well informed by the simple expedient of making a dumb show of eating and drinking, and indicating with his fingers how many minutes you will have for the repast.

Every account of rail travel remarks how slow the trains were; there were stops for loading fuel for the wood-burning locomotives, and country trains seemed to stop almost everywhere. North writes that 'the journey from Vuonislahti to Vaala – a matter of 164 miles – takes about eight and a half hours, and involves at least twenty-eight stops, with a possibility of twenty-one at intermediate halts'. Travellers would take an overnight sleeper for journeys which today take only a few hours. I have found little evidence of trains provided especially for tourists, but Wilmot Russell describes a train to Punkaharju which had 'an observation car attached'. When the trains were so slow, steamers were a genuine and practical alternative; the railway had replaced the post routes by this time, but had not displaced the steamers.

All of the Tourist Association's organised tours included travel by steamer, and it remained a favoured way of seeing Finland. These tours were nothing like the cruises which are so popular with modern holidaymakers; steamers, unlike those on the Rhine or on Lake Windermere, for example, were part of the public transport system, so that foreign travellers shared their journeys with local people as they were taken through the lake systems into deepest Finland. 'Humble folk and great folk,' writes Rothery, 'pass in juxtaposition':

> In the drizzle of an evening shower we pause at a landing whose rough logs indicate that this is no fancy summer pier but the primitive necessity of a primitive hamlet.

Atchley describes a journey by steamer through 'the wildest part of Savo' in the late 1920s:

> The whistle breaks the silence, and the stocks of the small pier creak and crack as the bows press into them. There may be twenty or thirty people there, for the arrival of the steamer makes an occasion for the people from the scattered farms to meet. They come down to the landing-stage to talk to each other and to see some life, not because they have any business with the steamer . . . A rope is thrown from the boat, someone makes it fast, and the gangway of two planks is pushed over the side. A little girl returning from school walks down it, and seriously shakes a hand with those who have come to meet her and drops a curtsey. There are no smiles or kisses. A sack of flour or some farm implement is thrown ashore from the bows, and an old woman pushes a cow up the gangway. Trivial happenings, yet every movement and every face is interesting. During the passage through the forest you have been longing to see some human life, then this small play is acted before you on an ideal stage, and you see all these people at a moment when they are living more intensely than normally.

The child with two fair plaits hanging across her shoulders lifts the mooring rope off the bollard without fear or excitement, and turns towards the path leading inland. The steamer pushes out into the silence of the lake again.

Some years later Robert Colville, taking the 'passenger boat' from Savonlinna to Kuopio, was more conscious of the touring possibilities of the route:

> the boat is tied up for a few hours during the night at Leppävirta village, but if it is summer the light evenings induce many people to go ashore and see the wonderful old church and the quaint village itself.

'Leppävirta' was actually the name of the lake-steamer photographed by North, built in a famous boatyard in Varkaus. Many of the travellers, from the 1890s onwards, describe memorable cruises on these steamers; North gives the details:

> a curiously top-heavy looking craft, rather like a two-storied house-boat, with a verandah to the upper story, and a chimney surrounded by life-boats on the roof . . . [S]mall as it is the vessel [has] its first class and its third, its lounge and its dining room, and, most surprising of all, a complement of cabins like those of ocean-going liners in all but size. The cabins open out onto the upper deck and serve as semi-private lounges during the long hours of daylight – a very useful feature since the deck is only a yard wide.

Dinner on board astonishes him: 'that a meal so varied and so good can be conjured up from the diminutive kitchen, and so daintily served in the narrow saloon has to be seen in order to be believed'.

Several of these steamers are still to be seen coming and going in Savonlinna during the tourist season.

By the 1920s most of those areas of the country still not served by railway or steamer had become accessible by motor bus, and public transport by horse was finally disappearing. Droshkies were now of retro-interest: Gilmour writes that '[a]musing old-fashioned horse cabs are found in several cities'; in Helsinki it cost a mark extra to hire one with a hood. Buses enabled any traveller who could read a timetable to visit easily even remote parts of the country. The railways, like the post routes of earlier times, were both limited and fixed, whereas buses covered nearly the whole country, and at the same time enabled travellers to sit side-by-side with the local people, and on occasion with their livestock. Ingram describes boarding in Sortavala: 'After they had packed the bus full of women with babies, and lean brown men who looked as though they had been left out in the sun for a long time, we started off.'

This was something that could never have happened in the age of posting, before the mid-nineteenth century, when British travellers typically moved and even slept in their private carriages. Railway trains, with their small compartments and different classes of accommodation, did not make it easy for travellers to mix with the local people, even if that was what they wanted. Several of the bus journeys described below take the travellers into the very heart of Finland. North admires the 'well-timed series of cross-country services', linked with an efficiency which some countries have not achieved more than seventy years later. His account of travelling to Koli gives the flavour:

> from time to time people got out, as often as not where there seemed to be no obvious reason for their doing so, until you noticed some inconspicuous track along which they disappeared into the woods.

In remote parts a bus stop, he wrote, like a landing stage, provided 'the day's diversion' for the locals.

Buses lacked many of the attractions and all of the comforts of trains and steamers. They were often overloaded – 'no vessel or vehicle proved to be full in Finland when there was anyone desirous of getting in,' wrote North. The roads were rough, the suspension of the buses primitive, and the ventilation non-existent. In Lapland, especially, with long distances between stops, bus travel was distinctly challenging. Despite all this, for many travellers this was the age of the bus. Not until 1939 do we read the account of our first modern tourist, Buckley, arriving by air and travelling by motor car.

'Motoring in Finland' was being promoted vigorously by Finland-Travel (*Suomen-Matkat*) during the 1930s in a thirty-two page booklet. 'To some motorists,' it reads, 'Finland may seem a very faraway country and one difficult to reach. This is not the case.' We learn that 'the steamers are specially equipped for carrying automobiles and used to handling them'. The motorist who dislikes sea travel might 'consider travelling to Finland by air 10 hours from London or Paris and sending his car by sea in advance'.

> Finland is a motoring country, even if the volume of motor traffic may seem small to those coming from thickly-populated countries. Even in the remotest villages, behind tracks the town-driver would never think of using, there are cars, the reason being that in a sparsely-populated country, with relatively few railways, the advantages offered by the automobile are more patent than ever. Hence Finland is not motor-shy, and there are filling-stations and service stations all over the country. The motorist need not fear that some breakdown will find him stranded and left to his own resources; on the contrary he is more likely to be struck by the prevalence of skilled knowledge of cars. Adequate signpost arrangements are another result of the prevalence of motoring.

Buckley provides the only published account of a motoring tour during this period, but there are indications that suggest

that they were not rare – J. M. Richards drove from Turku
to Vyborg with Alvar Aalto 'along dusty gravel roads, almost
traffic-free', and Harriet Cohen and Arnold Bax made several
excursions by car into remote parts of eastern Finland in 1932,
before their visit to Sibelius. Scott remarked that 'the roads are
not yet first class, but the drivers are'. This is perhaps the first
accolade to Finnish drivers, now so successful in the motor-
racing and rallying worlds, although their ancestors may be
identified among the many descriptions from the nineteenth
century of unsprung Finnish carts being driven at high speed
on dangerous roads by very small boys.

Many British visitors did not share Scott's opinion, and com-
monly saw the motor car from the pedestrian's point of view.
Fox gives the picture:

> Helsingfors, as indeed all Finland, has nowadays motor
> fever in an acute form: in an even more acute form than
> the countries of Western Europe. The Finnish motorist has
> directed his first care to getting a motor, and intends to
> learn how to use it prudently in the future. So the gen-
> eral recklessness of the driving constitutes a real danger
> to unwary pedestrians. Finland seems to recognize this as
> a nuisance, and the other day a special police detachment
> was sent to London to study methods of traffic regulation
> there.

Fox feared that viewing Finnish architecture in Helsinki was
putting his life in danger: 'we [are not] all as athletic as the
Finns: personally it disturbs my taste for a building if, in stopping to glance at it, I have to make a wild leap to escape a
motorist in a hurry'. Gilmour shared his fears:

> We leave our hotel in Station Square, crossing the square
> itself with the utmost care; for, though everyone in Finland
> drives to perfection, the speed of the traffic can only be
> compared with those early American cinemas in which

cars, by a quick-motion process, were made to cover incredible distances in the twinkling of an eye.

Even in Lapland safety could not be guaranteed, as Ingram discovered: 'some of my narrowest escapes were due, not to bears or wolves, but to motorists who nearly ran me down!' However, there were a few safe havens: Malleson records that she had been more than three months in Vehmersalmi before she saw a motor vehicle – and that was an army lorry.

This section should perhaps have begun with walking and cycling, neither of which was promoted by the Tourist Association. Walking seems to have been the last resort for nearly all travellers, except in Lapland, where there were few roads and where, as 'the last wilderness in Europe', it was already attracting hikers. Back at the turn of the century Harry de Windt had remarked that in Helsinki 'almost every fourth inhabitant cycles', and that the proportion was even greater in Tampere. During this period only two travellers described actually riding a bicycle in Finland: Newman, whose *Baltic Roundabout* describes a tour taken entirely on two wheels, avoided large towns, and the Finland he discovered was, he recorded, 'surprisingly deficient in cyclists'. Cycling was an urban activity, perhaps for reasons suggested by Barbara Cotton: 'the roads in Finland are rather bad for cycling,' she writes; the Great Arctic Highway 'turned out to be a very grand name for a glorified cart-track'.

Lapland

Lapland is a 'cultural region' in Finland, Sweden, Norway and Russia, as well as the northernmost 'region' of Finland. As early as the eighteenth century travel books about Lapland had included Finland as only part of a northern journey, sometimes starting from Norway. In the nineteenth century only four British travellers had described venturing north of Tornio, and these were all genuine explorers, not sightseers. Now the

extension of the railway to Rovaniemi in 1909, the completion
of the Arctic Highway in 1931, and the arrival of the motor
coach put Lapland firmly on the tourist map. Hirn complained
to Sutherland that writers 'ignore Finland except as a means of
getting to Lapland as quickly as possible.' You no longer needed to be either especially adventurous or intellectually curious
to venture there: Joan and Peggy Webster in the late 1930s
provide evidence of this.

The bus journey from Rovaniemi to the Arctic Ocean took
two days; first class passengers sat in the front, second class
at the back, and luggage and freight in the middle. Tourism
was not the purpose of the new road, although it became a
consequence. Ingram realised this when he wrote that 'Lapland
was a colony in the making, and everywhere men were hard at
work, constructing bridges, roads, settlements, building houses, barns, garages and shops'. It manifested, as a Finnish friend
remarked to him, 'civilisation marching north'.

Travelling from Britain to Lapland in order to see the midnight sun was a fairly short-lived eighteenth-century fad. Although in the twentieth century it could have been done in
comfort, I have read no description later than 1799. Gilmour
nonetheless describes it as a popular attraction, and gives exact
travelling instructions:

> From Kemi the traveller in search of the midnight sun con-
> tinues to Tornio, the small town on the Swedish frontier.
> From here, forty-five miles by rail, to the hill of Aavas-
> aksa, the most southerly point from which (from June
> 21st to 25th) the midnight sun is visible.

At Ounasvaara Hill, outside Rovaniemi, she writes, 'many
sightseers flock to view that magnificent spectacle'. It is a pity
that none of them seems to have published a description. Although 'Land of the Midnight Sun' is today the title of the
Official Travel Site of Finland, it is the Northern Lights which

are promoted for modern travellers: 'In Finland, nature's most spectacular light show, the Aurora Borealis, can be viewed in a range of purpose-built spaces from glass igloos to luxury suites.' After ticking Lapland off their lists, modern tourists can now, perhaps, set off to defile Antarctica.

By no means all of the travellers to Lapland were sightseeing tourists; there was plenty of scope for genuine exploration and adventure. It was easier to discover more primitive patterns of life in Lapland than it was further south – Ingram found his lost Karelian village only with great diligence. Lapland attracted the adventurous, the intrepid, and the foolhardy; for some the existence of the long border with the Soviet Union added further excitement to the adventure. The Public Schools Exploring Society promoted hikes through Lapland in 1933, with the avowed purpose of 'testing the boys'; the boys' own accounts of their different responses make unusual reading.

The Arctic Highway, hailed internationally as a marvel, opened up Lapland to summer and winter visitors. Tourism has, of course, continued to develop: Lapland, as well as northern Finland, is today promoted for winter sports. Rovaniemi airport, opened in 1940, is now 'Santa Claus Official Airport'; it is possible to fly there from England, visit 'Santa Park', and return the same day. Your children might prefer to meet 'Santa's Elves', in which case you will need to fly to Ivalo. You might prefer to stay at home.

Henry McGrady Bell

Finland has had few better British friends than Harry (as he was usually known) Bell; of all those featured in the following pages he alone spans the whole period, and indeed overlaps it. His *Land of Lakes* was published in 1950, exactly fifty years after he first set foot in Finland. Born in Dundee in 1880, he left school at seventeen to enter his family business, the timber firm of Bell and Sime. When at the turn of the century the company decided to develop its trade with Finland he was sent out to Helsinki. He quickly learned Swedish, and soon immersed himself in the cultural life of the capital, as well as travelling extensively in Finland on business. The Fennia Timber Company was wound up in 1903, on the death of Bell's father, and the next six years saw him in South Africa, Sweden and finally Russia where, in 1915, he was enrolled – seconded, effectively – by the British Embassy, and given the title 'Representative of His Britannic Majesty's Embassy in Petrograd', 'dealing with requisitioned goods and claims against the Russian government'. His German wife and their children found what he called 'sanctuary' in Vyborg, where he visited them whenever he could. After the second Russian revolution the British Ambassador 'decided to evacuate all British nationals', and the Bells found themselves back in Scotland.

In 1918 he was, at the suggestion of Rudolph Holsti, 'delegate of the Finnish Government then resident in London', unexpectedly appointed British Consul-General in Finland; 'I was certainly delighted at the prospect of returning to my beloved Finland,' he writes. His activities as Consul and his strenuous promotion of the Finnish cause are an important part of his book. Diplomats usually have elaborate training, and are parachuted into a different country every few years, learning about the local scene on the job. Bell, by contrast, had no diplomatic training at all, but knew Finland perhaps better than any other Briton did. 'Certainly,' he wrote, 'a better-trained Consul would not have dared do many things that I did in the service of my country; and a better-trained Consul could not, therefore, have got the results I did!' He was especially successful in handling the succession of spies and couriers who were toing-and-froing between Helsinki and Petrograd; Dukes and Agar were the only ones he mentions by name, since he 'knew most of them by their pseudonyms'. After the storming of the British Embassy in Petrograd in August the entire staff had been thrown into prison. Eventually they were released, and Bell was called at midnight to arrange a special train to meet them at Riihimäki, where his powers of organisation extended to providing a 'sumptuous meal' at the station restaurant, and two bottles of whisky.

Bell quotes from *Karjalan Aamulehti* (18 July 1919):

The Representative of Great Britain, although he has not had the full powers of a Minister, has already done great service in the development of the relations existing between England and Finland, both politically and economically. He has earnestly endeavoured to stimulate good feeling between Finland and Great Britain, and has done much to educate public opinion in his country, where, up to the present, very little was known with regard to Finland and conditions obtaining there . . . In every circle where Consul Bell's activity is known, it is hoped that he will continue to use his influence towards further successful development of the relations between England and Finland, and extend the work he has so efficiently commenced.

Bell worked hard to help secure British acknowledgement of Finland's independence, but until it was obtained had to suffer Mannerheim's disapproval, as described in the following interview:

> 'Herr Consul, do you bring me good news today?'
> I blushed and stammered:
> 'I regret, Your Excellency . . .'
> It was sufficient.
> 'Herr Consul,' he interrupted imperiously, 'if you do not soon bring me good news – that Britain has recognised the independence of Finland – your visits will no longer be welcome. Good-day.'
> It was typical of the great man that on the day the important news arrived, and I presented him with a copy of a telegram I had received from Mr. Balfour, in Versailles, confirming Britain's recognition of an Independent Finland, he thanked me courteously, and said:
> 'Herr Consul, I would like to see the *original* document.'
> And it was typical of me that I let him have it, and deposited the copy in my archives.

Since Bell was one of the few Britons to have recorded impressions of Mannerheim, it is worth including the following anecdote:

> As a diplomat, Mannerheim was inscrutable. In the Spring of 1919 Major Scale, our Military Attaché, came over from Stockholm to secure information on one of a number of colourful rumours which were then afloat; this particular project was that the Finns, under Mannerheim, would advance on Petrograd.
> Major Scale dined with General Mannerheim, but could not draw out the General at all. Eventually, when he was leaving and Mannerheim courteously helped him on with his coat, he resorted to a policy of desperation. He put his question point-blank.

'What will you do, General, when you get to Petrograd?'

Mannerheim looked at Major Scale in an old-fashioned sort of way and smiled behind his grey face.

'My dear Major,' he said, 'when I get to Petrograd I shall crown you King.'

One of Bell's last official duties was noted by Agar in his diary entry for 16 July 1919:

Today the British colony celebrated peace by a garden party at Brunnspark. Bell, who has now been appointed British Minister and Chargé d'Affairs, made a rather good speech just like John Bull & we gave three cheers for the King.

Bell returned to Finland as a trader in 1921, remaining for nearly twenty years as a private citizen. *Land of Lakes*, part history, part portrait gallery and part scrapbook, contains many descriptions of friends and acquaintances in Finland; there are chapters on Mannerheim, Sibelius and von Julin, with accounts of, among others, Walter Gräsbeck and Paasikivi. He did not become involved in Finnish public affairs again for twenty years.

CROSSING THE NEW RUSSIAN BORDER

Both the opening and the close of the inter-war period were very far removed from the leisurely interests which the British enjoyed in Finland during the 1920s and 1930s. The first British Ambassador, Lord Acton, claimed that the Finns had tried to assassinate him, and Gordon Vereker, arriving as ambassador in 1940, presented his credentials in a bunker during an air raid.

After the Bolshevik Revolution in October 1917 the British Navy established a permitted base for a squadron of light cruisers and destroyers under the command of Admiral Cowan at Björkö Sound, near Koivisto; their purpose was to patrol the Baltic and keep open the sea lanes to Estonia and Latvia, which had both, like Finland, newly become independent. At Terijoki, twenty-five miles east, Captain Augustus Agar set up his own headquarters with speedboats which were to penetrate the defences of Kronstadt.

Arthur Ransome (i)

Ransome is best known for his series of children's books set in the English Lake District, beginning with *Swallows and Amazons*, published in 1930 when he was forty-six. His earlier life had been very much more exciting than these idyllic stories would lead one to expect: it had in fact been revolutionary. His biographer, Roland Chambers, writes that he 'succeeded in concreting over his past brilliantly'.

At the age of eighteen Ransome had set off from his native Yorkshire to work for a London publisher. He quickly made friends among literary people, and within two years had published his first book; the final total was more than forty. In 1913, for professional and domestic reasons, he abruptly left for Russia, where he got to know many of the leading politicians. At this time his principal interest was folklore, but the outbreak of war in 1914 turned him quickly into a foreign correspondent, covering the war on the Eastern Front for the radical *Daily News*. He published several books describing those tumultuous times.

Ransome's first visit to Finland had taken place immediately after he arrived in Russia, when he crossed the border from St Petersburg to stay with an Anglo-Russian family, the Gillibrands, at their dacha in Terijoki. He describes the visit in his autobiography:

> I was no sooner in Russia than I was out of it again. I was driven straight from the quay to the Finland Station, and, after an astonished glance at the ikons and candles in the booking-office, was sitting in a suburban train on the way to my friends' *dacha* or country house, some thirty miles on the Finnish side of the frontier.
>
> The *dacha* was a pleasant wooden house among pine-trees, almost on the shore of the gulf. There is little work done in offices during the middle of the northern summer. Schools and universities are closed. I reached Finland in time to know the magical 'white nights' of the nearly Arctic summer. All night long I heard the nightingales.

The Gillibrand family encouraged him to take a crash course in Russian, and within a month, with help, he was translating Russian fairy tales.

Ransome welcomed the February and October revolutions, and quickly became their fervent and uncritical defender, blind even to the atrocities of the Red Terror. His understanding of Bolshevik policy was more than sympathetic; he was close to its leaders, notably Vladimir Lenin (whom he famously beat at chess) and Leon Trotsky. This infuriated the British Foreign Office, and made him a politically suspicious figure. The suspicions were strengthened when he began an adulterous affair with Lenin's secretary, Evgenia Petrovna Shelepina. Despite this, in the summer of 1918 MI6 recruited him in Stockholm; he became effectively a double agent when, towards the end of 1918, he joined the Bolshevik legation in Stockholm, headed by V. V. Vorovsky. He was expelled along with them in January 1919. 'I shall probably shift to Viborg, or some other abominable Finnish town,' he wrote to his mother, but in fact he got permission to return to Russia. With three other newspaper correspondents he 'crossed by boat to Abo, grinding our way through the ice, then travelled by rail', with numerous delays, to Vyborg. There the news from Russia 'sounded fairly lively'; they got to Terijoki by train, and headed for the border, pulling their luggage on sledges. Ransome's description of crossing the Russian border takes one back more than a hundred years, to the accounts of the bridge over the Kymen, the old frontier between Sweden and Russia. Sir Nathaniel Wraxall had made this crossing in 1774, and described

> a wooden bridge, one half of which is constantly repaired by the one, and the other half by the other nation. I was stopped by the guards on either side, and underwent a very minute search before I was permitted to proceed.

A century and a half later the pattern was still recognisable:

> A Finnish lieutenant walked at the head of the procession, chatting good-humouredly in Swedish and German, much as a man might think it worthwhile to be kind to a crowd of unfortunates just about to be flung into a boiling cauldron. We walked a few hundred yards along the line and then turned into a road deep in snow through a little bare wood, and so down to the little wooden bridge over

the narrow frozen stream that separates Finland from Russia. The bridge, not twenty yards across, has a toll bar at each end, two sentry boxes and two sentries. On the Russian side the bar was the familiar black and white of the old Russian Empire, with sentry box to match. The Finns seemingly had not yet had time to paint their bar and box.

The Finns lifted their toll bar, and the Finnish officers leading our escort walked solemnly to the centre of the bridge. Then the luggage was dumped there, while we stood watching the trembling of the rickety little bridge under the weight of our belongings, for we were taking with us as much food as we decently could. We were none of us allowed on the bridge until an officer and a few men had come down to meet us on the Russian side . . . At last, after a general shout of farewell, and 'Helse Finland' from Nina [Vorovsky's small daughter] the Finns turned and went back to their civilisation. And we went forward into the new struggling civilisation of Russia. Crossing the bridge we passed from one philosophy to another, from one extreme of the class struggle to the other, from a dictatorship of the bourgeoisie to a dictatorship of the proletariat.

The contrast was noticeable at once. On the Finnish side of the frontier we had seen the grandiose new frontier station, much larger than could possibly be needed, but quite a good expression of the spirit of the new Finland. On the Russian side we came to the same grey old wooden station known to all passengers to and from Russia for polyglot profanity and passport difficulties.

Later in the year he made a trip to England, returning in October as correspondent of the *Manchester Guardian*. He relocated to the Baltic states, from where he could report on Russia while avoiding Russian censorship.

Ransome's involvement with the Bolsheviks links him with two other British arrivals in Finland during the first years of independence.

Paul Henry Dukes

In September 1907 Paul Dukes, son of a Congregationalist minister in Somerset, eighteen years old and a talented pianist, had taken a one-way ferry ticket to Rotterdam, with a distant ambition of enrolling in the famous Conservatoire at St Petersburg. Working his way there took two years as he eked out a precarious living teaching English, and later German, in Rotterdam, Germany, Warsaw and Riga. Thirteen years later he was knighted by King George V, who called him the 'greatest of all soldiers'.

He finally arrived in Russia in 1909, was accepted at the Conservatoire, and after graduating in 1913 became assistant to Albert Coates, principal conductor of the famous – still famous – Mariinsky Theatre Orchestra. Two years later, after being rejected for military service, he was taken on by the 'Anglo-Russian Bureau', a nebulous organisation which, in the words of Ramsome's biographer, 'encouraged cooperation between Russian politicians and British diplomats'. His task was to 'monitor conditions inside Russia and at the same time engage in propaganda activities designed to keep Russia loyal to the allied cause'. He sent reports from many parts of the country, and summarised significant material from the Russian press. In 1917 he became a King's Messenger, carrying dispatches. Summoned urgently to London, he was informed by Lieutenant Colonel Browning, second in command of MI6, that 'it has been proposed to offer you a somewhat responsible position in the Secret Intelligence Service'. 'Briefly,' he said, 'we want you to return to Soviet Russia and to send reports of the situation there.' This was a large brief, both responsible and dangerous, and one for which Dukes had no experience or training whatsoever: his only relevant abilities were his fluent Russian and his close knowledge of the country, especially of Petrograd.

The responsibilities proved to be even greater than anticipated: on 31 August 1918 the Cheka (the Bolshevik secret police; forerunner of the KGB) were closing in on Captain Francis Cromie, 'the de facto chief of all British intelligence operations in northern Russia'. The British Embassy was stormed, the staff herded off at gunpoint, and Cromie's trampled corpse left on the staircase. 'It was,' wrote Dukes, 'the threads of his shattered organisation that I hoped to pick up.'

Travelling via Stockholm, Dukes was in Helsinki by mid-November:

> Helsingfors, the capital of Finland, is a busy little city bristling with life and intrigue. At the time of which I am writing it was a sort of dumping-ground for every variety of conceivable and inconceivable rumour, slander, and scandal, repudiated elsewhere but swallowed by the gullible scandalmongers, especially German and *ancien régime* Russians, who found in this city a haven of rest. Helsingfors was one of the unhealthiest spots in Europe. Whenever mischance brought me there I lay low, avoided society, and made it a rule to tell everybody the direct contrary of my real intentions, even in trivial matters.

After several weeks he moved to Vyborg; here he met Melnikov, one of Cromie's former agents, who drank most of his whisky, briefed him, and organised the Finnish border guards for him:

> Melnikoff wrote out a password on a slip of paper. 'Give that to the Finnish patrols,' he said, 'at the third house, the wooden one with the white porch, on the left of the frontier bridge.'

Boarding a train bound for Petrograd, he was, he wrote, 'obsessed with the inevitable feeling that everyone was watching me'.

At last the train stopped at Rajajoki, the last station on the Finnish side of the frontier. It was a pitch-dark night with no moon. Half a mile remained to the frontier, and I made my way along the rails in the direction of Russia and down to the wooden bridge over the little frontier river Sestro. I looked curiously across at the gloomy buildings and the dull, twinkling lights on the other bank. That was my Promised Land over there, but it was flowing not with milk and honey but with blood. The Finnish sentry stood at his post at the bar of the frontier bridge and twenty paces away, on the other side, was the Red sentry. I left the bridge on my right and turned to look for the house of the Finnish patrols to whom I had been directed.

Finding the little wooden villa with the white porch I knocked timidly. The door opened, and I handed in the slip of paper on which Melnikoff had written the password. The Finn who opened the door examined the paper by the light of a greasy oil lamp, then held the lamp to my face, peered closely at me, and finally signalled to me to enter.

'Come in,' he said. 'We were expecting you. How are you feeling?' I did not tell him how I was really feeling, but replied cheerily that I was feeling splendid.

'That's right,' he said. 'You are lucky in having a dark night for it. A week ago one of our fellows was shot as we put him over the river. His body fell into the water and we have not yet fished it out.'

This, I suppose, was the Finnish way of cheering me up. 'Has any one been over since?' I queried, affecting a tone of indifference. 'Only Melnikoff.' 'Safely?' The Finn shrugged his shoulders. 'We put him across all right *a dalshe ne znayu* . . . what happened to him after that I don't know.'

The Finn was a lean, cadaverous looking fellow. He led me into a tiny eating-room, where three men sat round a smoky oil lamp. The window was closely curtained and the room was intolerably stuffy. The table was covered with a filthy cloth on which a few broken lumps of black bread, some fish, and a samovar were placed. All four men were shabbily dressed and very rough in appearance. They spoke Russian well, but conversed in Finnish amongst themselves . . .

We sat down to the loaves and fishes. The samovar was boiling and while we swilled copious supplies of weak tea out of dirty glasses the Finns retailed the latest news from Petrograd. The cost of bread, they said, had risen to about 800 or 1000 times its former price. People hacked dead horses to pieces in the streets . . .

After supper we sat down to discuss the plans of crossing. The cadaverous Finn took a pencil and paper and drew a rough sketch of the frontier.

'We will put you over in a boat at the same place as Melnikoff,' he said. 'Here is the river with woods on either bank. Here, about a mile up, is an open meadow on the Russian side. It is now 10 o'clock. About 3 we will go out quietly and follow the road that skirts the river on this side till we get opposite the meadow. That is where you will cross.' . . .

There remained only the preparation of 'certificates of identification' which should serve as passport in Soviet Russia. Melnikoff had told me I might safely leave this matter to the Finns who kept themselves well informed of the kind of papers it was best to carry to allay the suspicions of Red guards and Bolshevik police officials. We rose and passed into another of the three tiny rooms which the villa contained. It was a sort of office, with paper, ink, pens, and a typewriter on the table.

'What name do you want to have?' asked the cadaverous man.

Dukes now became Joseph Hitch Afirenko, the first of more than a dozen pseudonyms which he was to adopt during the next few years; he became known as the 'man of a hundred faces' and 'The New Scarlet Pimpernel'. The guard selected 'a certain sort of paper', and took out 'a box full of rubber stamps of various sizes and shapes with black handles'. These were the 'Soviet seals'.

When the Finn had finished writing he pulled the paper out of the typewriter and handed it to me for perusal. In the top left-hand corner it had this heading:

Extraordinary Commissar of the Central Executive Committee of the Petrograd Soviet of Workers' and Red Army-men's Deputies.

Then followed the text:

CERTIFICATE

This is to certify that Joseph Afirenko is in the service of the Extraordinary Commissar of the Central Executive Committee of the Petrograd Soviet of Workers' and Red Army-men's Deputies in the capacity of office clerk, as the accompanying signatures and seal attest.

'In the service of the Extraordinary Commission?' I gasped, taken aback by the amazing audacity of the thing.

'Why not?' said the cadaverous man coolly, 'what could be safer?'

What, indeed? What could be safer than to purport to be in the service of the institution whose duty it was to hound down all – old or young, rich or poor, educated or illiterate – who ventured to oppose and sought to expose the pseudo-proletarian Bolshevist administration? Nothing, of course, could be safer! *S volkami zhity, po voltchi vitj*, as the Russians say. 'If you must live amongst wolves, then howl, too, as the wolves do!' . . .

'That is your certificate of service,' said the Finn, 'we will give you a second one of personal identification.' Another paper was quickly printed off with the words, 'The holder of this is the Soviet employee, Joseph Hitch Afirenko, aged 36 years.' This paper was unnecessary in itself, but two 'documents' were always better than one.

It was now after midnight and the leader of the Finnish patrol ordered us to lie down for a short rest. He threw himself on a couch in the eating-room. There were only two beds for the remaining four of us and I lay down on one of them with one of the Finns. I tried to sleep but couldn't. I thought of all sorts of things – of Russia in the past, of the life of adventure I had elected to lead for the present, of the morrow, of friends still in Petrograd who must not know of my return – if I got there. I was nervous, but the dejection that had overcome me in the train was gone. I saw the essential humour of my situation. The whole adventure was really one big exclamation mark! . . .

The two hours of repose seemed interminable. I was afraid of 3 o'clock and yet I wanted it to come quicker, to get it over. At last a shuffling noise approached from the neighbouring room and the cadaverous Finn prodded each of us with the butt of his rifle. 'Wake up,' he whispered, 'we'll leave in a quarter of an hour. No noise. The people in the next cottage mustn't hear us.'

We were ready in a few minutes. My entire baggage was a small parcel that went into my pocket, containing a pair of socks, one or two handkerchiefs, and some dry biscuits. In another pocket I had the medicine bottle of whiskey I had hidden from Melnikoff, and some bread, while I hid my money inside my shirt. One of the four Finns remained behind. The other three were to accompany me to the river. It was a raw and frosty November night, and pitch-dark. Nature was still as death. We issued silently from the house, the cadaverous man leading. One of the men followed up behind, and all carried their rifles ready for use.

We walked stealthily along the road the Finn had pointed out to me on paper overnight, bending low where no trees sheltered us from the Russian bank. A few yards below on the right I heard the trickling of the river stream. We soon arrived at a ramshackle villa standing on the river surrounded by trees and thickets. Here we stood stock-still for a moment to listen for any unexpected sounds. The silence was absolute. But for the trickling there was not a rustle.

We descended to the water under cover of the tumble-down villa and the bushes. The stream was about twenty paces wide at this point. Along both banks there was an edging of ice. I looked across at the opposite side. It was open meadow, but the trees loomed darkly a hundred paces away on either hand in the background. On the left I could just see the cottage of the Red patrol against which the Finns had warned me.

The cadaverous man took up his station at a slight break in the thickets. A moment later he returned and announced that all was well. 'Remember,' he enjoined me once in an undertone, 'run slightly to the left, but – keep an eye on that cottage.' He made a sign to the other two and from the bushes they dragged out a boat. Working noiselessly they attached a long rope to the stern and laid a pole in it. Then they slid it down the bank into the water.

'Get into the boat,' whispered the leader, 'and push yourself across with the pole. And good luck!'

I shook hands with my companions, pulled at my little bottle of whiskey, and got into the boat. I started pushing, but with the rope trailing behind it was no easy task to punt the little bark straight across the running stream. I was sure I should be heard, and had amidstreams the sort of feeling I should imagine a man has as he walks his last walk to the gallows. At length I was at the farther side, but it was impossible to hold the boat steady while I landed. In jumping ashore I crashed through the thin layer of ice. I scrambled out and up the bank. And the boat was hastily pulled back to Finland behind me.

'Run hard!' I heard a low call from over the water.

When Dukes had been recalled to London in 1917 he had briefed the head of the Ministry of Information, John Buchan, whose novel *The Thirty-Nine Steps* had been recently published. The adventures of his spy-hero Richard Hannay have been compared to Dukes's account of his experiences and activities in his 1922 book *Red Dusk and the Morrow: Adventures and Investigations in Soviet Russia*, from which these extracts are taken. Finland was, of course, only on the margin of his adventures, which saw him, in various disguises, infiltrating the Communist Party, and the Cheka, and being enrolled in both the Red Army and the Bolshevik army.

The information which he collected was taken over the border to Helsinki by couriers, but on several occasion Dukes found it necessary to go himself. Helsinki, full of Bolshevik spies, was little more than a relay station for the MI6 office in Stockholm, and Dukes was sometimes sent there for debriefing. Two of these journeys into Finland were as dangerous as any of his other experiences.

One of his contacts, a relic of Cromie's organisation, was John Merritt. The Cheka was close on his tail when Dukes contacted him, and they had already arrested his wife. While Merritt escaped to Finland, Dukes boldly promised to arrange her release and bring her over. Amazingly, he managed to keep both promises. They were part of a small party guided by Fita, a sixteen-year old Finnish boy whose father has been shot 'for conspiring against the proletarian dictatorship'. After fifteen miles by horse-drawn sledge they had a long trudge on foot through deep snow to the Finnish border.

> The 'bridge' we found to be a rickety plank, ice-covered and slippery, that threatened to give way as each one of us stepped on to it. One by one we crossed it, expecting it every moment to collapse, till at last we stood in a little group on the farther side.
>
> 'This is Finland,' observed our guide, laconically, 'that is the last you will see of *Sovdepia*.' He used an ironical popular term for Soviet Russia constructed from the first syllables of the words Soviets of Deputies . . .
>
> 'It's all right for you,' the peasant went on, suddenly beginning to talk. 'You're out of it, but I've got to go back.' He had scarcely said a word the whole time, but once out of Russia, even though 'Sovdepia' was but a few yards distant, he felt he could say what he liked. And he did. But most of the party paid but little attention to his complaints against the hated 'Kommuna'. That was now all behind.

Dukes's journeys to and from Helsinki put him in mortal danger. On one occasion he set out from the outskirts of Petrograd on the sledge of a homeward-bound Finnish smuggler; it would be about forty miles over the ice before they could hit the Finnish coast. They managed to evade the searchlights, but were spotted and pursued by a band of Russian cavalry. The sledge overturned, and Dukes, who was wearing dark clothing, quick-wittedly lay flat on a large patch of black ice and managed to stay undiscovered. 'He was carrying maps and documents,' wrote Bell, 'which would have assured his being shot without compunction had he fallen into Russian hands.'

Was the sombre expanse of frozen sea really deserted? Cronstadt loomed dimly on the horizon, the dark line of woods lay behind me, and all was still as death except for the sea below, groaning and gurgling as if the great ice-burden were too heavy to bear.

Slowly and imperceptibly I rose, first on all fours, then kneeling, and finally standing upright. The riders and the sledge were gone, and I was alone.

It must have been a weird, bedraggled figure that stumbled, seven or eight hours later, up the steep bank of the Finnish shore. That long walk across the ice was one of the hardest I ever had to make, slipping and falling at almost every step until I got used to the surface. On reaching light, snow-covered regions, however, I walked rapidly and made good progress. Once while I was resting I heard footsteps approaching straight in my direction. Crawling into the middle of another black patch, I repeated the manoeuvre of an hour or two earlier, and lay still. A man, walking hurriedly toward Cronstadt from the direction of Finland, passed within half a dozen paces without seeing me.

Shortly after daylight, utterly exhausted, I clambered up the steep shore into the woods. Until I saw a Finnish sign-board I was still uncertain as to whether I had passed the frontier in the night or not. But convincing myself that I had, though doubtful of my precise whereabouts, I sought a quiet spot behind a shed, threw myself on to the soft snow and fell into a doze.

It was here that I was discovered by a couple of Finnish patrols, who promptly arrested me and marched me off to the nearest coastguard station. No amount of protestation availed to convince them I was not a Bolshevist spy.

The assertion that I was an Englishman only seemed to intensify their suspicions, for my appearance completely belied the statement. Seizing all my money and papers, they locked me up in a cell, but removed me during the day to the office of the Commandant at Terijoki, some miles distant.

The Commandant, whom I had seen on the occasion of my last visit to Finland, would, I expected, release me at once. But I found a condition of things totally different from that obtaining six weeks earlier. A new commandant had been appointed, who was unpersuaded even by a telephone conversation conducted in his presence with the British representatives at the Finnish capital. The most he would do was to give me a temporary pass saying I was a Russian travelling to Helsingfors: with the result that I was re-arrested on the train and again held in detention at the head police office in the capital until energetic representations by the British Chargé d'Affaires secured my release, with profuse apologies from the Finnish authorities for the not unnatural misunderstanding.

Bell confirms this story, and describes his own part in it: 'I got to work with all the weight I had.' After Dukes 'had had a bath, a sleep, and a beard-trimming, we had a good dinner together and a good laugh over the whole adventure'.

A further trip to Finland by the 'ice route' was uneventful, but the return was anything but. For complex political reasons he decided to evade danger by crossing the border much further north, close to Lake Ladoga, heading for the border village of Rautta, and relying 'on finding some peasant or other who would conduct him to the border'. On the train north he made friends with a young Finnish lieutenant who arranged safe conduct for him to the border, and into Russia.

Nothing could be more truly proletarian than Finnish administration in regions where neither German nor *ancien-régime* Russian influence has penetrated. It is the fundamentally democratic character of the Finnish people that has enabled them since the time of which I speak to master in large measure their would-be foreign counsellors and controllers and build up a model constitution. The elder of the village of Rautta, who was directed by my friend the lieutenant to show me hospitality and procure me a guide, was a rough peasant, literate and intelligent, living with his wife in a single large room in which I was entertained. His assistants were men of the same type, while the guide was a young fellow of about twenty, a native of the village, who had had a good elementary education at Viborg. In the hands of people of this sort I always felt myself secure. Their crude common sense – the strongest defence against nonsensical Red propaganda – made them as a class trustier friends than a spoilt intelligentsia or the scheming intrigants of the militarist caste.

My guide produced half a dozen pairs of skis, all of which were too short, as I require a nine- or ten-foot ski, but I took the longest pair. About eleven o'clock our skis were strapped to a *drovny* sledge, and with a kindly send-off by the elder and his wife, we drove rapidly to a lonely hut, the last habitation on the Finnish side of the frontier. The proprietor was roused and regaled us with tea, while a scout, who chanced to come in a few moments after our arrival, advised my guide as to the latest known movements of Red patrols. Our peasant host possessed no candles or oil in this solitary abode, and we sat in the flickering light of long burning twigs, specially cut to preserve their shaky flare as long as possible.

About midnight we mounted the skis and set out on our journey, striking off the track straight into the forest. My companion was lightly clad, but I retained my overcoat, which I should need badly later, while round my waist I tied a little parcel containing a pair of shoes I had bought for Maria [Merritt's housekeeper] in Helsingfors.

By the roundabout way we were going it would be some twenty-five miles to the village that was our destination. For four years I had not run on skis, and though ski-running is like swimming in that once you learn you never forget, yet you can get out of practice. Moreover, the skis I had were too short, and any ski-runner will tell you it is no joke to run on short skis a zig-zag route across uneven forest ground — and in the dark!

We started in an easterly direction, moving parallel to the border-line. I soon more or less adapted my steps to the narrow seven-foot ski and managed to keep the guide's moderate pace. We stopped frequently to listen for suspicious sounds, but all that greeted our ears was the mystic and beautiful winter silence of a snow-laden northern forest. The temperature was twenty degrees below zero, with not a breath of wind, and the pines and firs bearing their luxuriant white burdens looked as if a magic fairy-wand had lulled them into perpetual sleep. Some people might have 'seen things' in this dark forest domain, but peering into the dim recesses of the woods I felt all sound and motion discordant, and loved our halts just to listen, listen, listen. My guide was taciturn; if we spoke it was in whispers. We moved noiselessly but for the gentle swish of our skis, which scarcely broke the stillness, and the stars that danced above the tree-tops smiled down upon us approvingly.

After travelling a little over an hour the Finn suddenly halted, raising his hand. For some minutes we stood motionless. Then, leaving his skis, he walked cautiously back to me and pointing at a group of low bushes a hundred yards away, visible through a narrow aisle in the forest, he whispered: 'You see those farthest shrubs? They are in Russia. We are about to cross the line, so follow me closely.'

Moving into the thickets, we advanced slowly under their cover until we were within a few yards of the spot indicated. I then saw that before us there lay, crosswise through the forest, a narrow clearance some ten yards wide, resembling a long avenue. This was the Russian border-line, and we stood at the extreme edge of the Finnish forest. My guide motioned to me to sidle up alongside him.

'It is to those bushes we must cross,' he whispered so low as to be scarcely audible. 'The undergrowth everywhere else is impassable. We will watch the shrubbery a moment. The question is: is there any one behind it? Look hard.'

Weird phenomenon! – but a moment ago it seemed that motion in the forest was inconceivable. Yet now, with nerves tense from anticipation, all the trees and all the bushes seemed to stir and glide. But oh! so slyly, so noiselessly, so imperceptibly! Every shrub knew just when you were looking at it, and as long as you stared straight, it kept still; but the instant you shifted your gaze, a bough swung – ever so little! – a trunk swayed, a bush shrank, a thicket shivered; it was as if behind everything were something, agitating, toying, to taunt you with deceits!

But it was not really so. The forest was still with a deathlike stillness. The dark trees like sentinels stood marshalled in sombre array on either side of the avenue. Around us, above, and below, all was silence — the mystic, beautiful winter silence of the sleeping northern forest.

Like a fish, my companion darted suddenly from our hiding place, bending low, and in two strides had crossed the open space and vanished in the shrubbery. I followed, stealing one rapid glance up and down as I crossed the line, to see nothing but two dark walls of trees on either hand separated by the gray carpet of snow. Another stride, and I, too, was in Russia, buried in the thick shrubbery.

I found my guide sitting in the snow, adjusting his ski-straps.

It is soon after this, the last of his recorded journeys to Finland, that Dukes's fortunes become entwined with those of Augustus Agar. His hair-raising career as a spy ended with the conferring of his knighthood; he remains the only person ever to have been knighted for espionage. After the war he spent much of the rest of his life in other fields – music, and yoga. His last words on Finland came some thirty years later, in his Foreword to Bell's *Land of Lakes*; he acknowledges that Bell had 'extricated me from difficulties with the Finnish frontier authorities'. Bell's book, he hopes, will 'help to accord belated recognition to an heroic people to whom all Europe, and therefore all civilisation, undoubtedly stands in debt'.

Augustus Agar

'Gus' Agar's connection with Finland, like that of Dukes, was entirely unsought. He had joined the Royal Navy as a boy of fourteen in 1904, and by 1919 was a lieutenant based at HMS Osea, a top-secret island base off the Essex coast. He was captain of a Coastal Motor Boat (CMB), known as a 'skimmer'; these boats were revolutionary hydroplanes, which could reach a speed of 45 knots. They had a crew of three, with two Lewis machine guns, and were capable of carrying a torpedo.

Early in February 1919 he was called in by his chief, Captain Wilfred French: 'Well, Agar,' he said, 'would you like to go on Special Service?' On replying that he certainly would, Agar was immediately warned:

No-one must know where you are going until you are under way, not even your crew. This special mission is a highly dangerous one to the Baltic Sea and the Gulf of Finland. The work will involve use of two C.M.B.s because great speed at sea will be an essential. You alone will be in charge, and you will have no-one but yourself to rely on. It is of the utmost importance that not a soul, either here in England, on the journey out, or even when you arrive in those waters, shall have any suspicion of your activities.

The next day Agar was in London, first at the Naval Intelligence Division at the Admiralty, then in the office of the Head of the British Secret Service, Captain Mansfield Smith-Cumming, the first Director of MI6; a legendary figure, known as 'C', he was later made famous in Le Carré's novel *Tinker, Tailor, Soldier, Spy*. Since the shutting-down of the British Embassy, Smith-Cumming explained, 'Russia was now a closed book and hostile country with which we were virtually at war.' There was 'a certain Englishman' (in fact Dukes, known then only as ST-25) who

had remained in Russia to conduct Intelligence, whose work was of vital importance, and with whom it was essential to keep in touch. It was necessary to help him get out alive, as he was the only man who had first-hand reliable information on certain things which was required by the Government.

Agar was to pick his own band of young men, and they were to travel to the Baltic as private individuals, masquerading as yachtsmen or as agents for the selling of motor boats. 'Our destination,' wrote Agar, 'would be Finland.'

Although it was urged on them that time, as well as secrecy, was 'of the essence', it was not until 30 May that the Finnish ship *Fennia* landed Agar and his crew – Richard Marshall and John Hampsheir – at Turku. Agar's diary records:

May 30. Arrived Abo 7.30 pm. Took the luggage to the station and ordered calls at 6am to catch the 7.10am train to Helsingfors. Skipper had a pal, the harbourmaster, on board [who] opened a bottle of whisky in our honour and to wish us goodbye.

There followed a bad day in Turku. They got to the station in good time, only to discover that the Helsinki train had left at 6.45am. There was not another until 4.30 pm, so they took a cab back to the hotel. Agar's diary continues:

We adjourned to the Hotel Grand for breakfast and lunch. Everything is a ruinous price. Our cab fare came to 140 marks (nearly £4). The British Consul was away and we were rather left to the wolves – I tried to have a row with the blighter but the police backed him up & said that the fare was correct.

They eventually got to Helsinki after midnight, and established headquarters at the Hotel Fennia. 'It was a funny little place and in spite of the primitive plumbing and bathing, quite clean and comfortable. It was here that we held our meetings and made our plans, like conspirators in a private sitting room.' Here he was briefed by two local agents (ST-30 and ST-31), and by Bell, as well as being taken to Tallinn to liaise with Admiral Cowan.

Because couriers were no longer getting across the border, and several had been captured and shot, it was proposed to employ speedboats to rendezvous at a prearranged spot near Petrograd. On the face of it this looked like mission impossible. As far back as 1854 the British Navy, after surveying the fort on the island of Kronstadt, which defended the harbour and city of St Petersburg, had decided not even to attempt to capture it. All these years later its defences were even more impregnable: in addition to Kronstadt itself there were fifteen fortresses spread across the whole Gulf, all with batteries of guns. There were also mines, breakwaters, gunboat patrols, submarines, searchlights, and even even some air cover. It was through all this that the CMBs were to pass, depending entirely on their shallow draught and their speed, to drop a courier who would locate ST-25 and return with him to the pick-up spot some days later at a fixed time.

Scanning a map, Agar spotted Terijoki, where a few years earlier Arthur Ransome had spent those idyllic summer days. It lay in a sheltered cove, only three miles from the Russian border, and twenty-five miles east of Björkö Sound and Admiral Cowan's squadron. 'The small harbour,' wrote Agar, 'which had, in the old, pre-revolutionary days, been used as a sailing club by the aristocracy of St. Petersburg, was simply ideal for our purposes.' 'The Cowes of Petrograd' it might have been called. One of Agar's contacts (ST-31) had prepared an abandoned *dacha*, formerly 'the summer home of a wealthy Russian nobleman', for the party. The commandant of the local Finnish garrison was Colonel Sarin. Agar describes him as 'an extremely courteous man', but his requests and activities stretched this courtesy to its limits during the ensuing weeks.

Agar depicts the melancholy situation of 'aristocratic refugees' from Russia in this Finnish village, eking out 'a primitive life of near starvation with dreadful memories, a wife waiting for her missing husband, another for her son . . .' All of them 'were imbued with the firm belief that the British Navy had arrived to succour them, and that therefore Petrograd must fall and they would soon be able to regain possession of their estates'.

It was mid-June before Agar was able to set off past the forts with Pyotr Sokolov (known as Peter), Dukes's regular courier, and drop him off in the delta of the Neva. The journey was tense but reassuringly successful, passing without detection. The Finnish coast, whose beauty was usually extolled by travellers, for Agar reflected only the terrible events unfolding just a few miles away:

The sun had already set over the silent pine forests that lined the Finnish shore. In the long twilight mysterious shapes appear, long shadows, spreading like tentacles in the curious mirage, giving birth to strange apparitions.

Two days later they picked Peter up, again without being detected. He brought dispatches: 'precious documents, the contents of which must be at once transmitted to London'. Dukes had now decided that he needed to travel to Moscow; the urgency of four months earlier had for some reason evaporated. This meant that Agar would have to stay on for another month or more, until after the White Nights. He had not been entirely candid with Colonel Sarin, passing off these expeditions as 'reconnoitring trips', but he now carefully established 'cordial relations' by handing on valuable information about the position of the Russian ships, and the extent of the minefields. Sarin, in gratitude, gave him access to the fine lookout post 'on the top of the high church steeple overlooking the harbour of Terijoki'.

From the steeple he was able to ascertain that outside Petrograd a Russian cruiser, the *Oleg*, was shelling the White Russian – that is, the anti-Bolshevik – garrison which was trapped in the nearby fortress of Krasnaya Gorka. Agar worked out that if he could disable or sink the *Oleg*, or just worry it into retreating back to Kronstadt, the fortress might be saved. So, disobeying specific orders from London, he boldly anticipated the permission of Admiral Cowan, and decided on the exploit which was to earn him the Victoria Cross.

At 11 p.m. on 16 June his CMB set off through the Russian defences. Just after midnight, having slipped between three destroyers to get within a quarter of a mile of the *Oleg*, Agar launched his torpedo. As he headed for home at top speed he looked back and 'saw a large flash abreast of the cruiser's foremost funnel, followed almost immediately by a huge column of black smoke reaching up to the top of her mast'. Back in

Terijoki the next day he had a great deal of explaining to do to Sarin, and finally took him fully into his confidence.

*

The sinking of the *Oleg* had excited Admiral Cowan to the extent that he summonsed Agar and grilled him about the feasibility of 'getting from England a whole flotilla of CMBs and using them, as I did against the *Oleg*, in a full-scale attack on the Russian fleet in Kronstadt harbour'. What came to be known as Operation Kronstadt was set in motion, and took place on 18 August. It is described in detail by Harry Ferguson in a book of that title published in 2008. The news that the Bolshevik fleet was no longer a threat to the coast of Finland made the Finns 'grateful to England for their share in the attainment of Finnish national independence'.

In the month needed to bring CMBs from England, and to prepare for the operation, Agar was refitting one of the boats in Helsinki, where, as always, he kept a very low profile. Although he hardly describes the city, he does give one glimpse of a Finland which seems to belong to the previous century. One of his crew, John Hampsheir, already mentally frail, had broken down completely after the stress of the *Oleg* episode; Agar and Peter paid two visits to him in his sanatorium, a 'magnificent building . . . tucked away in the pine forests many miles north of Helsingfors.'

> We travelled in the oddest of trains driven by the oldest of engines, and I doubt if our speed reached twenty miles an hour, but there was a wonderful fascination in the journey. The beautiful green colouring of the fields and the pine forests must, I felt sure, act as a sedative to Hampsheir's broken nerves. We were in the depths of a primitive and unspoiled country. At each little wayside halt, flowers, both wild and planted, grew in profusion. After the few passengers had alighted from the train and packages for the

next halt had been placed in the van, the guard, who wore a quaint, old-fashioned uniform not unlike those worn by German foresters, never failed to visit our compartment in the train, and, with head respectfully uncovered, ask permission for the train to proceed to the next halt.

I enquired the reason for this, and was told that according to an old Finnish custom only officials of the Tsarist aristocracy were allowed to travel first class, and as we occupied the only first class carriage in the train we were in consequence regarded by the guard and local inhabitants as privileged travellers.

Darkness disappeared completely only for a very short while as the train progressed northwards; and the whole unspoilt countryside seemed to be transformed by nature into one immense conservatory open to the sky. Innumerable lakes of all shapes and sizes (known in the Finnish language as 'ponds') showed up in beautiful relief against the background of green formed by the forests and fields.

The rickety old train, grinding along the rough permanent way, was a symbol of the simplicity of country life and the privations and hardships the people had passed through, since it was all that was left for them to use after the Bolshevik ravages and German exodus. It was easy then for me to understand, after one or two of these journeys into the interior, that the Finnish people desired nothing more than to be left in peace and given time and facilities to reconstruct their country according to their own ideas of national independence. The last thing they wanted was another war or a war party no matter what price the reward for their services might be.

In the meantime 'London's demands for the return of the head of our British intelligence organisation in Russia had become insistent'; it was, for obvious reasons, urgent to get

Dukes out of Russia before the attack on Kronstadt harbour. Gefter, Agar's 'second courier', was already in Petrograd making the arrangements to bring him out on 8 August. They failed, waiting in vain at the pick-up point; Agar learned later that 'through a series of misfortunes Dukes and Gefter had to forsake their small rowing boat and swim towards the shore to save their lives, and were lying exhausted on the shore, actually in sight of our signal'.

Despite all the increased dangers after Operation Kronstadt, Agar decided on one last last attempt to bring Dukes out. Under fire, and blinded by searchlights, he lost control and drove the boat at full speed onto a rocky breakwater. They managed to get the wrecked boat clear, and with frantic baling efforts drifted slowly towards the Finnish coast. As dawn broke they were still in range of the Russian guns. They were saved by two 'Red soldiers from one of the forts' who were out fishing. Encouraged by a machine gun, they gave a tow towards Terijoki, and were sent on their way with what food was left, and a little rum. Agar's last trip had been nearly fatal, and would in any case have been unsuccessful, as Dukes, with the Cheka closing in on him, had no chance of making the rendezvous. The next day the Bolsheviks proudly announced the sinking of the speedboat; Dukes assumed that Agar must be dead, and that he would have to make his own way out of Russia. This he did; his perilous journey through Latvia is described in 'Escape', the penultimate chapter of Red Dusk.

Operation Kronstadt had resulted in British losses, one of whom was buried on Finnish soil, like the British fatalities of the 1854–5 war who lie buried in Åland, Kokkola and elsewhere:

> We buried 'Mossy' Reed next day in the tiny Finnish cemetery at Koivisto with full naval honours from the Fleet. It was most moving for all of us, especially when

two little girls ran out from the crowd of village spectators with posies of wild flowers for his grave.

Agar's achievements in Terijoki would earn him the Victoria Cross, as well as the Distinguished Service Order for his part in Operation Kronstadt, but his mission to bring Dukes out of Russia had finally failed. He never forgot his last sight of Finland as he left Helsinki on 17 September:

> The next day I sailed for Stockholm and to my surprise found amongst the passengers on board the steamer no less a person than General Mannerheim himself, the late Regent also bound for Stockholm as a result of his recent resignation. He looked a sad yet impressive figure standing at the stern of the small steamer with his gaze fixed towards the receding shore as we wound our way in and out of the islands and past the impressive battlements of the fortress of Sveaborg . . .
>
> It was late in the evening and the setting sun threw up the red roofs of the summer *datchas* in beautiful relief against a background of green pine forests giving the same effect as a searchlight. Not for a moment did that figure standing in the stern of the ship take his eyes off this exquisite evening panorama which to him was his native land. He watched until the coast faded away into a thin black line, and finally out of sight altogether. Then, as the twilight disappeared, he gravely removed his hat and bending his head, stood motionless for a few moments – it seemed to me that he was saying a prayer – after which he walked straight down below to his cabin.

Back in England Agar went straight to the Foreign Office, and as he waited outside C's 'sanctum' a man, 'tall, darkhaired, and lean', came out of another door. In 'a flash of intuition' he asked,

'Are you Dukes?'

'Yes,' he replied.

'Well,' I said, 'how strange that we should meet at last like this, and here of all places. I suppose you know I am Agar.'

At this they both 'laughed and shook hands and entered "C"'s office together.'

Soon after this he was he was ordered to present himself 'without delay at Buckingham Palace', where King George V presented him with his Victoria Cross and DSO.

The first question His Majesty asked me concerned my parents, and when I told him they were both dead, he said: 'I am so sorry – so very sorry, they would have been so proud of you today if they were now alive.'

Agar's naval career continued until 1942, when HMS *Dorsetshire*, which he was commanding, was sunk in the Indian Ocean and he was badly injured. He retired to farm in Hampshire, and there, nearly fifty years after he had left Finland, and just a year before his death, he stood at salute by his garden gate as the last surviving CMB was transported past his home on its way to 'a new berth in Southampton'.

'EVERYTHING PROGRESSES WELL'

Arthur Ransome (ii)

Ransome had always been a keen fisherman and chess-player; now a man of some leisure and means living mainly in Tallinn, he began to learn navigation so that he could indulge on the Baltic the love of sailing he retained from his childhood. His dream of having his own boat built could now be realised. The story of his first extended trip, from Riga to Helsinki and back in September 1922, with 'the Ancient Mariner' (his Estonian friend Mr Wirgo), 'the cook' (Evgenia) and himself as crew, was recounted in *Racundra's First Cruise* (1923), which is described by his biographer as 'the obvious precursor of *Swallows and Amazons*'.

Delayed by poor charts and the bewildering number of islands, they arrived at Helsinki after dark, finally getting to Nylands Club with the help of a pilot who, well primed with vodka, told them with a laugh that they had been under suspicion: 'Do you know, we reported you by wireless to Helsingfors as a likely smuggler and told them to look out for you! Yours was the very last boat we thought would need a pilot.'

> Next morning I came on deck to find *Racundra* in the delightful anchorage of the Nylands Yacht Club. The Club House is itself on an island, and with other islands of pink and grey rock and a cliff on the mainland close above the water, gives perfect shelter to the little fleet that lie to mooring-buoys in this southern corner of Helsingfors harbour. The harbour proper lay before us, with white steamships along the quays, on which were the low Customs houses, the booths of a busy market, blue trams slipping

swiftly by – a lively, comfortable scene – while over all were the great domed church and the cathedral spires that I have often admired from the sea when in ships bigger but not better than *Racundra*. Wirgo and I went ashore in the dinghy, he to hurry back to Reval by steamship and I to look for the friends who, after waiting for us last night in the Club House, had supposed that the fog had kept us on the other side of the Gulf.

In comparison with Riga and Reval, Helsingfors seemed not to have suffered from the war. The shops were full of all the things which for the last few years most Baltic towns have had to do without. With its clean white steamers and blue trams, it seemed more Swedish than Finnish. Finland, real Finland, is to be found in the country, not in the capital; and walking through the streets of this modern western town, with its restaurants and taxi-cabs, I kept thinking of the simple country life I had tasted in Finland years ago. Near Hittola, by Lake Ladoga, paddling with a friend in a canoe-shaped boat, I remember finding a little ancient steam-yacht lying covered in on the reedy bank of a river. I was told that in its day it had made a voyage to Edinburgh and back. It was dropping into decay, that aged little steamer; those who had sailed in it were dead; the elk snuffed round it in the winter snow and wandered north to tell the reindeer, who perhaps, on the shores of the Arctic, has seen similar strange things. Looking north from that place to the Pole was nothing but wild country, lake, marshes, ragged forest and ice-infested seas. The little steam-yacht did not seem more foreign to it than this trim stone-built capital.

So far as *Racundra* was concerned, I wasted all that day in friendship. But early next morning there was a coughing and spluttering and spitting alongside, and I tumbled out to find that by that friendship *Racundra* was to profit after all. Commander Boyce had brought his little motorboat, *Zingla*, to take me for a run round the harbour to show me the way through the buoys and out into the fairway, which I had missed by falling asleep as we were coming in. We ran out one way and ran in another through well-marked channels between the uncompromising rocks. The Finnish coast is not a coast on which to make mistakes, and I was glad I had not attempted the foolishness of trying to find the Club for the first time in the dark. Once you know where it is, however, it is easy enough . . .

After introducing me to a score or so of spar-buoys, eloquent in the language of up-turned and down-turned brooms, Boyce brought the *Zingla* back to *Racundra*, and the Ancient, for the first time – indeed, for the only time on the whole cruise, except for getting water – made up his mind to come ashore. He wanted a special size of sailmaker's needles, besides some scrubbing-brushes and mops which he did not trust me to buy. He was not in the least interested in the town. 'Towns,' said he, 'are all one and all dirt.' This was a manifest libel on the spotless Helsingfors, but the Ancient had been a little embittered by the thick fringe of black grease which our waterline had acquired while lying in the harbour of Reval.

Alexander MacCallum Scott

Scott was a Liberal Member of Parliament when he became the first President of the Anglo-Finnish Society in 1911. *Suomi: The Land of the Finns*, published in 1926, was the culmination of several decades of his close interest in Finland. A prolific author, he had written the first biography of Winston Churchill (1905), and in 1908 published *Through Finland to St. Petersburg*, an informed and informative book, but written *for* travellers rather than *by* one. *Suomi: The Land of the Finns* is not a travel book either: its thirty-one chapters range from 'Origins' to 'Sonck', and from 'The Skärgård' to 'The Story of Petsamo'. As well as giving well-informed descriptions of Finnish painters, architects and writers, the book is full of out-of-the-way information, some of it transmitted by the ever-helpful Professor Hirn. Here you can learn the story of E. D. Butler of the British Museum, an eccentric bearded figure who alleviated his personal unhappiness by throwing himself into the study of Finnish, perfecting his writing without ever having a chance of speaking it. He kept the British Library well stocked with Finnish books, and without ever leaving London became the most extreme Fennoman that Hirn had ever encountered. There is an account of Matti Pohto, a self-educated Finnish peasant who travelled into the remotest parts of Finland in the mid-nineteenth century and collected about three thousand rare books and manuscripts for the University Library. Scott saw himself as a minor Pohto figure, and had, in 1926, collected about two hundred books connected with Finland. He has a chapter on English writers on Finland, and another devoted entirely to Edward Daniel Clarke.

Scott is a passionate advocate of Finland; there is even an occasional whiff of eugenic fervour when he sees the Finnish race as potentially the regenerators of an enervated and debilitated world. For Scott Finland evokes a classical age of innocence; one has to go back to the eighteenth century to find other British travellers extolling Finland in such Arcadian terms:

> On many of the islands, sunning themselves on the rocks or plunging into the clear cool water, are to be seen bathers, naked and unashamed, as innocent and unconscious as the nymphs and fauns of a younger world. Vague memories of classic idylls float through the mind – of Theocritus and Anacreon, and even something of the epic simplicity of Homer. In summer people live in the open air,

and ams, legs, and shoulders are tanned as brown as Indians. Here is the young world of the North, close to nature, untrammelled by the conventions of civilisation. It is like the Garden of Eden, with steamers and motor boats and telephones, and wireless, and hammocks between the pine trees, and comfortable villas with verandas for all meals.

One of the few parts of the book which describe his own travels is an account of a bus journey to Tampere:

At six o'clock on an August morning I set out by autobus from Koto, Pälkäne, for Tammerfors, a thirty miles journey. Pälkäne is a nodal point in the great western system of lakes in Finland. The land here is a mere filigree of dark-green setting between the shining jewels of crystal-clear lakes. The high road to Tammerfors seems to be borne on stepping stones across the surface of the water, upon a high and narrow ridge piled by a race of giants. It undulates like a switch-back railway, affording a panorama of ever-varying views, each surpassing the other in some peculiar feature of beauty. These ridges, which in Ireland are called *eskers*, and in Sweden *åsar*, are one of the most striking features of the Finnish landscape. They form a natural causeway over lake, marsh and dry land, and the road system of the country is based upon them.

On this early mid-August morning the sun was shining strongly. The dewdrops sparkled like millions of diamonds in the grass, among the meadow-sweet, blue-bells, clover, and cornflowers. On the low land by the lake side were long strips of rye, barley and oats, yellowing towards harvest, and patches of potatoes all in bloom. Cow-bells tinkled from the forest. In this part of Tavastland is some of the best agricultural land in the country, and the farmers are prosperous and comfortable.

We picked up passengers at various points as we went

along. From a villa like a Swiss chalet came a smart business man with a portfolio under his arm. He was escorted
to the garden gate by four merry children. At the cross-
roads were waiting two bronzed, fair-haired peasants,
with hands like shoulders of mutton. From a cottage came
a young woman, dressed in the fashion of the towns, with
a baby in her arm, and a large wooden bandbox. A sweet-
faced old grannie, with bare feet, and with a shawl over
her head, kissed the baby through the carriage window
and waved them adieu. I was puzzled by a portly, jolly-
looking, elderly gentleman, with gold-rimmed spectacles,
who was waiting at the end of a farm lane with a large
milk-can. He only travelled with us a few miles. A week
later I saw him again in Helsingfors, walking along the
pavement with the aplomb of a bank-director. He had
been re-visiting the ancestral farm and re-enacting the
tasks of his boyhood.

Scott made several visits to Finland. In 1924 arriving in
Helsinki by boat from Tallinn, he observes an interesting little
episode in Finnish history, caught quite by accident:

At Reval I boarded the *Ariadne*, from Stettin. As we
neared Helsingfors, after four hours of perfect voyag-
ing, signs of unusual excitement became manifest. I was
watching two torpedo destroyers manoeuvring near the
spirit-smuggling fleet, which anchors outside the three-
mile limit, and was wondering whether they were oper-
ating with the coastguards, when suddenly they wheeled
about and began to follow us up, one on the left and the
other on the right, till they came abreast. The bluejackets
lined up on the decks, and as they came within hailing
distance we could hear them shouting, 'Hei! Hei! Hei!
Suomi! Suomi! Suomi!' Only then did I learn that we had
on board a large contingent of the Finnish athletes who

had so greatly distinguished themselves at the Olympic Games a week before, at Paris. They were receiving an official welcome.

We approached the capital with a naval escort. Presently a hydroplane, emblazoned with the swastika on both wings, appeared and began to gyrate round us. Then a motor launch dashed past, throwing up a flashing wave of foam on either side. As we neared the grim gates of Sveaborg other craft appeared in great numbers – coastal steamers, small vessels that ply, like motor 'buses, among the island suburbs, motor boats, yachts, and little rowboats, with the rowers labouring frantically to gain a position to make their cheers heard. Every boat was decorated with bunting and overloaded to a degree that would have shocked Mr. Plimsoll. They all fell in to a procession behind the *Ariadne*, which displayed all its flags in acknowledgement of the welcome. As we entered the inner harbour, whistles, horns, hooters, blew until it seemed the heavens must rend.

Every place of vantage near the wharf was crowded with spectators, and there were dense rows of people all around the landing place. Cinema operators and camera snapshotters worked zealously. A civic potentate stepped forward and read a fervid oration out of his silk hat while the cameras were focused on him. A general took his place, and make a speech like a statesman addressing the House of Lords. The leader of the team descended the gangway amid delirious applause, and hat, kerchief and flag waving. He was immediately garlanded with a laurel wreath like a life-belt and shaken by the hand till all his bones must have rattled. The others landed and were likewise greeted with flowers and handshaking. Then, heroes though they were, they were led to the Customs Office, to make sure that they were playing no tricks on a grateful and adoring country. Finally they were conducted by twos to waiting automobiles, into each of which climbed four or five damsels, dressed in white and laden with flowers, 'to every man a damsel or two,' and carried off in triumph through the streets. It was two hours after our arrival before we could land.

These festivities were certainly not overdone. Finland had penty to celebrate, with eleven gold medals: Paavo Nurmi for the 1500m and 5,000m (which were held with only an hour between them) and for the cross-country; Ville Ritola for the 10,000m and the 1500m steeplechase; Albin Stenroos for the marathon; and the Finnish team (including Nurmi and Ritola) for the 3,000m and cross-country team events. There were twelve silver and seven bronze medals in addition.

Scott's account continues:

From the harbour one drives over well-paved streets, through the market place; past Ville Vallgren's beautiful fountain with four seals spouting jets of water towards a bronze Spirit of the Wave, who rises in the centre; along Norra Esplanade, with its attractive shops and its promenade shaded with lime trees; up a side street of high buildings with glittering shop-fronts; into the wide railway station square, with its clamantly modern architecture; and so to a luxurious hotel, which, in accordance with the ancient tradition of the country, is called the House of Society, *Societetshuset*. The Briton feels at once at home in Helsingfors. It is the civilisation with which he is familiar.

Scott is, for the moment, the last of the travellers for whom the Hotel Societetshuset represents civilisation.

Kay Gilmour

During the 1930s a stream of British visitors echoed Ransome's recognition of 'the spirit of the new Finland' and Dukes's admiration for Finland's 'model constitution'. Among them was Kay Gilmour, who calls Finland 'the Pioneer Republic'. She reveals fleetingly in her pocketbook *Finland* (1931) that she travelled with a group of journalists, probably in 1930. She shows a good sense of what visitors would want to know, but the information she gives, and even her statistics and figures, are comfortably digested into her narrative; it describes government, and many 'Aspects of Finnish Life', including social life, Finnish grammar, the sauna, and so forth. All this reveals a journalist of considerable skill, but what is striking about her book is its enthusiasm for *modern* Finland. She praises the Finnish Tourist Association, and the way in which it smooths the path of the traveller, but her real interests are clearly the social institutions. In particular it is childcare and education that attract her admiration; she calls Finland the 'Children's Paradise'.

A chapter on 'Europe's most up-to-date orphanage' (Sofianlehto) shows nicely her way of combining accurate description and admiration: after noticing 'the ultra-hygienic arrangement of separate chutes for clothes, and lifts for clean laundry', she describes 'the spacious kitchens where special food suitable for infants of such tender years is prepared under the direction of experts. The nurses' sunny dining-room . . . is situated next to its own kitchen.'

> Ascending to the first floor we come to the babies up to one year old. Here they may have artificial sunlight if required, though in that blaze of real sunlight it is impossible to conceive of its being necessary. Here on a balcony they take their fresh air and sleep as rhythmically as little

automatons. In fact, so entirely harmoniously does the system work, so automatically do the babies fall asleep at the right moment, and so exactly alike do they all look in their gingham crawlers, that I found myself wondering whether, after all, they had been live babies or merely contented dolls!

The second floor is built on the same principle as the first, but houses the children up to two or two and a half. All nurseries face due south and thus enjoy every available ray of sun. The cots lie ten on each side, and between the night nurseries are the day ones, provided with every possible toy suitable to the age. On the opposite side of the long corridors are bathrooms, sink-rooms, and kitchen, each bathroom so superlatively equipped for twenty children that it would take a volume to do their ingenuity justice.

The very top floor is all devoted to the nurses' quarters and sitting-room, housemaids' domain, and a quarantine wing.

Another chapter, entitled 'Where Children know no Tears', describes in comparable detail a visit to the Kindergarten Training Centre in Helsinki. 'As we traversed the various light and airy rooms it became apparent that the Finnish educationalists had taken the German idea and developed it to the highest point,' she writes, remarking that Helsinki alone has twenty-seven Ebenezer nursery schools. Each room at the Centre, she claims, 'merited a day's study'.

There was only one aspect of the New Nation which did not at all appeal to Gilmour: prohibition. She does not appear to have been a drinker herself; her objections are largely ideological. She describes an evening at a 'smart hotel in Helsinki' where her party 'declined all drinks' and noted the antics of those who did not:

The scene was a supper dance. The visitors, well-dressed and sober, might have been found in the best hotels of any civilised country. The orchestra was good, but a trifle un-inspired. That was at nine o'clock.

By ten the orchestra had 'warmed up', as is the wont with orchestras. One could not fail to be surprised at the extent of their exhilaration acquired on mere coffee. The dancing too grew more spirited, as the *tempo* quickened. People who before had kept sedately to their own tables were now mixing with complete strangers. Would-be partners besieged us as if we were the only guests left in Christendom. Dimmed and many-coloured lights alter-nated with the brilliancy of the massive chandeliers. The din grew.

By eleven o'clock the musicians had left their platform and were dancing among the audience. Astonishing to re-late, the quality of their music improved with their gyra-tions. Presently the *chef d'orchestre* waltzed over to our table, and having serenaded us with a haunting melody, took a sly peep into our coffee-pot. Then, with a wink – as one who would say, 'You can't hoax me' – danced away.

Inquiries explained his behaviour. We learned that beer was being served in milk-jugs, whisky in soda-water si-phons, wine in lemonade-bottles, and cocktails, etc., in coffee-pots.

Prohibition in Finland, many of the keenest temperance advocates admit, is a fiasco. What temperance societies had gained in peaceful propaganda they have lost by for-cible legislation. If this was introduced with a view to ob-taining a more all-round efficiency it has had the converse effect.

Gilmour introduces and describes virtually every area of Fin-land, but so skilfully does she write that it is not always clear whether her descriptions are first- or second-hand. With her account of Lapland there is no doubt: she came, she saw, she was conquered.

In Helsinki there had been 'nothing but discouragement'. The 'polite young man in the travel bureau' 'heaved a deep sigh, and with true Finnish politeness asserted "I will follow you with my thoughts."'

> And so, luggage in hand, we stood at the railway's end on an early October morning, at the Gate of Lapland, wondering if we, too, should be ultimately caught up by the wizardry of its silent beauty, which is said to magnetize the traveller so completely that in due course he abandons the complications of civilisation for Lapland solitude.

'Autumn was at her richest' as they set off from Rovaniemi in 'post-coach Number 66'; it was soon clear that the wizardry was going to work. At one level Gilmour describes practical details: the 'acrobatic feats' by which the driver dropped the postal packages into the roadside post boxes; the coffee break at 'Ornela', where, on finishing, each guest 'turned down his cup and placed thereon a two-mark piece'; the skill of the driver on 'so deeply rutted a road, across narrow bridges and on to primitive ferries'; reaching the 'spotless hostelry at Ivalo' 'illuminated only by the Northern Lights'.

The journalists' mission – travelling the full length of the Arctic Highway – was accomplished with their arrival at Pet-samo. Gilmour, though, had experienced something more: no traveller could have been more completely captivated. Her book concludes:

> Long after you are sitting in a London office – senses deadened by the ceaseless roar of traffic, nerves frayed by the vibration of an automatic drill in the road beneath – there will come back to you the memory of an intense still-ness which is nearer to God than anything you knew – the

exhalation of crystal clear air unpolluted by human inventions – the inspiration of the adventure of the only High Road in the Universe that leads to the magnetic Arctic.

Jim Ingram

With the arrival in Finland of Jim Ingram in 1931 we meet one of the travellers who were never going to go near a Seurahuone or any other grand hotel. Ingram was embarrassed even by the bank where he changed his money on arriving in Helsinki:

> . . . a huge palace of granite and marble, where I became uncomfortably aware that my size nine, hobnailed boots were hardly in keeping with the polished floor.

Clutching the two thousand marks for which he had exchanged his life savings of eight pounds, he went straight to the railway station, 'eager to be off into the wilds'.

Although born in Manchester, Ingram had grown up in Canada, which is where he got his taste for the carefree outdoor life. In particular he developed an 'interest in tramps and tramp life'. Back in Manchester in his late teens he became an obsessive autodidact; 'the instinct to write gripped me like a fever'. He was trying without success to make his way as a journalist when a newspaper editor gave him the advice he needed: 'you have not enough experience to draw on. Stories won't just come to you. You have to go out and get them.'

> The advice 'Never argue with editors – they know' prevented me from contradicting him, so instead I explained my plan of seeking adventure in far-off lands. When he asked which country I planned to visit first I replied:
> 'Finland.'
> 'Why?' he asked.
> I told him how once in Birkenhead docks I had seen a

big white sailing-ship moored to a quay, and, wandering on board, had spoken with big, laughing-eyed men who told strange tales of a little-known land of lakes and forests. It was the wildest land possible for me to reach with my scanty capital. Europe could wait until I had reached the bath-chair stage.

'Then this ought to interest you,' remarked the editor.

He gave me a newspaper cutting headed: 'GOVERN-MENT OF FINLAND COMPLETES ONLY ROAD IN WORLD LEADING TO THE ARCTIC OCEAN'. The paragraph announced the completion of the 'Great Arctic Highway', the most northerly motor-road in the world. This road, it was stated, was driven across the wilderness country of Finnish Lapland, and ended at a mysterious port on the Polar Sea, hundreds of miles north of the Arctic Circle.

'Now there should be a story in that road,' continued the editor. 'Why not go to the Arctic and get it?' That is what Ingram did:

I knew very little about Finland, and hardly a word of the language. I had no letters of introduction, nobody to vouch for me, and should be entirely 'on my own.' If I got into difficulties I must rely upon myself to get out of them . . .

So I started out, a pack on my back and eight pounds in my pocket, determined to reach the Polar Sea.

Ingram travelled very light, and slept in all sorts of unusual places. His travelling clothes were 'a Canadian lumberman's jacket, red sports shirt, khaki riding breeches, black boots and leggings'.

On the boat to Finland he had met a Finnish journalist who persuaded him that he should visit Valamo, the Orthodox monastery on an island out in Lake Ladoga; the train from

Helsinki took him to Sortavala, where he took the monks' steamer to Valamo. Two chapters of his book are devoted to this expedition. Valamo had changed since Clive-Bayley's description from the early 1890s: Ingram had imagined a relic of 'pre-soviet Russia', but it was now more of a holiday destination than a place of pilgrimage; 'like a plant whose roots have died,' another visitor remarked. Ingram was perhaps the last British visitor to record the view from the bell-tower:

> Below us was a most magnificent scene, an amazing tangle of buildings, where fantastic blue-and-gold Tartar domes, red roofs, green onion-shaped cupolas shimmered in the sunshine with a semi-barbarous, half oriental splendour.

It was here that he heard about Manssila, a 'forgotten place' where, he was told, primitive Karelians still really lived in 'the old style'. The fact that it was in the forbidden frontier area made a visit all the more appealing. It required a trip to Vyborg to obtain a pass, but within a few days he was on his way.

Tiny red houses and chalets, each perched on its own hill-top, lined the road. Grey wharves jutted out forlornly into Lake Ladoga, where blue and yellow double-ended boats were drawn up among the rushes. At first there were sweeping vistas of little well-tilled fields, and small villages where the red houses lay scattered about anyhow like bricks from a child's toy chest. Behind the houses the little cultivated patches of land went up the hillsides to where the bare rock showed; beyond were fenced-in scrubby areas where cows grazed. Women were working in the fields, bare-legged girls in white skirts and pink aprons, gathering in the hay with long wooden rakes.

Civilization was gradually left behind and the country became wilder. Karelia is a land of pine-clad moors and fir-covered bogs and swamps. The farms were concentrated in villages, islands of civilization in the forest, with miles of wilderness between. In Finland civilization was brought into close contact with the wild.

Our journey ended at Samli, a real frontier town, consisting of a single street lined with wooden buildings and a few lumbermen and soldiers lounging about. I spent the night at the inn, and having stored my rucksack there, started out the following morning to tramp through the woods to Manssila. 'Where the forests go on for ever' is a local saying. A man presently overtook me, an old fellow with a white beard and an axe slung at his hip. We came to a house, a rough log cabin, strong and sturdy like the brown-faced man who brought me a glass of water.

A couple of peasant carts came along and one of the drivers stopped to give me a lift. The other cart contained two women and a man. The men were dressed in blue shirts and trousers, the women in pink or blue dresses, knee-high leather boots, and had white handkerchiefs knotted round their heads. They laughed and chattered continually, chuckling at my attempts to reply to their questioning. The carts were long flat boxes mounted on wheels, drawn by horses resembling Suffolk punches. The carts had no springs but the box was filled with rags and old clothing, which absorbed the vibration – but not all of it!

On through the hot afternoon we journeyed till we came to a lake where they drove the horses straight over the bank into the water and up the other side, and here by a cross roads I left them. A few miles farther on I came to a clearing in the forest, and there before me lay Manssila, 'the forgotten place'. A wooden gate like those used at level crossings barred the road, with a military post on one side and a sentry box on the other.

Ingram was immediately arrested because of political suspicions caused by his red shirt. After being released he began a period 'out of time', as he worked for his food and keep, and adopted the patterns and rhythms of the life of the village.

It was late in the day when I started looking around for a place to sleep. The village contained neither inn nor lodging-house, so I studied the nearby farmhouses reflectively. Finally I walked up to the nearest one and knocked on the door.

A big pleasant-faced man answered my knock. In halting Finnish I asked if I could sleep there for the night. 'Passport,' said he. Obviously a lone stranger without any baggage – for my pack has been left at Salmi – and I had not even the proverbial toothbrush – needed investigating. I handed him my military pass and we squatted down on the front doorstep. He was so long examining it that I was just considering the advisability of going elsewhere when he made a move.

He led me into the house, which consisted of two rooms up and two down, and introduced me to his wife and daughter. Then he opened a door and bowed me into the best room of the house. It was a large square room, one corner of which was occupied by a large, white brick stove. Pots of geraniums stood on the window sills, and gilt-edged pictures depicting hunting scenes hung on the walls.

We sat down at the table and his wife brought in an enormous rye loaf, at least two feet long. She cut off several thick slices – one was nearly a meal in itself – and placed them on a plate, together with cold meat, jellied fish, and a jug of milk. Ruotsi – thus my host introduced himself – motioned to me to eat, and while I ate the family stood round watching me. Afterwards the woman brought glasses of tea, very pale and very hot, which we drank without milk in the Russian fashion. When we had finished our meal the women and children had theirs in the kitchen.

Ruotsi was a man of ideas, eager to learn, so I taught him the English names for the objects on the table, and he repeated these to everybody with whom he came in contact, as pleased as a child with a new toy. He got out an atlas and made me point out my route, from Manchester to Manssila. 'Maanchasttare – Manssila, Manssila – Maanchasttare,' he repeated solemnly.

Somebody had gone out into the fields and announced my arrival, and Ruotsi's two elder sons, sturdy lads as big as myself, came trooping in. In twos and threes other neighbours joined the party, and everybody was laughing and talking at once. And I, who had once suffered from an inferiority complex, sat there in the middle of them and laughed and talked and explained, not in the least self-conscious.

We crossed the fields to the next farm where a man who was chopping wood greeted me in broken English. His name was Yrjö – or George – and he was a timber-cruiser by trade, his job being to select suitable trees for felling. While we were talking his wife brewed coffee, which we drank in the best room. We went the round of the village, stopping at several more houses for coffee and cakes, so that by the time we started back for the farm I was full to capacity.

I slept with the boys in the hayloft above the byre, a big roomy place smelling of men and animals. Half workshop, half bedroom it was, with a big bench littered with machinery on one side and two beds on the other. I slept soundly on a big sleigh filled with straw, while beneath us in the bottom storey the cattle slept noisily and cowbells clattered every time they moved. Chickens wandered in and out, and whenever an egg was laid in the straw we knew about it . . .

The problem of what to do was solved for me because

when I returned to the farm I found all the family engaged in haymaking, so I joined in. The hay had already been cut and now it had to be stacked. We were divided into three parties. The first party, of which I was one, gathered the hay into piles with the aid of long wooden rakes. The second party drove six-foot wooden stakes into the ground. The third party, armed with pitchforks, stacked the piles of hay round the stakes.

A break of a few minutes was made for breakfast when everybody trooped into the house to partake of the bread, cheese and milk standing on the table. The children had finished the chores, chopping wood and drawing water, taking the cattle to pasture, and now they joined us. Then back to work, under a sun so hot that the men worked stripped to the waist. Soon the field looked as though an army of monoliths had been planted on it.

At twelve o'clock – by the sun – we stopped for dinner. On the table stood a big bowl of fish soup and a pile of plates. As guest I helped myself first, then Ruotsi took his share, then the boys, and finally the women and children. An appetizing pudding followed, made of rye baked brown, eaten with sugar and melted butter. Food was wholesome and plentiful and nobody was overburdened with table manners. Everybody sat down just as they were, the men clad only in trousers, and dipped into anyone else's dish if they fancied it.

There was still work to be done after dinner, so the mistress of the house carefully locked the front door and then hung the key on a nail outside. I learned that this custom originated to keep bears from entering the house if the doors were left open or unfastened. The Carelians were a lighthearted, cheerful crowd, and the work was accompanied by songs and jokes. During the hottest part of the day we rested in the shadow of the hay, watching the activities of our neighbours. A metal water tank mounted on wheels with a soldier squatted on top came lumbering along behind a sleepy horse. Once a motor-car full of students came roaring out of the blue. They were visiting the frontier under the auspices of the educational authority. After watching us work, and asking questions, and making notes, and scrutinizing my red shirt, they went roaring off again.

Twice a day we went down to a small lake to swim, and undressed on a jetty while various spectators, male and female, sat on the bank and watched. When we went there the first time the men, ever polite, waited until I was bare before indicating that I go first. I did not fancy the idea but dived in, through water deep and cold, and put up the best show possible. Afterwards we lay on the grassy bank and sunbathed. Soon the whole male population of the village was sprawled naked on the grass, including half a dozen soldiers whose uniforms were piled beside a signboard prohibiting soldiers from bathing in the lake. Nearby a few optimists were fishing, though what they hoped to catch with all that splashing going on was problematical.

About this time the women would quietly disappear and by the time their menfolk had leisurely dressed and ambled home the evening meal would be prepared. Evening was the time for paying social calls, shopping and amusements. The Carelians lived up to the old Finnish proverb 'There is nothing so much as time'. I became friendly with Toivo the storekeeper, who was proud of his collection of books.

This was a modern frontier, a rifle in one corner of the room and a radio loudspeaker in the other. Here, while the Moscow station was blaring propaganda I would sit eating *siika* or jellied fish, and drinking *must*, which is like the blackcurrant tea which they make in Suffolk. Toivo had an English phrase book and by its means we were able to carry on intermittent conversations.

Finally Ingram returned to Sortavala to begin his journey to Lapland. He took the train to Vaala and then, like so many travellers before him, travelled down the rapids to Oulu on board a 'tar boat' (the tar, he notes, 'is carried by rail'). He continued by train to Rovaniemi, 'a peculiar blending of back-woods settlement and modern city'. From there he finally set out for the Polar Sea, a journey which involved many further detours and other forms of diversion.

In a shop on the main street I bought bread, butter, sug-ar, coffee, corned beef in tins, a *rankinen* or tent-shaped mosquito net, and a bottle of vile-smelling mosquito-tar which was guaranteed to keep even the most ferocious insects at bay. I walked along the river till I came to a red bridge, where a signpost stating POLAR SEA 531 KILO-METRES marked the beginning of the Great Arctic High-way. I turned my back on Rovaniemi and started north along the Arctic road.

I doubt if ever again I shall recapture the thrill which I felt when I first started out for the Polar shore. The fasci-nation of the wild place gripped me, so that I walked as if under a spell, till there was only me and the road, the for-est and the sunlit sky. Yet I was not alone, for this friendly trinity marched with me, and most diverting companions they proved to be. For this was one of those rare magic days which we remember all our lives, when the whole world is bright and gay and beautiful and nothing can go wrong.

I came across a signpost with 'Arctic Circle' inscribed on it in four languages. A yellow motor-bus passed me bound for the Polar Shore, which it would reach in fifteen hours. How many days – or weeks – it would take me to reach the same destination I did not know, but I would not have exchanged my adventure with its delightfully uncertain future for the most comfortable seat on that north-bound bus.

His first lift was by lorry to Sodankylä, and next day he was well on the way to his first Lapland objective, the gold-fields at Laanila.

The landscape became sterner as we approached the Maanselkä watershed. The woods began to thin out. The road climbed over a high, bare plateau, where wooden posts marked the way. This was the *tundra*, the barren, stone wastelands of the Lapps. We came to a lone red bridge in the heart of the wilderness and the lorry halted. 'Lannila,' said the driver laconically, so I asked him how many kilometres it was to the nearest village. '*Neljäkym-mentäydeksän*,' he replied with a grin, and by the time I had figured this out to be forty-nine kilometres he was miles away.

I followed a track through the woods and came upon several log cabins clustered about a grass-grown road. The camp was surrounded by tall woods and exploring these I came upon more buildings lost in the trees, piles of rusty machinery, and deep shafts covered with rotting boards. From a hillside I looked down into a deep valley through which ran a brawling stream that was evidently a tributary of the Ivalo River. I heard men talking down below, heard the clang of their metal tools against rock.

At Laanila he met Vilho, 'a long, lean individual with an old felt hat pulled low over his eyes. He had a face the colour of old saddle leather and a pair of startling blue eyes.' Vilho taught him how to prospect for gold and pan for it. The two of them embarked on a prospecting trip along one of the tributaries of the Ivalo river. They stayed in a Lapp encampment for some days before, without explanation, Vilho vanished. Next he met Carl, a young itinerant German artist who had been wandering in Lapland for three years. He decided to join Ingram on the next leg of his adventure: his second objective was 'to tramp overland to the Tana [in Norwegian Finnmark] and watch the migration of the great reindeer herds'. After numerous adventures Ingram dropped out, fell seriously ill with fever and bronchitis, and struggled, eventually on all fours, to the orphanage at Riutula (today the Youth Centre Vasatokka), and from there was taken by boat and car to hospital in Ivalo. It was 'staffed wholly by women, who spoke only Finnish. Whenever I wished to explain what was wrong with me I had to resort to dumb show.'

After a fortnight in hospital I was discharged, so immediately I looked for a lorry to take me north. I had less than a pound in my pocket, and the sensible thing, of course, would be to turn back, but I was more than half-way to the Polar Sea and was determined to go on.

His final night on the outward journey was spent in a pearl hunters' tent in Petsamo. He escaped from their drunken fight to fulfil the ambition which he had conceived in Manchester. He heard

the rumble of an approaching lorry, and a few minutes later it came roaring out of the darkness. I stood by the crimson glow and waved my hand for a lift, and the big vehicle stopped long enough for me to scramble on board and then went into the darkness again. We passed through a wild region of small lakes and rocky peaks and lichen-covered rocks, where grim grey hillsides rose out of a straggling growth of dwarf birches and creeping juniper.

The nearness of the coast became evident in the greater frequency of the settlements. Villages slipped by – Näsykkä – Parkkina – Trifona – in quick succession. Now we were rumbling along beside Petsamo Fjord, through which the main river of the territory empties its water into the sea. We hurtled through a rock gorge, the last kilometre post on the Great Arctic Highway – Liinahamari, fishing village in Seventy North!

I had reached the Polar Sea!

A few minutes later the manager of the inn was surprised to find himself accosted by a dirty unshaven apparition who demanded a bed, and a few minutes later that same apparition was snugly asleep in a bunk in a big dormitory. I was so very tired!

At midday I walked over the hills to Nurmensätti. It was a vast treeless land of grey rock and bog. I came to a sheltered bay with a few sheds, a pier and rack for drying fish. A small turf hut served as a chapel. Inside was an iron box on a plank, and outside were a few graves with broken oars and axes on them. Once during the fishing season a priest came from St. Trifon's Monastery to say Mass. I stood for a long time looking at the waters of the Arctic Ocean. Here ended the road, the most romantic road, which I followed so far. Now I stood 333 miles north of the Arctic Circle, on the very edge of the world. I said to myself proudly: 'Well, *that* job is done!' Then I turned back.

Unable to get a lift, he borrowed a pound to get him to Rovaniemi by bus. Here the final stage of his travels began:

That evening I boarded the train to Helsinki, using the last of the ticket entitling me to fifteen hundred miles of travel which I had bought in Viborg weeks before. What I should do when I arrived in the capital I had not the slightest idea, but I had the vague notion that the British Consul might be able to help me. The train was crowded, and I was sitting there reading one of Miss Lipponen's books when a voice asked: 'May I sit in this seat beside you?' and I looked up to find a young Finnish student standing beside me . . .

Michael was a tall, bespectacled young man of studious appearance who had just returned from a tramping trip among the high mountains on the Norwegian border. He was feeling sick after the long bus journey across Lapland, so I dosed him with a couple of aspirins and we then discussed philosophy, he from the academic, I from the severely practical point of view. When he heard that I was studying life in Finland he invited me to spend a few days at his home in Oulu.

'I should be glad to have you as my guest,' he said.

It was past midnight when we arrived at Oulu, and we had to walk three miles out to the Anttilas' summer home (their town house being closed during the summer), but by this time I was used to arriving at people's homes at odd hours of the day and night and it did not seem incongruous to sit down to a meal at two in the morning. Then to bed under the rafters of this big old wooden house, with the roaring of the great Oulu River to lull us to sleep . . .

I spent several pleasant days at Michael's home when Fate solved a problem which had been puzzling me: how to return to England when I had only a shilling in my pocket? We were wandering about Oulu harbour one day when I saw an English cargo steamer moored to a wharf so I promptly went on board to inquire whether I could work my passage home. But Captain Southcombe of the *Cedartree* was not very hopeful, for he was already carrying two passengers and had no room to spare.

'Sit down and have a cup of tea, lad,' he invited. 'Tell us where you have bobbed up from so suddenly.'

So with a cup of tea on one knee and a plate full of bread and jam on the other, I told him of my long pilgrimage to the Polar Sea, of Palamo and Ruotsi's farm on the forbidden frontier, of life among the gold-miners and the Lapp reindeer-herders, of hospital and Petsamo, all the things you have read of in this book. Soon I realized that in addition to the captain and the steward I had an appreciative audience which included the mate, the chief engineer and a couple of seamen.

When I finished Captain Southcombe sighed, and said:

'What a yarn you can tell. Oh, well, I suppose we can find a corner for you somewhere. You'll be the rummest ordinary seaman that's ever been signed on this ship.'

'You're a sport,' I said.

'Better get ashore and collect your kit, Captain South-combe added. 'We sail in an hour.' . . .

Late that night I peered out through one of the *Cedar-tree's* port-holes; but saw only a vast expanse of water stretching far away. Finland had vanished.

This was the end of Ingram's first adventure, but it is not the end of his book, nor was it the last view that he had of Finland. Soon after his return to Manchester he set off again, this time working as a deckhand aboard Sven Erikson's four-masted barque *Herzogin Cecilie*, sailing from Belfast to Uusikaupunki, on what was destined to be that famous ship's last passage to Finland. He went to Mariehamn to pay homage to the remaining great sailing ships, and then set off for Lapland again, finally reaching Kirkenes, and working his passage home from there on a freighter. But that is another story.

F. J. North

Only a few years separate the Finnish travels of F. J. North from those of Ingram, but a greater contrast could hardly be contrived than that between a solitary, carefree, impecunious adventurer who thinks nothing of sleeping in a barn, and a rather pedantic academic geologist on a family holiday. North covers many of the same routes as Ingram, but never duplicates his experiences.

Leaving school at fourteen, North had studied geology in evening classes, and finally taken an external degree from London University with first-class honours. He worked for forty-two years at the National Museum of Wales, for the last thirty as keeper of the Department of Geology. Among his 200 scholarly, geological articles and dozen books was *Finland in Summer*, which came out in 1938. Markedly different from all his other published work, it nonetheless contains a good measure of geology: no other British traveller is so attentive to terrain and rocks.

'I have tried to portray the country,' North writes, 'as it appeared to a perfectly ordinary English family on holiday bent, but sufficiently inquisitive to enquire into he meaning and significance of what it saw, during fifty long summer days.' We learn nothing about the family, which he refers only as his 'companions'; he writes in the first person plural, but mentions his wife only once, when he describes her problems with a Finnish teapot. From the 1890s the regular steamer service from England had made summer tours in Finland popular, so it is puzzling that North's book seems to be the only published account of a British family holiday.

Whereas Ingram's writing is at times almost conversational, North's style is formal, and even severe: 'So well is the city concealed by the irregularities of the coast that you come upon Helsinki rather suddenly,' he writes. A seasoned academic author, he explains as well as describing: 'Many other features of the Finnish scenery assume significance in the light of our enquiry into the geological history of the land.' For all its austerity, *Finland in Summer* is full of interest. The range of North's knowledge is amazing – not just a clear and accurate knowledge of Finnish history, but a highly appreciative account of Finnish art and literature. (It was, he reveals, his second visit to Finland.) He has, refreshingly, provided his own photographs rather than the predictable gallery supplied by the Finnish Tourist Board. Typical subjects are 'Washer women at Porvoo', 'Suursaari: getting water from a shallow well', 'Fuel for the railway engines, at Vaala', 'Droskies at Kuopio' and 'A fence and an ant-hill in the woods near Vaala'. There is even an illustration of a Helsinki tram ticket, with an interpretation: 'issued at 18 o'clock on the fifth day of the month'. The ticket indicates all the stops.

Fifty days took the family first from Helsinki by boat to Porvoo, then out to Suursaari. This island, 'where foreign visitors seldom come', he thought 'a little primitive', and for that reason all the more worth visiting; North's description makes it sound very like Sark, yet within a few years it would become the most heavily fortified island in the Baltic, with Finland, Russia and Germany in contention. The steamer took them round several other islands before heading for Koivisto, 'a convenient landing place for Viipuri'. From there they headed north, including popular tourist spots in the east, then onward to Kuopio, Kaajani and Oulu. The final leg took them right up to the Norwegian border, which they crossed but which 'has no place in this account of Finland'. North was at times overwhelmed by the beauty and peace of the lake district; a calm evening on a lake steamer moves his scientist's prose towards poetry:

> The reflections are beautiful at all times, but superlatives fail to describe their charm in the evening, when the sun shines right into the heart of the forest, throwing into sharp relief the inner trees, and making their bark – the rich red of the pine and the silvery white of the birch – appear to be almost luminous, picking out the detail of every single leaf, or cone, or needle.

He is aroused especially by Imatra, where 'the Rapids were altogether too great to be comprehended'; the bridge, 'as a symbol of man's triumph over nature . . . seems positively impudent'.

North provides the first English description of Koli. I remember Koli as being perhaps the most beautiful place I ever visited in Finland in the 1960s; North's experiences suggest that before the age of the motor it was virtually inaccessible. Sir George Renwick wrote early in the century that getting off a boat there was 'like being put down on a desert island'. This was the furthest off the beaten track that the North family ventured.

> The day was wet, and the road to Koli, part of which had not long been constructed, was muddy and rutty, and the signs of human habitation seemed to be even less frequent than usual. We started . . . with a 'bus full of people; but from time to time folk got out, as often as not where there seemed to be no obvious reason for their doing so, until you noticed the inconspicuous track along which they disappeared into the woods . . .

> At last the 'bus was empty, save for ourselves, and when the forest seemed to be at its densest, the road at its muddiest, and the rain at its heaviest, the vehicle stopped, and without a word, except words of surprise on our part which were not understood, the driver indicated that we must alight, and putting our bags on the stones at the side of the road, he drove away.

> Recollections of things that had happened to travellers in unfrequented regions came crowding into our minds, and we wondered what was coming next, for some of those who had got out before us had guns and some had particularly efficient-looking axes. We had no idea where we were, for the road we had followed for the last hour or two was not on the map we carried, and even if anyone had been in sight, it is hardly likely that we should have been able to explain our plight. To 'sit tight' and see what

happened seemed to be the wisest course to adopt, and almost before we had had time to arrive at that conclusion, our troubles were over. A second 'bus came along and drew up beside us: the driver jumped down and began to stow our bags in the little saloon-like back compartment of the vehicle, to the obvious discomfort, albeit not annoyance, of the occupants, smilingly bowed us in, and away we went, at full speed along the muddy road.

After a very few minutes we swung away into a side lane and swished along through forest that seemed more nearly virgin that any we had traversed earlier in the day, and then, after a time, we drew up at cross roads where there were a cottage, a general store, a petrol pump and about a dozen people. The latter all began to help unload the 'bus, and once more our bags lay on the roadside.

Was *this* Koli, we asked ourselves – in some consternation, it must be confessed – for it seemed hardly a spot in which to make a lengthy stay in such weather. We were evidently understood, because one man went to our bags and patted them as if to indicate that it was quite in order for them to be where they were, and then he pointed down the road, in the direction from which we had come. Hardly a minute elapsed before along came a very small 'bus with a very full complement of passengers, and it was marked Koli. Were all these people by the roadside hoping to travel? If so who was to be left behind? Actually, no one was marooned, for it transpired that the little crowd had merely gathered at the cross roads for the day's diversion – the passing of the 'buses – and we had a send-off as cheery as if we had been highly esteemed local residents. On this 'bus we found a time-table, and the mystery of the morning was explained: instead of being the victims of inefficiency, we were saving hours by an extremely well-timed series of cross-country services.

The road got worse as we passed on to more recently made portions, consisting principally of large stones and mud, and at last, after a stiff climb towards the mist that descended as low as the tops of the trees, we drew up at a smooth gravelled clearing in the woods, with a petrol pump (in such circumstances a welcome sign of civilisation) on one side, and on the other a flight of concrete steps that seemed to fade away into the mist. The driver now asked for our fares – hitherto the question of payment had not arisen at all, and no one had asked to see our tickets.

From the bus stop they climbed the steps into the mist to the '*Upper Koli Inn,* and a delightful temporary home it proved to be'.

Their departure was as eventful as their arrival, and they came close to missing their train at Vuonislahti:

As we approached the bottom of the hill we were met by a woman and a girl who indicated in an unmistakable manner that we should hurry, but we could see no necessity for this, as there was still a quarter of an hour before the scheduled time for the departure of the boat. Moored at the landing stage was a small but smart-looking motor-boat, together with a smaller and anything but smart-looking rowing boat with a motor attachment; the former was empty but the latter was full to overflowing – at least so it seemed, but no vessel or vehicle proved to be full in Finland when there was anyone desirous of getting in, and the anxiety to accommodate the newcomer contrasted strongly and pleasingly with the air of sole-ownership like that so frequently displayed by the occupants of a railway compartment in most other countries.

We made our way towards the smart empty vessel, but found that it was out of order and that somehow or other we must drop into the shabby full one, floating quite three feet below us. This gymnastic feat accomplished, the heavily-laden craft chugged out into the lake. Once well away from the landing stage we realised that the lake was larger than it seemed, for although the shore we had left slipped rapidly away, a long time elapsed before the opposite shore seemed to come appreciably nearer. Seen from the lake, the Koli hills rise magnificently from above the forests which clothe their flanks, and in the almost total absence of anything that by comparison could suggest their size, the looked as impressive as many of the Swiss and Austrian mountains – those with rounded contours, not frost-serrated ridges – seen in similar circumstances: it was possible then to understand the esteem with which Koli is regarded by the Finns, and to realise that metres are not of necessity a measure of magnificence.

From the furtive glances which passengers made at their watches it was apparent that doubt was being entertained as to whether the journey would be made in time, and from the frequency with which first one person and then another would peep into the box that contained the motor, and tinker with the works, it was evident that everything was being done to increase the speed – here, at last, was the explanation of the apparently unreasonable anxiety to expedite our arrival at the Koli landing stage. Eventually, after about an hour, we drew up alongside some smooth rocks at the edge of the forest, and in almost less time than it takes to write, the passengers, all save ourselves, had jumped ashore and had disappeared among the trees. The boat quickly made off again in the direction of Koli, and we, with our bags, were left alone at the edge of the woods, except for one solitary man sitting upon a log.

Beyond the fact that there was obviously only one path to take, we did not know in which direction the station lay, or how far away it was: two things were certain – our train was to leave in less than a quarter of an hour, and the man on the log was trying to tell us to hurry after our fellow passengers. There seemed nothing else to do but to take his advice and hope for the best – which we did. Soon a man approached us with a little hand-cart, and with the comprehensive smile that serves when speech is not possible, relieved us of our luggage, went off at a trot, and was quickly out of sight.

When the path brought us at last clear of the forest, the porter was nowhere to be seen, and there was a choice of three country roads with nothing to indicate which was the one we should take. Fortunately a man was working in a nearby field, and a shouted enquiry *Rautatie* (railway) produced an indication of the road we were to follow, and very soon we came in sight of the station, where our bags awaited us, and where the train was arriving punctually to the second.

The North family would have a very different experience today. 'Near the top,' Wikipedia tells us, 'there's the Heritage Center Ukko and Hotel Koli. In the summer, two long scenery lifts are working in Koli.' They could also try 'Finland in Winter', which benefits from the four ski lifts and six ski slopes.

The train took them, eventually, to Vaala, a journey taking eighteen and a half hours. From there they took the shortened tourist version on the rapids boats, heading north again from Oulu. In Rovaniemi, 'a very wooden town – even the pavements are of wood', they were 'accosted by a man who who said, "You are English? Can I help you?"' This was a local shopkeeper, who became their 'self-constituted guide' for the morning. When they later visited his shop he explained that he had never been outside his own country – his knowledge of England was derived entirely from books and magazines, no opportunity of reading which he ever lost. In a little room upstairs was his collection of books – a collection which would not have looked out of place in a professor's study; most of them were very substantially bound, for he believed that the cover of a book should have some relation to the esteem in which its contents were held. It is through such men – men who have shown that culture, and earning one's living by manual labour or by conducting a small business are not incompatible – that the Finnish nation has been able to grow from a down-trodden and largely illiterate peasantry into a cultured and progressive people.

The Norths went more or less as far north as it was possible to go:

> The road to Inari – about twenty-four miles from Ivalo – is interesting in the extreme: it goes past little lakelets and waterways, mostly with boulder- strewn shores, between tree-clad hillocks, past pools so still as to look like mirrors spread upon the ground, past conical erections of poles that are the frameworks of Lappish winter huts, and, perhaps most interesting of all to the foreign visitor, past reindeer more numerous than he has seen them farther south.

From Inari they went north to Liinahamari, and then by way of a thrilling journey on the Paatsjoki river to Kolttaköngäs (both places now belong to Russia, and are no longer accessible to travellers). This was North's last image of Finland.

> At last, just above the magnificent Kolttaköngäs Rapids the steersman makes for the bank on the left, the luggage and the parcels that have been sent by the boat are loaded

onto the cart, the motor-boat driver puts on a new hat and becomes the postman, while the passengers are left to walk through the birch woods to the inn, about half a mile away. Here in homely, comfortable, and topical surroundings, a stay of any length will pass too all quickly.

Halliday Sutherland

Soon after completing his medical studies at Edinburgh University, Sutherland came under the influence of Sir Robert William Phillip, a pioneer of modern anti-tuberculosis schemes. He had published two books on the subject, and in Finland he gained further first-hand experience of the disease and of its treatment. In middle age he turned his experiences in medicine and in travel to good account to become a popular author, while remaining in medical practice. There are few second-hand bookshops in Britain where you do not come across copies of his two autobiographies, *The Arches of the Years* and *A Time to Keep*. His *Lapland Journey*, first published in 1938, was immediately reprinted and went through four more editions. It is easy to account for Sutherland's success: he has an attractive anecdotal style, and an unusual ability to be informative and personal at the same time. 'He explored no new pathways of human experience,' writes his biographer, 'but his idiosyncrasies and pugnacious judgements were highly entertaining.'

Having an interest in the incidence and treatment of tuberculosis, Sutherland visited hospitals and pondered over medical statistics, noting that the 'death rate in Finland is more than double that of Britain'. Something which ought to be of particular interest in Britain today is his account of how Finland had dealt with the problem of TB in cattle; the unpasteurised milk he enjoyed there was one of his particular pleasures. In Helsinki he admired 'the four most modern hospitals in Europe', comparing them to those in London with their 'antiquated buildings . . . in the midst of petrol-laden air'. It was not only in the hospitals that the cleanliness impressed him; 'you could eat food off the pavements of Helsinki,' he writes. He is alert to social conditions, to the 'relatively small' discrepancies between the rich and poor, the absence of slums and of any 'submerged tenth' or 'problem class'.

Sutherland was another of the travellers who was indebted to Professor Hirn as guide, raconteur and source of information. He spent some time with him in Helsinki, and records their conversations in great detail. Describing a sightseeing trip, he tactfully claims to be 'no judge of railway stations', but considers the Diet House 'one of the world's finest buildings'. He was taken to sign the visitors book at the Academic Bookshop, where there was a display of his own books, two of them in translation.

Lapland, not Helsinki, was Sutherland's goal, and he was fortunate to find in Helsinki a guide and companion:

> At the Tourist Association a Finnish girl, speaking perfect English (so perfect that some of our island race sometimes ask, to her annoyance, 'Are you really a native?'), explained that the Great Arctic Highway had been cleared of snow and that buses were now running, although in places the banks of snow were twelve feet deep. She added that if I could wait for a few days their Director, Mr. Wolter Stenbäck, was going north and would cross Lapland by reindeer sledges.
>
> 'A great opportunity!' added Professor Hirn.
>
> 'Of course I'll wait. When does he start?'
>
> 'I don't know, but – oh, here is Mr. Stenbäck.'
>
> I turned and was introduced to a spare man of medium height, clean-shaven, with iron-grey hair, strong features, and penetrating eyes. His expression was serious, and in his smile there was something, I know not what, that re-

minded me of De Valera. Both had been revolutionaries. He led the way to a large roller map on the wall, 'I am going to Kauliranta, the railhead on the Swedish frontier, then by bus 118 miles to Muonio, and from there with reindeer to Enontekiö and across to Inari. If you'd like –'

'I'd like nothing better.'

He turned and gave me a swift intent glance. I knew of old that look. It was the 'once over' that is usually given by sergeants-major and inspectors of police. 'It's going to be rough,' he said.

I nodded.

'Do you understand? Definitely rough.'

'Yes, I understand – and I want it.'

'Very well, what kit have you got?'

'A pair of gum boots –'

'Useless! In fact, dangerous! What else?'

'A leather flying coat.'

'Also useless, in that cold! What else?'

'A woollen Balaclava helmet and leather flying helmet.'

'That may be useful, and I'll lend you whatever else you need. Don't bother about your kit.'

'Thank you very much. And when do we start?'

'On Sunday week by the 11.15 train. Meet me at the railway station.' He bowed formally and disappeared into an inner office. I say disappeared, because our short interview had left me with the impression of a man who could appear and disappear with equal facility.

Explorations of Helsinki, and studies of Finnish history, architecture and food occupied Sutherland for the intervening time.

On my last evening in Helsinki I had supper at the Royal restaurant, where my companion was a Finnish girl-graduate, aged twenty-five, who had specialised in

Social Science. To her I remarked that there seemed to be
no night-life in the capital.

'There's night-life if you know where to look,' said she,
'and I'll take you there, if you like.'

So off we walked through a maze of narrow and badly
lit streets to a doorway above which red neon lights spelt
the name of the café. As we ascended a steep straight staircase my companion said archly, 'What about your reputation?' to which I made the obvious retort, 'What about
your own?' for I knew her to be a respectable girl and
engaged to be married. I pointed out that if by chance we
were recognised in such a place, we had as much right to
be there as the person who knew us.

This café is on the first floor, and glass partitions, rising
from the stair landing to the ceiling, partially divide the
place. On a small platform between the front wall and the
partition a pianist and violinist played to the customers
on either side. These are musicians whom we should pity,
as only an unrequited love of music could lead to their
playing in places such as this. All around the walls and
alongside the glass partitions were tables and chairs for
two. We took the only vacant table, and an elderly wait-
ress brought the list of wines, beers and soft drinks. No
spirits are sold in the café. On each table was a telephone,
and on the otherwise undecorated wall the number of the
table was painted in large figures. This was new to me,
and my companion explained, 'If you want to talk to a girl
you telephone to the table where she's sitting. She doesn't
know who is telephoning, and so you can have quite a
long flirtation before inviting her to your table – if you
decide to do so.'

'Wouldn't it be quicker to go to her table?'

'That would be considered very bad manners, and the
management forbid it. There is etiquette in these affairs.'

Sutherland's interest in social medicine did not slacken even in such attractive company. He asked his 'guide' about the shop-girl prostitutes they could see in the café; she explained the economic background to their activities, adding 'we've got twice as much V.D. as they have in Denmark'.

On the train to Lapland Sutherland was fascinated to discover that the restaurant-car was a relic of the 'Compagnie Internationale des Wagon-Lits'. Since there was no covered gangway to get to this car, he was glad that the speed did not exceed thirty-three miles an hour, and said so to Stenbäck. 'Well, so far no one has ever fallen out of these trains,' he replied comfortingly. They reached Kauliranta after more than twenty-five hours travelling, and immediately boarded a bus for Muonio. (It is a challenge for a non-geographer to follow Sutherland's route through Lapland, despite – and partly because of – the end-paper map. His names of places, rivers and lakes bear only intermittent resemblance to anything that is found on modern maps.) In Muonio Stenbäck gave him his first lesson about Lapland:

> The bus, seated for twenty passengers, after frequent stops now contained thirty, some of them sitting on the floor and others on each other's knees. Yet there was a limit to overcrowding, and the driver smilingly refused a man who stopped the bus with the intention of putting on several hundredweight of loose machinery.
>
> 'In Helsinki,' said Stenbäck, 'an overcrowded bus would be stopped by the police. Here we are in the wilds, and it does not matter. In this land people are accepted or rejected on their merits. Titles or degrees may be used, but only to distinguish one person from another. In themselves they carry no privileges. There is only one law here – the Law of the Wild.'
>
> 'Yes, and what other law could there be – with only twenty policemen in a country the size of Scotland? What's

the use of a policeman if he's two hundred kilometres away? The Law of the Wild is more effective.' . . .

At 8pm and in darkness we reached the inn at Muonio. In some countries it is difficult to define the difference between hotels and inns, but in Lapland I found a clear line of demarcation between the two. At hotels there is indoor sanitation, whereas at inns the latrines are out of doors. At Muonio there was a door on the ground-level from which fourteen steps ascended to a platform on which were two seats side by side. Far below was the manure heap from the cattle byre, and so the height of the latrine saved labour. At the Orphanage at Riantula there were steps to ascend and six seats side by side. For the benefit of those who have experienced the dreadful outdoor sanitation of southern France and Spain, be it said that in Lapland these places were scrupulously clean. Moreover, in the dark winters days and nights many adults of the same sex and all children prefer to go in the company of others. There are dangers of being over-refined, and if children are taught that in this natural function there is nothing of which to be ashamed, they escape many physical and psychological troubles in later life.

At supper – consisting of oatmeal porridge, cold reindeer meat, bread, butter, cheese and milk – Stenbäck announced that we would start for Hetta in reindeer sledges at six o'clock next morning.

'The guide wanted to start at ten to-night, but I though we had better have a good sleep. You will be up at five.'

Then and then only did I realise that I was expected to drive my own reindeer. Up to that moment I had visualised a sledge with a driver, preferably a beautiful girl, and a passenger . . .

From Muonio the plan was to sledge with reindeer to Inari. Stenbäck proved to be a strict and meticulous instructor.

Sutherland gives very detailed accounts of the practical aspects of travelling – of the special sort of hay used to line their boots, the ointments to prevent frost-bite on the face, and so forth. He has a whole chapter on the techniques of reindeer-driving, enlivened by descriptions of his successes and failures. Among the places where they stopped was Stenbäck's home, a Lapp farm where he was building a house for his retirement. Earlier they had arrived at a house at 3 a.m. to find it locked – a thing unheard of in Lapland.

'They're probably away from home,' I suggested.

'No,' said Stenbäck, 'this door is locked from the in-side,' and he banged on the wall with a stone. This woke at least one of the occupants, and a woman opened the door to let us in. She then roused her husband and they lit a fire on which we could make our coffee. He had a small reindeer farm and was also the local postman. Twice a week at his house the post-sledge in winter, and the post-rider in summer, left the local mail, which the farmer-post-man delivered.

As coffee was being made I looked out of the kitchen window and saw what gave me some anxiety – the snow was yellow.

Sutherland was afraid that he was 'in for snow-blindness', but Stenbäck diagnosed tiredness:

I removed my fur coat, made a pillow of the R.A.F. hel-met, and was asleep before I had time to calculate that during the past forty-six hours I had only slept for four. When Stenbäck awoke me the others had finished their supper and were asleep. I rose, drank a cup of coffee, ate a slice of reindeer tongue in aspic – very good indeed, a great delicacy – and returned to the deep dreamless sleep of physical exhaustion.

They made a brief detour to visit to Riantula, the orphanage on the shore of Muddusjärvi, where Ingram had crawled to safety some years before.

Often in London, poring over maps of Lapland, I had wanted to see this Children's Home to which, according to the guide-book, it was difficult for fishermen to make their way in summer. It stood on the top of open rising ground above the level of the lake, and at the foot of a hill covered with pines. A one-storied wooden building, it was larger inside than one would have thought after seeing the out-side. A dozen or more children, boys and girls, were play-ing on the snow outside the front door, and curtsied when they saw us. The eldest, a fat boy, aged about eleven, came forward, placed the toe of his right boot behind the heel of the left, bobbed a curtsey, and smilingly shook hands. All these children appeared to be self-possessed and quite at ease with strangers. Indoors the rooms were large, well warmed with stoves, and in the dormitories the cots for in-fants and the bunks for older children were in double tiers – as I understand are all the sleeping-rooms in barracks on the Continent. The Home is supported and managed by the Finnish Y.W.C.A., and takes orphans or children who are motherless, and whose father, especially if he be tending reindeer, is unable to look after his offspring. The older children attend a State boarding-school, within a few hundred yards of the Home, as day scholars, and the boys when over twelve go there as boarders. There were about thirty children in the Home. The matron gave us coffee, bread and butter and cake. Afterwards we saw the children in their dining-room, and I gave them some choc-olates and sweets that I had brought from London in the hope that one day I would see this Home in the Arctic.

From there they made as straight a track as the reindeer

permitted for the new tourist hotel at Inari. It was late April; the thaw had set in early, and sledges were about to give way to carts and buses. Stenbäck moved on, while Sutherland remained, waiting until the bus service began, and spending the time learning how to drive a *pulkka* (reindeer sledge) on the still-frozen lake.

On 5 May he left Inari by bus for Ivalo, staying in the old posting inn in preference to the modern hotel. The next day he continued by bus to Virtaniemi, visited the Petsamo Greek Orthodox monastery, where he had an amusing encounter with a bogus hermit, and arrived finally at Liinahamari. He was greeted at the hotel by General Wallenius, 'who had heard from a friend in London about my visit'. The General was now Manager of the Petsamo Deep-Sea Fishing Company, and with him Sutherland made several excursions by boat, the longest being 'in a small steamer of 120 tons to the Russian frontier at Vaitolahti on the Arctic Ocean'.

> The captain, a pleasant, good-looking Finn in his early thirties, spoke excellent English and made me free of the bridge and the chart-room, in which he slept. 'If a man has to live in Liinahamari,' he said, 'it generally means that he has a past. This is the place where the bad boys come,' and then he added, 'I was divorced.'
>
> 'Is that all? I expected murder, and surely divorce is not uncommon in Finland?'
>
> 'No, but it's not so usual here as in Hollywood.'
>
> 'Does anyone take Hollywood as a standard of anything?
>
> 'In my case I think it was her fault. She refused to have children, and I wanted children. Anyway, this is my last trip in this damned ship and I'm going back to Helsinki.'
>
> 'If you'd known beforehand, perhaps you wouldn't have come. There's a hole in the stern as big as your head.

That's not so bad, because it's been filled up with concrete, but the plates are loose and she leaks like a sieve.'

The number of interesting people he met during his stay at Liinahamari is a reminder that Lapland was now (1936) firmly on the tourist map, with modern hotels, and a regular bus service during the summer. In his Lapland hotel Sutherland listened on the radio to the Coronation of George VI, broadcast from Westminster Abbey.

After an unsuccessful salmon-fishing interlude near Yläluostari Sutherland continued to retrace his route back to Salmijärvi, then took the bus north to Kolttaköngäs where – for the first time in his life – he caught a salmon, which was served ceremonially at his hotel, 'so well garnished that I wish I had asked for the recipe'. He continued his journey into Norway; when he re-entered Finland at Onnela, a round of misunderstandings began. He was planning to spend the next night at the Utsjoki Rectory, but was led by an elderly Lapp (who suffered a heart attack on the way) to a forest house which turned out to be an inn presided over by a rotund woman. 'Her languages were Lappish and Finnish, and she yo-ooed at me without understanding a word of what I was saying. We were joined by a young clean-shaven man in a lounge suit, and in German he told me that he did not speak French.'

All I wanted to know was the way to the Rector's house. 'Où est Monsieur le Curé, le Prêtre, Herr Pastor, Papa, Rector, Clergyman, Minister, Vicarius?' He shook his head, the woman whimpered yo-ooh, and Lapps from the kitchen crowded round the doorway. I decided to walk off to the church in the hope that the Rector's house was adjoining. Yet as soon as I made a move to leave, they shook their heads and indicated that I should stay where I was. It was twelve hours since I had eaten, and I was feeling most annoyed with everything in general when the telephone rang. The old woman answered, beckoned to me, and to my relief I was talking English to the manageress of the Inari Hotel. She told me that I was at the inn and post office of Onnela, where I must stay until Friday morning, when the post boat left at 10 a.m. . . . The Rector had friends staying in the rectory and could not put me up. On Friday at 8 p.m. I would reach the foot of Lake Mierash. 'Follow the path for twelve kilometres until you come to the Red Autiotupa, where men will be waiting to make coffee. The first autiotupa is five kilometres from the lake, but go on to the red one. You will have less distance to walk next day. On Saturday you will find a telephone in the inn at the end of Lake Syys. If you are too tired to walk the last twenty kilometres to Kammenen, telephone to me, and I will arrange for a horse to go and meet you. Mr. Stenbäck's letter did not reach you in time.'

Everything was clear, and I assumed that the man in the lounge suit was the postmaster. To make sure I pointed at him and said, 'Posti?' to which he replied, 'Jo, jo.' I then pointed at myself and said 'Dr. Sutherland', at which he shook me warmly by the hand and led me into a bedroom next the dining-room. This bedroom had two doors, one opening into the dining-room and the other into the hall. There were also two beds, and he indicated that one of them was mine. On a table in the centre of the room were butterfly nets, dead butterflies, and small glass jars. The postmaster cleared half the table for my use, and I thought that butterfly collecting was an excellent hobby for a postmaster in a lonely place. Next day, when he had recollected some French, I learnt that he was not a postmaster, but a Professor of Entomology on holiday. 'C'est trés amusant,' he remarked on realising my mistake. The postmaster I never saw. He was apparently in bed upstairs, and the old woman from the foot of the staircase frequently conversed with him.

For supper, and indeed for all other meals, we had salt
salmon, potatoes, rye bread, butter and coffee. At meal
times the professor would point to the coarse fare and
shake his head sadly. To such straits had the lure of butterflies reduced him. At 12 p.m., in broad daylight, he took
his net and went out to catch more butterflies. I went to
my bed, but not to sleep. The bed was clean and fairly
comfortable, but the old woman had dragged a rocking-
chair into the hall. There at the foot of the stairs and just
outside the bedroom door she rocked herself, and talked
to the man upstairs. The man did most of the talking and
the old woman yo-ooed. Still worse, the rocking-chair
creaked. There were also mosquitoes in the room. They
bit me. I rose and donned the felt hat to whose brim a
yard of circular mosquito netting was glued. With the veil
tucked under the collar of my pyjama jacket I returned to
bed and lay with my hat on the pillow . . .

On Friday morning I indicated to the round old woman
that I wanted my bill. She fetched pen, ink, an old envelope, and sat down at the table in the bedroom. For
some minutes she sat looking at the back of the envelope.
'Yo-ooh,' she whined. 'Yo-ooh,' then wrote rapidly on the
back of the envelope in large figures 78 M. She was over-
charging me, but I was glad to be going away and handed
her a 100 mark note. 'Yo-ooh,' and she waddled swiftly
out of the room. I knew what was going to happen, as I
had seen the professor pay his bill on the previous afternoon, when sharp words had passed between them.

Somewhere in the inn the old woman must have had a
collection of good Finnish notes. There did not appear to
be any notes in the old hand-bag with which she returned
to give me change. Sitting down at the table with the bag
in front of her and its mouth turned away from me, she
opened it, peered inside, and extracted an öre. This she

pushed across the table and yo-ooed in parting with the the coin. The copper Norwegian coin was followed by a pre-war Austrian coin, a French franc, and by other coins with square holes punched in the centre. She seemed to be an expert on foreign exchange, but yo-ooed because the money on the table was not quite the equivalent of the 22 Finnish marks she owed me. What it was actually worth I have no idea. Yet apparently it was short, because she seized the pen and added 2 marks 50 pennis to the bill, 'Yo-ooh, telefony.' At that moment the servant came into the room and I gave her all the change. She curtsied and ran to the kitchen with the round old woman in pursuit. Then the kitchen door was shut, and I wondered if the change would soon be back in the bag.

From Onnela Sutherland travelled south by post boat, through the long series of lakes. At one point he arrived at the next lake to find an empty boat waiting. 'Soon the boatman and his wife arrived, wheeling the bicycle with the out-board engine on the carrier.' The sights he recorded here included a grim piece of medical observation:

At the southern end of Lake Kenish we stopped at another Lapp house to eat sandwiches of reindeer meat and rye bread. In this house was a family of father, mother and two grown-up daughters. The father was lying alongside a wall of the kitchen. He lay on one reindeer skin and was covered by another. Beside him was a bucket. Every minute or so he raised himself on his hand and expectorated into the bucket. I glanced at the contents and knew the diagnosis. Nobody in the room spoke to him, and only the postman who limped asked about his health. 'Tuberkuloosin' replied the wife. In all languages that word is almost the same.

After a ten mile walk to the next lake Sutherland was rowed

further south, finally to the southern end of Syysjärvi, where a horse and cart was sent from Kaamanen to meet him. As he jogged on through Kaamanen towards his night's rest he reflected on the words of Linnaeus:

> Ovid's description of the Silver Age is still applicable to the inhabitants of Lapland. Their soil is not wounded by the plough, neither is the iron din of arms to be heard, neither have mankind found their way into the bowels of the earth, nor do they engage in wars to define its boundaries.

Sutherland's Lapland journey had been, mainly thanks to Stenbäck, not just an adventure but an education.

Young Pioneers

Education as well as adventure was also what had taken a group of twelve public-school boys to Lapland a few years before Sutherland. Their leader was George Murray Levick, who had accompanied Scott as surgeon and zoologist on his Terra Nova Expedition in 1910–13, and whose significant writings on penguins were rediscovered and published in 2012. *Young Pioneers in Northern Finland: A Record of the Second Expedition of the Public Schools Exploring Society 1933* was written by Levick, but includes descriptions of different parts of the journey by each of these young men. It is not surprising to discover that none of them found a career in writing:

> The journey proved interesting from both a geological and forestry standpoint. Some of the views proved magnificent and many fine photographs were obtained.

> They had some fun and games on the train from Helsinki to Oulu, and then headed towards Kuusamo. The principal

purpose of the expedition was 'testing the boys', and their progress through bogs and over fells certainly did that. Levick was as much concerned that their mental as well as their physical stamina should be developed, and the boys' little contributions to the *Record* often confirm that they are feeling the benefit in both these departments: '[a] fire was soon lighted and after a good lunch we all bucked up considerably'.

On one expedition they for some reason expected to get dinner at 'the poverty stricken little group of log houses which is Alakurrti', which is now beyond the Russian border. (After 1940 an air base was established near this tiny hamlet. As Russia stepped up its military activity in the Arctic region in 2014 a brigade comprised of 7,000 soldiers was moved there, with motorized infantry arriving by train.) Approaching the school house Levick met 'a pretty young lady . . . dressed in spotless white'.

Then followed quite a pleasant little chat, neither understanding a word of the other's language, but I was trying to tell her that there were eleven more of us and that we wanted a meal. She was beginning to understand this, and that we were English, when another very attractive young lady, with blue eyes, came on the scene. This one spoke a very little English, enough for her to tell me that that she was staying with the first lady who was the wife of the schoolmaster.

It appeared that they were unable to cater for so large a party and then there was a good deal of talk between the two in the Finnish language. We were all very friendly and amused with each other and I forgot how hungry I was and that we had already marched twenty kilometres. Then a man appeared with a gun. He turned out to be the schoolmaster, Lassi Kolehmainen. who had been down to the river after wildfowl. He also was charmingly friendly. After a few words of explanation from the others he said (interpreted by the other lady) that he would take us to a farm-house for a meal. So we all four set off . . . [W]e collected the boys and all went to the largest of the farm-houses. To cut a long story short, here in its great kitchen, we got our hearts' desire. Great bowls of boiled potatoes and butter *ad lib*. Jugs of milk, chunks of rye bread, then bowls of porridge. Our gigantic feast was watched by a crowd of children and a goodly collection of adults. The women of the household vied with each other in plying us with food. At length even we could eat no more and pulled out our pipes and passed cigarettes round to the audience.

A good deal of consultation ensued between our kind schoolmistress and the farmer's wife as to the bill. When it came, it was so small that we felt obliged to add to it. All the signs showed how poor these good people were, but it never entered their minds to charge us strangers a mark more than the standard price for the actual food consumed. For kindliness and honesty, these Finnish peasants are the salt of the earth. Wherever we went we found the same thing. They are kind to strangers, kind to children and kind to animals. Their horses and dogs are their friends. All the time I spent in Finland I have never seen a blow administered to any of these, or heard a harsh word spoken to them.

On the walls of the kitchen hung the rifles of the men who were in the native military reserve. One old man, probably over seventy years of age, fetched his military cap and put it on, evidently in our honour, and he wore it with dignity and manifest pride.

After this meal we were taken to the little village store where we bought cigarettes and tobacco and peppermint drops. Then our friends from the school, not satisfied with all they had done for us, took our whole party back with them to the school-house for tea and cakes, by special invitation of a government engineer, Lauri Karsta, who was staying there.

The British Exploring Society, as it is now called, has moved with the times. Its current website states that it draws from 'different schools, universities and many other walks of life', and it makes no mention of smoking.

Norah Gourlie

In 1896 Mrs Tweedie had planned to extend her tour of Finland as far as Lapland as 'a fitting finish to our summer jaunt', but was dissuaded by 'the horrors we should have to encounter' from mosquitoes. It was not until the 1930s that we find any accounts of English women travelling in Lapland; most of them wisely went in winter.

Norah Gourlie's first idea was to ride through Lapland in summer by pony. Wolter Stenbäck soon talked her out of this madcap notion, and successfully talked her into a carefully researched three-month excursion. With Ivalo as her base (where she was the only guest during the first winter opening of the tourist hotel), she travelled by bus, horse sleigh, reindeer, sea, and finally on foot; she provides a map of her route to show where she used these different modes of transport. Stenbäck met her at Ivalo, appearing 'resplendent, in the beautiful and decorative costume of an Inari Lapp, strangely reminiscent of a medieval court jester'. Her book is dedicated to Stenbäck, 'known and beloved through the length and breadth of Lapland', 'who made all things possible'. Gourlie proved worthy of him, overcoming with little fuss several daunting difficulties.

One of the most memorable things he made possible was seeing the annual reindeer round-up, near Kaamanen:

Making our way to the outer corral, we found we had to crouch in the snow against the fence, not moving a muscle, as once the beasts begin to come in, any sudden movement can make them take fright and bolt, thereby undoing the weeks of patient herding required to catch them.

Presently we heard a bell tinkling. A Lapp driving a fine reindeer came through as leader. Slowly, at first in single file, and gradually *en masse*, the herds trooped after, driven by the dogs and shepherds who had previously concentrated them into one area; ringing them round, and now drawing them fanways. As the men ski they can move very quickly. From where we were crouching it was like watching a moving frieze . . .

There were about twenty thousand reindeer. The calves leapt and gambolled beside the mothers, the males kept throwing up their heads and sniffing the air. When between two and three thousand had passed through, the inner gate was closed, and we followed. The Lapp with the bell reindeer and a few companions stood in the centre, and the reindeer began to circle round sunways. There was something curiously mechanical in their action. The snow, which had been over our knees when we first ploughed our way across the enclosure, quickly became a hard beaten mass. The only sound was the thudding of hooves and heavy breathing, with occasional lowing when a mother got separated from her calf. A cloud of steam filled the air from their breath; it is a curious fact that reindeer do not perspire or bite. The sight of thousands of antlers milling round and round made me dizzy; the circle kept breaking away at the edges, as a lasso momentarily split the mass, but quickly wheeled into place again.

There was no shouting, the men stood quite quietly, throwing the lassos with lightening speed; I never once saw a man miss, even in poor light they recognised their own ear-markings from 20 or 30 feet distant. I could not see the marks on the ears at all. Each owner had his own pen to which he took the deer when thrown. There are two methods of lassoing: the Hill Lapps aim at the antlers and drag the reindeer by these to the pens, while the Wood Lapps, who lasso the legs, half carry them. Both methods call for strength, and it often takes two men to get an animal penned. The calves are not dragged, but carried bodily. The action of throwing the lasso is peculiarly graceful, the poise rather that of a Greek disc thrower. I did not see any women casting, but quite small boys were trying their hand at it, frequently bringing down their target, to be thrown sprawling to the ground, their father immediately coming to their aid.

Later on her journey she came across a less picturesque aspect of the reindeer economy at a farmhouse: 'a gruesome sight, being entirely plastered over with deer skins stretched out to dry, bloody side outermost'.

Most of Gourlie's accommodation was far from the tourist hotels, in comfort as well as in distance. With communal sleeping quarters quite common she got used to not undressing at night. Near Pasijärvi she faced probably her most severe challenge when after a dispute she was abandoned by her guide. She walked on until she 'saw a glimmer of light ahead':

when I got there I was past speech, not that it mattered, for the Lapp owners would not have understood. They were more than surprised to see me; the woman helped me out of my peski, and the man went outside to see who I was with. He came back looking puzzled.

When she indicated that she wanted to sleep there, a woman took her 'up a hen-roost stair to the second stor[e]y'. Her husband brought up her bags, 'followed by four boys and two little girls'.

In spite of her assertions that her husband never drank, he was certainly pretty tight, as were the children. I offered him cigarettes, and the children sweets, which they refused. To my disgust, he emptied my cigarette case for them, and they all started smoking.

The little maid now came up with a tray of coffee, buttered bread and a tin of sardines. I filled my wash bowl with water, putting it on the stove to heat, so by the time I had eaten I had a nice quantity of warm water and tumbled into bed feeling comfortably clean, and fell asleep at once.

Much further north she arrived at Suonikylä (now Suonjel, in Russia).

We dashed up to the village in fine style, bells ringing, dogs barking, and heads watching at every window. There are forty families living in Suonikylä, and the wood dwellings are built in two long straight rows, with the schoolhouse and the dwelling for the Frontier Guard at one end.

I was greatly struck by the schoolmaster and the matron, as splendid a pair of young young people as one could wish to find, intelligent and kindly, beloved by the children and obviously on most happy terms with the parents – both tremendously proud of their job, and what they were making of it. It seemed to me that they were indeed courageous to bury themselves in this isolated spot. Their homes being in the south of Finland, neither of them were able to go home more than once a year. Both had very good quarters, Jaako Pohjolo's being in the school, and very delightful he had made them, with Finnish rugs, wireless, and quantities of books; these I found were on a Government Educational Loan system, for teachers in remote places. The matron, Neiti Takalampi, had her rooms in the children's house. The children are left in her care when the parents migrate in April, rejoining them not later than 1st June, and reassembling in the autumn. The house had a large kitchen, dining-room, matron's room, and three dormitories. For furniture there were only benches, tables, and wash-stands. Neiti Takalampi did all the cooking with two Lapp children to help clean, all the girls receiving cooking lessons. The children came in every day at 11a.m for breakfast, oatmeal or rice porridge with milk. The were a splendidly healthy-looking group and very clean. Here toothbrushes were also the order of the day.

When I arrived Neiti Takalampi was baking, and the room was full of the delicious odour of hot gingerbread, pepper cakes, and Swedish pancakes, as there was to be a dance that night in my honour. These Lapps have several folk dances, and in winter spend many evenings dancing to accordions. They do not dance modern dances. One of the dormitories had been cleared, and about eight o'clock they began to file in. They all shook hands with us, the women greeting each other by rubbing their cheeks together, first right then left, while holding hands.

Gourlie visited the Orthodox monastery at Yläluostari, and continued by bus to Liinahamari; there, during a few days aboard a coaster, she gained new insights into what the weather could do in Lapland. Even stormier weather followed when she spent time aboard a trawler; this gave her a new perspective on all her hardships on land:

The result of my experience on the trawler was to fill me with an undying admiration for men who willingly brave the elements during the Arctic winter at sea. The life is hard beyond all conception.

A Winter with Finnish Lapps reveals a combination of intelligence and tenacity; Gourlie was a student as well an observer of Lapland. Her tour ended finally at Muonio, where winter too was ending. There was no snow, so to get to the bus station 'we were obliged to get out and walk, my Lapland journey ending ignominiously on foot'.

Joan and Peggy Webster

Further evidence that Lapland was no longer a male preserve was the journey undertaken by two English girls, Joan and Peggy Webster, whose *Footprints in Finland* was published in 1940. They were neither adventurers like Ingram, nor professional writers like Sutherland, but describe themselves as 'two very amateurish travellers'. What they present is a personal, occasionally gauche account of what they saw and did, combined with a lot of rather poorly digested background information. Despite its limitations their book has at times an engaging freshness; they do not mention the Tourist Association, and the photographs are all their own. Their book represents another new voice (or two, rather) among the British travellers.

After some time in Grankulla, where they learned and practiced skiing, and made brief visits to Helsinki, they took the train for the twenty-four-hour journey to Kauliranta in the company of a German girl, Kirre Henschel, who was fluent in English and Finnish. They observed characteristic details not always noted by other travellers:

> it is the custom of the inhabitants of these northern towns to use the station restaurants in the evening as social gathering places. There we saw girls dressed in their best clothes conversing with older women, children, and men over beer and coffee.

From Kauliranta, 'a scrubby little station with one restaurant building, a station office, and a few odd sheds', they took the post bus north to Muonio. Like Sutherland, they provide vivid descriptions of the idiosyncrasies of this mode of transport:

> The post-bus had all good intentions of departing at half-past one, but whether it left then or an hour later did not seem to trouble either the driver or the passengers. This may have been a matter of mutual understanding and, perhaps, even consideration, for long after the driver was safely installed and the engine ticking over patiently, all sorts of odd people – mainly 'friends and relations' – continued to pile in at haphazard, how, when, and where they liked. The last comers, looking rather disgruntled, seated themselves disconsolately on the conglomeration of *rucksacks* piled up behind the partition . . .
>
> At long last the driver, without the slightest warning, jammed his foot on the accelerator, the passengers rose as one man from their seats, and we were off – very nearly off the road, for the bus skidded wickedly on the frozen surface. We had had our warning of 'things to come,' but in common fairness to the man at the wheel it must be said that he was a splendid driver up against difficult circumstances. The road was nothing but a glittering sheet of ice in some parts ; in others the surface was rudely broken by blocks of ice and deeply furrowed where the snow was soft.

There were two stops for coffee, bread and ginger biscuits on the eight-hour journey. The second of these was at Kolari, where 'not a little amusement was caused by the postman, an extraordinarily ugly youth, producing from his pocket a broken mirror and a piece of haircomb'. Arriving at Muonio they found no room at the inn, and were charitably taken in by the pastor's wife, Mrs Kaupyynen. They stayed long enough in Muonio to get to know some of the people, and to be known themselves. From the church tower they saw how 'far away across the forest the white slopes of the fourteen peaks of Pallastunturi broke the even horizon', while closer at hand the village seemed 'utterly deserted' until they discovered the shop, 'the communal centre of village life', where a dozen people were 'all talking solemnly and evidently discussing local affairs at length'.

One afternoon whilst we were staying in Muonio we visited Alvar Salovius, the local chemist. We had heard that he was a great character and loved by all who knew him. He was a bachelor well over seventy years of age, but still viewed life with enthusiasm.

He was delighted, we were told, to hear that foreign visitors had come to the village, and when we went to his shop one morning to buy several things we wanted, he at once came hurrying through from his house at the back, made us welcome with both hands stretched across the counter, and asked if we would do him the honour of taking coffee at his home that evening, to which, of course, we agreed. Later we heard that there had been a great discussion in his house as to whether he should change his suit for the occasion.

When we first met him he had been wearing at his neck a bright scarf drawn through a ring of reindeer-bone, a check coat, knee breeches, and long fawn leather boots, pointed at the toes and beautifully embossed. He had a shock of long brown hair brushed upwards, which occasionally flopped over his forehead as he talked. In his mouth he had a large cigar, which he usually smoked as far down as possible and then finished off in the bowl of his pipe.

We arrived at Mr. Salovius' dwelling that evening after a long walk through the snow with Kirre and Mrs. Kaupyynen, who continued to talk English together, although both were far more fluent in many other languages. This was really very considerate of them, as it enabled us to follow and take part in the conversation. Our host greeted us on his doorstep and we noticed that his suit was unchanged, but he was wearing an ordinary necktie instead of the gay cravat we had seen that morning.

Inside we were introduced to his housekeeper and some of his friends who had gathered there for the evening. The table was laden with all sorts of delicacies, but there were apparently certain ceremonies to be performed before coming to that part of the entertainment. The first ceremony was that of signing the Guest Book; we all felt this to be rather an honour and lost no time when invited to look at the name of other honoured guests who had preceded us. We began to wonder a bit, however, when we saw that most of the guests had indicated that their home town *was* Muonio, and we smiled to ourselves still more broadly upon finding Mrs. Kaupyynen's name appearing with almost monotonous regularity. Her kind heart, we thought, had probably inspired her to please the old fellow by putting her name in his book almost every time she went to the shop.

The girls travelled on north by 'self-drive' reindeer sleigh, learning as they went from their guide and teacher, the imperturbable Toivo Ranta. It was some hours before they saw another human being, 'a little Lapp boy with his sleigh and reindeer, quite alone and certainly not a day more than six years of age. He looked like some little elf . . .' They got lost in a snowstorm, stopped to rest and warm themselves at a homestead where six men sat silently on a bench, hardly acknowledging the newcomers, and watching 'the centre of the floor, where a hunch-back dwarf was roughly fingering the broken leg of a young boy'. At their last homestead stop 'a delicious aroma of cooking greeted us' and they enjoyed 'true Lapp hospitality'. Finally, lost after a blizzard, they were guided to Enontekiö by the church bells. The only previous British account of this remote village was in 1799, when Edward Daniel Clarke, on his famous travels, recuperated at the vicarage.

The inn at Enontekiö was clearly not one approved by the Tourist Association: it 'consisted of one large living-room in which cooking, eating, sleeping, and everything else, including the waxing of skis, took place'. This was the area where they stayed for the remainder of their holiday, going out on skiing expeditions every day. Exploring these remote regions without map or compass led them into unnecessary danger on one occasion. The finest episode in the whole book is the chapter about Lyyli Laakso, his wife and nine children, and a visit to their one-roomed dwelling in a forest clearing. Seven of the eight sons, 'all of whom looked to us as though of identical age', were at home, and each 'bowed solemnly, held out his hand in greeting, and murmured a polite "Paivo"'. 'The tiny room [twelve feet by nine] was filled with different types of Lapland men, women and children', and Mrs. Laakso managed to make coffee for everyone. Lyyli was very curious to learn about England and London:

> So great indeed was his interest that he settled himself cross-legged on the floor and asked further questions with the persistence of a small child. Our statement that in London trains run under the earth was received with obvious incredulity, but, then the matter having been explained at greater length, he called one of his sons to sit by him and listen to these strange stories of another land.

The next chapter is titled 'Easter-tide at Hetta'. The girls set off on their skis to 'the little district church of Enontekiö' in neighbouring Hetta, mingling with groups of other church-goers. The Lapps in their brightly coloured costumes 'made a strange contrast to the dark gaunt figures of the Finns'. In the church, when they 'saw the full beauty of the Lapp costumes massed together in the pews, we felt extraordinarily untidy in our ski-ing trousers, *anoraks*, and helmets'. The service terminated with 'a very long sermon'. It was such a scene, and indeed such a sermon, that Clarke had experienced in the church here in 1799, although this was not the original building in which he had also constructed and tested the balloon which so alarmed the natives.

Before they left they wanted to buy a reindeer pelt, and this led to the most striking experience which they record; generally naive and inclined to condescension, they were here for once quite unable to misunderstand the criticism of their behaviour:

At last we succeeded in persuading the apparently reluctant Lapland woman to produce her husband's store of reindeer-skins for our inspection. She did not seem any too pleased at being thus hurried, but nevertheless, went through the communicating door and came a few moments later carrying two large pelts. These she had fetched from an attic reached by a wooden ladder. Twice she climbed up to the store-room, and each time returned with several skins which she spread out upon the floor for us to see.

The skins were of various sizes and colours, some dark and some almost pure white. The pelts, unlike some we had seen already at the local shop, were beautifully cured and dressed on the under-side. After examining each skin in turn with every evidence of care but, in reality, with most unprofessional eyes, we chose one and Kirre another. The price, we were told, was eighty Finn-marks for each pelt, which is the equivalent of about seven shillings. This price was, of course, most reasonable, but unfortunately we were at that time distinctly short of money. Stupidly enough, although we did not realize this just then, we endeavoured to strike a bargain with the Lapp woman. To our no small surprise she promptly flew into a terrifying temper which was accompanied by a long tirade and evil scowls and shaking of fists.

Kirre translated the outburst of animated speech as best she could and from her translation we gathered that the woman had declared indignantly that she was a Lapp, not a Jew, and knew perfectly well what was a fair price. Nor would she, she added, ask a fraction of a Finn-mark more for the skins than they were honestly worth.

Feeling rather small and truly sorry for ourselves, we gladly accepted the pelts at the price named without any further quibbling.

The Webster girls were, apart from the schoolboy explorers, the youngest British travellers to have ventured an account of Finland. Being young and female gave them at times fresh responses not matched elsewhere; they responded acutely to 'the intensity of the silence' of Lapland: 'we stood speechless, just listening and listening. The stillness of these almost uninhabited wastes seems terrifying at first.' Their book is at other times youthfully condescending and banal, nowhere more than in their concluding remarks:

Our Lapland journey had come to an end, leaving behind many memories of a hardy race of people, who care little for the toil and bustle of civilization, a people contented with their meagre lot in life and who are happy among the fields and fells of their native land.

VISITS TO SIBELIUS

Shortly after his seventieth birthday in 1935 Sibelius wrote to Rosa Newmarch to thank her for her greetings: 'It was like a tender memory of old and precious days, which were so precious to me and, thanks to you, of so much importance to my music.' Certainly no one in England had promoted his work for as long or as faithfully. From the beginning of the century she had recognised the significance of his music, and wrote as early as 1906 of her discovery in *Jean Sibelius: A Finnish Composer*:

> I began to realise that it was not merely a large packet of new music, but a new country and the representative of an unfamiliar culture I had undertaken to interpret.

Newmarch, described by Sibelius as 'une femme incroyable', was an early champion of Russian and Slav music, frequently visiting Russia, and learning the language. She not only wrote about the music of Sibelius, but helped to organise all five of his visits to England. She provided English translations (*via* German) for many of his songs; her own poetry is only now being discovered and revalued. She had spent a month in Finland back in 1910, largely in his company, when he showed her some of his favourite places in Karelia. Because Imatra 'savoured too much of excursionists'

> Sibelius took us to an old-fashioned inn by the lakeside, Rauha, clean and unpretentious, from which we could wander at will along the sedgy margins of Saima or in the adjacent woods.

Her memoir of their friendship was published in 1939.

As Sibelius's reputation grew during the early twentieth century his name became almost synonymous with Finland: he was, wrote Cecil Gray, 'virtually the uncrowned king of Finland and a living symbol of her culture and independence'. He was never more highly regarded in England than in the 1930s: Walter Legge, who supervised the recordings made for the Sibelius Society, wrote to him in 1934 'the English world is more than ever "Sibelius mad"'. A year after visiting him he published 'Conversations with Sibelius' in *The Musical Times* in 1935. 'On any subject except his own music,' he wrote elsewhere, 'Sibelius is a brilliant, illuminating and amusing talker.' In 1937 twenty-eight of his works, including all the symphonies, were played at the Promenade Concerts in London, and in the following year Sir Thomas Beecham organised a Sibelius Festival. Musicians and other travellers sought him out, and for his part he kept up many British friendships until the end of his life. Bell wrote that 'he is a great admirer of this country, which he delights to refer to as Old Albion'. 'His dress is that of the smart man about town,' wrote Legge, adding, 'he is an almost embarrassingly generous host, and he would rather discuss literature, painting or politics than talk of music'. Bell and Gray each remarked that he emulated Churchill as 'a lover of large cigars'; Legge, making another visit after the war, was greeted with, 'Ah, you're the young man who likes Mumm's champagne and corona cigars.'

Cecil Gray

Gray first became known during the 1914–18 War, as a contributor to the Socialist weekly *New Age* and as a neighbour and intermittent friend of D. H. Lawrence, who portrayed him in several novels, notably as Cyril Scott in *Aaron's Rod* (1922). His career as a music critic began in 1920 when he and Philip Heseltine founded a musical journal called *The Sackbut*, and he began to make a name for himself writing on music in the *Manchester Guardian* and the *Daily Telegraph*. His first important book was *Survey of Contemporary Music* (1924), an epoch-marking work which remained influential for a generation. As well as dethroning old gods, it enthusiastically promoted Bartók and Sibelius. Some of the ideas were expanded in a later book, *Sibelius* (1931; second edition 1934). He was a particularly articulate admirer both of Sibelius and of Finland. He condemned critics who

> consider Sibelius's comparatively restrained and traditional
> style of writing to be merely old-fashioned in consequence

of his belonging to what they fondly imagine to be a backward and primitive race beyond the pale of civilisation and
at least a century behind the times. The truth is precisely
the opposite . . . [a]nd if it is true that he does not share
in the contemporary love of experimentation for its own
sake – which is only a phase which is already passing – the
reason is not that he is behind the times but rather that he
is ahead of them, in the same way that Finland is, in many
ways at least, ahead of other European countries.

Gray's autobiography *Musical Chairs* (1948) recalls a life
lived at top speed. He was a composer as well as a writer; an
energetic, sociable man who lived in a bohemian world, he
counted leading writers, artists and dancers among his friends.
He died in his mid-fifties of cirrhosis of the liver. In 1931 he
had declined a proposal to write about his meetings with Sibelius, having 'a deeply rooted aversion, whole-heartedly shared
by my subject, to the vulgar and impertinent curiosity which
the modern public displays with regard to the private life of
eminent persons'. By 1948, though, this aversion had evidently
subsided.

At Christmas 1929 he had an engagement to visit Sergei Ma-
montov, the director of opera in Tallinn, and he proposed to
the *Daily Telegraph* that he travel on to Finland to interview
Sibelius. This was approved, and the experience was one which
Gray never forgot.

Our first meeting had a very sticky start. His English not
being good, and my Finnish and Swedish non-existent, we
floundered about in a curious macaronic language com-
pounded of French and German. After a few minutes of
polite, but strained, conversation in this idiom, I must have
made some observation which pleased him, for he suddenly exclaimed in wonderment: 'But, Mr. Gray, you are not a
journalist – you are a musician! Why did you not say so at

the start?' He became a different man, jumped up, shook hands with me warmly, produced a bottle of whisky from the cupboard, and from that moment onwards all went well. When we parted it was arranged that I should lunch with him the next day at the hotel where he always stayed on his visits to the Finnish capital. (Normally he lives in the country, some twenty miles away, at Järvenpää, where he leads a life of complete solitude and seclusion, in striking contrast to his visits to Helsinki.)

The occasion will always be one of the memorable and agreeable experiences of my life. Not only did he prove to be the perfect host in all that pertains to the table, but the intellectual feast he spreads before his guests is even more magnificent, if that were possible. Most musicians are apt to have one-track minds. However interesting their conversation may be in speaking of their art, and more particularly in speaking of themselves and of their own achievements, they are, as a rule, singularly uninteresting and unilluminating on other topics.

Sibelius exhibits precisely the opposite tendency – of himself and his work he speaks diffidently and unwillingly. One quickly realizes that he prefers to discuss any and every other subject on earth, and does – literature, philosophy, psychology, painting, politics, science. The time passed as if by enchantment. Suddenly, on looking around the restaurant, I noticed that we were the only people present and, glancing at my watch, discovered that it was about six o'clock. Murmuring a few words of apology for having outstayed my welcome, I made as if to depart; but my host appeared mildly surprised at the suggestion and prevailed upon me to stay for dinner, which we duly consumed at the same table. We did not separate until seven o'clock in the morning.

This was my first, but by no means my last, experience

of such prolonged sessions, which, I subsequently learnt, were a normal feature of Finnish social life and a particularly favourite predilection of Sibelius, in connexion with which many entertaining stories are told. I cannot resist the temptation of telling one of them here.

On a similar occasion to that which I have described above, the conductor Kajanus, one of Sibelius's most intimate friends, sought to excuse himself and take his departure, as he was due to conduct a concert at Petrograd next day. The others present protested that the occasion was not one to be sacrificed to such sordid material considerations, and pressed Kajanus to telephone through to Petrograd and cancel the engagement. Seeming to comply with the suggestion, Kajanus left the table, but went to the station, took train to Petrograd, conducted the concert, and returned to Helsinki, where, on re-entering the restaurant, he found the company still seated at the same table, engaged in the same animated discussion. On seeing him, Sibelius mildly expostulated with him, saying: 'That was surely a very long telephone call of yours, Kajanus!'

Finnish hospitality, as already indicated, is, or was in these days, a formidable proposition, especially at the time – New Year – when I first visited the country. Lunches imperceptibly merged into dinners, and dinners into lunches, and as it remained dark until eleven in the morning and became dark again by two-thirty in the afternoon, I completely lost all sense of time, not knowing whether it was a.m. or p.m. or what day of the week it happened to be. As often as not, I would be up all night and in bed all day without knowing which was which, and it really did not matter, since they were virtually indistinguishable. After what must have been about ten days of this hectic, phantasmal existence it was with a certain sense of relief that I succeeded in extricating myself from it and recuperating from the effects of Finnish hospitality in the comparatively sane and normal land of Sweden, in Stockholm, whence I returned *via* Copenhagen and Hamburg.

When I re-visited Finland some two years later, with the commission for the book, in order to obtain biographical material and to study the unpublished and otherwise inaccessible works of the master, I travelled by sea, from Hull to Helsinki. It was an appalling voyage, with a fierce gale blowing all the way. The ship arrived some twenty hours late, but Sibelius was waiting for me on the quayside. 'You must be very tired after your terrible journey,' he said; 'we shall have a quiet evening and meet again for lunch to-morrow, after you have had a rest.' Alas, for good resolutions! It was again seven o'clock in the morning before we separated, and so it went on as on the former occasion, except that, as it was only autumn, it was possible to distinguish day from night. What I should like to know is this: do (or did) the Finns live like this all the time, or only when offering hospitality to foreign guests? Whichever the answer, they are a race of supermen, and the fact that Sibelius had attained to the age of eighty and more without showing any ill effects, is a living proof of it. But even so, when or how do they ever get any work done? That is the mystery to me.

Harriet Cohen

Cohen was a concert pianist of international fame. Described by the musicologist Percy Young as 'one of the outstanding women of her time', her interests extended far beyond music: she was one of the most talked-about and photographed musicians of her day. Her friends included figures as diverse as Arnold Bennett, D. H. Lawrence, Albert Einstein and Ramsay

MacDonald. Arnold Bax was her long-term but by no means her only lover; all his piano music was written for her. 'My friendship with Sibelius,' she wrote, 'is part of the very stuff of my life', and she was certainly a favourite with him: 'challenged once with her presence in his house in Järvenpää Sibelius . . . had exclaimed, "Ah, but she is my daughter!"' They had been introduced in London in 1912, and their friendship lasted until his death in 1957. Some of their meetings in Finland are described in her autobiography, *A Bundle of Time*.

In 1932 she made a series of broadcasts in Oslo, Stockholm and Helsinki. She spent several days – 'dallied' is her word for it – in Stockholm with Bax and Balfour Gardiner:

> At last the time came to take the steamer for Finland which berthed the following morning at Turku, or Åbo as they called it then. In the saloon, thick with tobacco smoke, the whole atmosphere subtly changed, and what I can only describe as a growing excitement pervaded the small ship.
>
> In Helsinki I bought a camera and we wandered around. The town rather brought to mind the turrets and towers of Scotland; 'downright Aberdeen,' said Arnold with a pleased twinkle.

They decided on a 'a little trip into the country', to include 'Imatra of the wild, dashing Falls.' She records how they 'came upon the scene of a country wedding. The smiling bride and her groom in their complete peasant regalia . . . were coming across some fields in an ox cart.' On arriving back in Helsinki they found a telegram:

> J'ARRIVERAI LUNDI HELSINGFORS J'ESPÈRE VOUS TROUVER UNE HEURE A VOTRE HOTEL MES COMPLIMENTS SINCERES.   SIBELIUS

> Balfour having to go off to Tampere, Arnold and I had the gayest meeting with Sibelius at an outside restaurant

sitting in the sun where I took their photographs, together and separately. We laughed and ate and drank, and the two composers, who liked each other on sight, got on famously.

As the lunch extended itself into the following day Bax dropped out, leaving her alone with Sibelius.

> During the twenty-four hours we were together, Sibelius smoked ten cigars, and I two. We drank four magnums of champagne between us (our companion [Bax] preferred whisky which sent him to sleep). I remember Sibelius sending out, at about midnight, for some Enos fruit salts: he was rather worried what the acid wine would do to me. I took that bottle home and kept it for years. While Bax slept, Sibelius told me of the marvellous times he had while young in Vienna . . .

After Bax's death Sibelius accepted the honorary presidency of the Bax Society.

The last time that Cohen visited Sibelius was in 1956, about a year before his death. Again she arrived in Turku, and visited the Sibelius Museum.

> As I sat waiting for the train to depart for Helsinki, the press sought me out and gave me a great welcome. They were surprised I had chosen to go this rail journey of some hours detour by Porkola [sic], at that time in Russian hands. But my curiosity was aroused, and it was tremendously interesting to see, when a few miles out, how shutters were placed over the windows, doors were locked with Russian soldiers standing at each one, and to hear and feel the Russian engine being attached to the train. Somehow, the weird unreality of this experience heightened all the more my longing to see once again the great Finnish patriot.

After recording her broadcast she drove out to Järvenpää. 'After a kiss and the gripping of hands' they sat and drank brandy, and Sibelius again lit a cigar for her:

> Striding across the room to show me his books in the cosy little library tucked away behind the dining-room, Sibelius appeared to be sixty and not ninety-two years. His smile was still wide and his carriage upright, although he was somewhat thinner than I remembered. What a commanding presence he had, and yet what gentle and exquisite manners. He was quite magnificent in his dress, and my heart turned over when I saw how he had arrayed himself for my visit, with such care and attention, regardless of fatigue.

Noël Coward

The author of *Private Lives* (1930) and *Blithe Spirit* (1941), Coward was one of the best-known English actors, playwrights and song-writers of the era. He spent a short time in Finland on his way back from a tour of Russia in 1939, recording his experiences in his autobiography *Future Indefinite* (1954). Coward was not one of those who had expected to be impressed by the Socialist miracle in the Soviet Union, nor was he. He sensed that his very lifestyle – the fact that he was gay and debonair – had put him in a criminal class, and when his train finally pulled out of the Finland Station, he felt, he wrote, 'exactly as though I had been let out of prison after serving a long term'.

He was not yet free, since they still had to cross the border, where '[t]he station on the Russian side was dirty and uncomfortable and swarming with small officials'. Coward was full of foreboding, as he 'was again questioned and cross-questioned, and made to wait about interminably while a yellowish gentleman with a cropped head and a spectacular wart on his chin thumbed through my passport and handed it in turn to several of his colleagues'. Finally the train began to move and, Coward records, 'I lit a cigarette with trembling nonchalance and left the Soviet Union, I hope, for ever.'

No other British writer – in two hundred years – has more vividly and eloquently described the sense of relief at crossing the border. It comes over in the heightened sensuousness of his description of Finland as a vision of paradise:

> The Finnish frontier station was most beautiful in my eyes; most beautiful and gay and clean. The officials were smiling and courteous, and one of them even seemed to like my passport photograph. The Customs men, god-like creatures with blond hair and gleaming teeth, marked my baggage without even looking at it, and I was ushered into the buffet, where a waitress, who was a cross between Marlene Dietrich and Lady Diana Cooper, brought me some ambrosial bacon and eggs and a bottle of Lea and Perrin's Worcestershire sauce. My fellow passengers – most of whom were Finns – appeared to be as sensitive to the change of atmosphere as I was. They chattered and laughed and made jokes with the waitresses and there was a holiday feeling in the air. There was a lovely smell too, compounded of roasting coffee, frying bacon, the geraniums in the window-boxes and the heady, intoxicating scent of freedom.

Coward was attracted by the air of culture, and by the complete absence of ugliness or of anything which might vex an epicurean. He describes 'social occasions . . . . that I enjoyed immensely', and records that 'the people I met were uneffusive and genuine'.

> Sadly enough I have little to say about Finland beyond the fact that I found it enchanting and its people hospitable

and kind. I say 'Sadly enough' because it is a dreary comment on human nature that recorded pleasure inevitably makes duller reading than recorded irritation and criticism. I found nothing to criticise in Finland and much to admire. I stayed in a comfortable, well-run hotel. I visited a charming country house belonging to the Baronesss Vrede, in which there was some lovely furniture and several large tiled stoves. The food was simple and good, and marred by only one discordancy: the threat of Russian invasion. Madame Vrede discussed this, as Prince Radziwell had done, with detached resignation, as though she had steeled herself for what was to come and had prepared her mind to accept the inevitable with fortitude.

Probably nothing was further from Coward's mind than paying a visit to Sibelius. In terms of musical significance they were, to put it mildly, at different ends of the weight scale. Coward's slightly self-ironic account of their meeting is something to be treasured, and rivals scenes in his plays.

During my stay in Helsinki someone suggested that I should pay a call on Sibelius, who, although he lived a life of the utmost quiet and seclusion, would, I was assured, be more than delighted to receive me. This, later, proved to be an overstatement. However, encouraged by the mental picture of the great Master being practically unable to contain himself at the thought of meeting face to face the man who had composed 'A Room with a View' and 'Mad Dogs and Englishmen', I drove out graciously to call upon him. His house was a few miles away in the country and my guide-interpreter and I arrived there about noon. We were received by a startled, bald-headed gentleman who I took to be an aged family retainer. He led us, without any marked signs of enthusiasm, on to a small, trellis-enclosed veranda, and left us alone We conversed in low, reverent voices and offered each other cigarettes and waited with rising nervous tension for the Master to appear. I remembered regretting bitterly my casual approach to classical music and trying frantically in my mind to disentangle the works of Sibelius from those of Delius. After about a quarter of an hour the bald-headed man reappeared carrying a tray upon which was a decanter of wine and a plate of biscuits. He put this on the table and then, to my surprise, sat down and looked at us. The silence became almost unbearable, and my friend muttered something in Finnish to which the bald-headed gentleman replied with an exasperated nod. It then dawned upon me that this was the great man himself, and furthermore that he hadn't the faintest idea who I was, who my escort was, or what we were doing there at all. Feeling embarrassed and extremely silly I smiled vacuously and offered him a cigarette, which he refused. My friend then rose, I thought a trifle officiously, and poured out three glasses of wine. We then proceeded to toast each other politely but in the same oppressive silence. I asked my friend if Mr. Sibelius could speak English or French and he said 'No'. I then asked him to explain to him how very much I admired his music and what an honour it was for me to meet him personally. This was translated, upon which Sibelius rose abruptly to his feet and offered me a biscuit. I accepted it with rather overdone gratitude, and then down came the silence again, and I looked forlornly past Sibelius's head through a gap in the trellis at the road. Finally, realising that unless I did something decisive we should probably stay there until sundown, I got up and asked my friend – whom I could willingly have garrotted – to thank Mr. Sibelius for receiving me and to explain once again how honoured I was to meet him, and that I hoped he would forgive us for leaving so soon but we had an appointment at the hotel for lunch. Upon this being communicated to him, Sibelius smiled for the first time and we shook hands with enthusiasm. He escorted us to the gate and waved happily as we drove away.

After the visit Coward was furious with the friend who had exposed Sibelius to this intrusion, and did his civilised best to make amends.

Later, troubled by conscience, I wrote a brief note of apology to Sibelius, who, despite the fact that his seclusion had been invaded and the peace of his morning disrupted, had at least received me with courtesy and given me a biscuit.

*

Malcolm Sargent, his biographer wrote, 'had been a loyal advocate of Jean Sibelius since the 1920s', and visited him many times over the years. Sadly, there is no published account of any of these meetings. Sibelius knew his recordings and approved of the interpretations. Sargent 'spoke often of the happiness he knew in the old man's presence; how they used to walk the grounds of Ainola, Sibelius's villa at Järvenpää and in the tall forest beyond, "which," he would say "is so essential a part of his music."' His last visit to Sibelius was during a Scandinavian tour in 1956, when Sibelius was ninety. The following year, on 19 September, Sargent was in Finland again, to conduct the Helsinki Philharmonic Orchestra, and he and Sibelius spoke on the telephone. The next day Sibelius suffered a haemorrhage, and during the evening lost consciousness.

When the broadcast of Sargent's concert was due, Aino [his wife] wanted to turn the radio on in the hope that the sound of the Fifth Symphony would bring him back to consciousness, but decided against it. An hour later, at 9.15, the doctor confirmed that death had taken place.

I recall Nils-Erik Enqvist telling me that the British government asked Sargent to stay on in Finland to represent Britain at the state funeral, where he laid a wreath. He was furious at being stranded in Finland for more than a week, and as part of its attempt to pacify him the British Embassy sent him to Turku for a visit. In desperation Enqvist took him out to the Resurrection Chapel, where immediately he was at peace.

J. M. Richards

While it was music and Sibelius which took Gray to Finland, it was architecture and Alvar Aalto which attracted James Muade Richards; his *An Introduction to Modern Architecture* (1940) holds a position broadly comparable to Gray's *Survey of Contemporary Music*. Both writers interpreted and promoted modernism. Richards edited *The Architectural Review* from 1937 to 1971, was architectural correspondent of *The Times*, and is regarded as the principal British architectural critic and writer of the last century. His *Guide to Finnish Architecture* (1966) was revised and greatly enlarged in 1978 as a magnificent volume entitled *800 Years of Finnish Architecture*. He describes Aalto as 'one of the hero figures of modern architecture . . . Finland basked in the limelight his reputation brought to his country.'

Richards first met Aalto at an exhibition of his work in London in 1933. 'Nearly a year afterwards,' he writes, 'I had an unexpected letter from him about a pupil in his office who was learning English and wanted a holiday companion to practise on. The holiday would be spent sailing, and it would give a chance, Aalto said, to see something of Finland.' The pupil was Viljo Rewell (who 'was to become the best-known Finnish architect after Aalto'.) Richards's account of his visit to Finland

in 1934, the first of about a dozen – the ninth was in 1977 –
is taken from his autobiography, *Memoirs of an Unjust Fella*
(1980). Perhaps only a writer steeped in architecture could
have produced this wonderful and evocative description of arriving in Helsinki by sea:

> The early morning arrival at Helsinki was a delight
> and an astonishment. Like Venice, Helsinki is a city that
> should be approached from the sea. Arms of the sea extend
> from the wide still water of the harbour deep into the city.
> As you sail in, past the dismantled fortress of Suomen-
> linna, the outline of the city slowly lifts itself into the clear
> northern light. Far above the dark line of cranes and sheds
> along the waterfront hangs the dome of Engel's Lutheran
> cathedral, catching the morning sun. The roofs and pedi-
> ments of the surrounding neo-classical buildings lie still in
> shadow. They step down to a broad paved market-place,
> open to the South Harbour and thus displayed to the ship-
> board passenger like a scene in a theatre.
>
> The market is crowded with stalls of produce, barrows,
> trams and people. For a backcloth it has a pale wall of
> stucco buildings, the foremost edge of the neo-classical
> town: the city-hall, a hotel, an embassy or two, the presi-
> dent's palace set behind a pavilioned forecourt. Framing
> the scene from the wings, as it were, are on one side a line
> of buildings in the newer town, tailing into greenery; on
> the other the dark silhouette of the Orthodox cathedral,
> its gilded cupolas likewise catching the morning light.
> The wider panorama, before it closes in with the ship's
> approach to the landing-stage, includes smaller islands
> offshore, one crowned with a pointed church, and yachts
> rocking gently at their moorings.

There was no time to see any more of Helsinki on this occasion. They immediately boarded a train for Vaasa, Viljo's home

town, where, he explained, they had to sail across to Sweden in order to 'take part in the sailing regatta that was starting next day at Örnsköldsvik'.

It sounded a busy programme, but I was in his hands and off we went. From his attempts at conversation in the train it was clear that he was an expert and dedicated sailor. Many years later, in 1956, he was to be chosen for the Finnish sailing team at the Olympic Games. I thought it best not to disclose my own limited experience of sailing. On arrival at Vaasa late in the afternoon he took me straight to the harbour, where his boat was lying beside a jetty, and asked me to wait there whilst he went into the town to collect provisions for our voyage. He returned before long in a car, accompanied by another young Finn, Nils, who it turned out was sailing with us as skipper. From the car they unloaded case after case of beer and bottles of aquavit, whisky and rum. These we stowed carefully in the bottom of the boat under Nils's supervision. He was particular how this was done, as the liquor was to serve the secondary purpose of ballast while we crossed the open sea.

Here was my first introduction to the strenuous drinking habits of the Finns. After admiring the ingenious way space had been found for so much liquor, I inquired rather anxiously whether we were taking any food. Yes, Viljo reassured me, he had a packet of sandwiches in the pocket of his oilskins. I discovered later that there was also some tinned food already on board. Nevertheless during our all-night voyage our sustenance was mainly liquid. Bottle after bottle was emptied, carefully refilled with seawater and stowed in the same place so as not to upset the trim of the boat. I was quite unable to keep up, but felt I had to appear to do so. It was not difficult, while the other two were busy consulting charts or trimming sails, to pour the contents of a bottle over the side. It would have been wrong to waste good liquor, but I was able to pick out for myself bottles that had already been used and took care to be seen refilling them.

After the regatta, in which they had mixed fortunes, they returned to Finland. 'Viljo's family had closed their town house in Vaasa for the summer and were living in their summer house, which stood on a promontory overlooking the gulf.' Here they relaxed for a few days, exploring the archipelago. 'Never since,' Richards wrote, 'although I have taken saunas in many parts of Finland, have I met one to match the Rewalls' at Vaasa for combining all the pleasures.'

It was soon time to begin the second part of our programme. Alvar Aalto had told Viljo that he wanted to show me his newest buildings and they had made plans accordingly. We were to meet at Turku, where Aalto had been working until the previous year – in fact ever since leaving his home-town Jyväskylä in 1927. We therefore travelled to Turku, found Aalto waiting for us, and with him met Erik Bryggman, who had been his ally and associate and had himself designed a number of buildings in Turku – not as remarkable as Aalto's, but calm and disciplined in what seemed to me a modernized version of Finland's neo-classical vernacular.

Aalto showed us one of his own buildings, a new headquarters for the local newspaper *Turun Sanomat*, completed in 1929, a fairly orthodox modern design with a flat façade and long horizontal windows. Only in the large subterranean chamber housing the printing presses was there evidence, in the profile of the columns and their elongated capitals, of the capacity to conjure sculpturally expressive shapes out of technical necessities which was to be so much admired in Aalto's later buildings.

Then we set off eastwards by car across the whole width of southern Finland. We drove along dusty gravel roads, almost traffic-free, through pine-forests so tall and dense that it seemed like dusk in the middle of the day, and along the boulder-strewn shores of lakes – or they might have been deeply penetrating arms of the sea, there was no telling which. Aalto was a relaxed and entertaining companion. Although only thirty-six he had an infectious self-confidence, a mature sense of what his contribution to architecture was to be. He already knew his own value. In his eccentric but expressive English he talked about what was waiting to be done with the new techniques and resources that were becoming available to architects. At the same time his evident respect for human needs left no room for the arrogant imposition of doctrinaire solutions of which some of the pioneer modern architects were already guilty.

I saw this exemplified when we reached our first destination: Aalto's tuberculosis sanatorium at Paimio, planted deep in a pine forest, with its narrow cliffs of white concrete crisply modelled to form windows and balconies and spreading out to embrace the sun and the view. It was a spectacular structure and was soon to be recognized as one of the classics of modern European architecture. Yet it was based on a studious analysis of the routines of patients, doctors and nurses: in all the boldness of invention their needs, the qualities they could be expected to respond to, had never been lost sight of.

The Paimio sanatorium was the subject of a competition which Aalto had won in 1928. When I saw it in his company it had been finished for about a year. It was the first of his buildings to be equipped with the birchwood furniture he had exhibited in London, and this gave it a freshness and gaiety not usually associated with buildings of this purpose. Aalto's handling of concrete was fresh in the same way. When I looked at the Paimio sanatorium I realized for the first time that reinforced concrete could be used not only functionally, economically and dramatically, but wittily. Wit is a quality that bubbles out of Aalto's early work and gives it a stimulating sense of providing aesthetic entertainment as well as possessing architectural worth. It made it clear that there was no need to associate the new, socially responsible modern architecture, to which young men like me were committed as much for moral as for aesthetic reasons, with humourless solemnity . . .

From Helsinki we continued our journey as far as Viipuri (Wiborg in Swedish) in the extreme east of Finland, but now in the Soviet Union since it is in the strip of territory that Finland was compelled to cede to Russia in 1940. Our route took us through a more populated region than before, and through farmland rather than forests. Soon after setting out we passed through a couple of small towns: Porvoo and Loviisa I think they must have been when I look now at the map. They gave me a closer view of the Finnish urban vernacular whose acquaintance I had made at Vaasa. The wide streets – wide not only to prevent the spread of fire but to leave room for snow to be banked up on either side when they were swept clear in the winter – were lined with rectangular blocks of wooden buildings no more than one or two storeys high, raised on stone basements and painted various shades of ochre. The flat façades and the bracketed cornices and moulded window surrounds are enriched with naïve and ingenious carpenters' ornament. It is only in the smaller Finnish towns that this wood vernacular predominates today but in 1934 the bigger towns too, except in the central areas of Helsinki, Turku and Viipuri, were all built of wood.

Aalto showed himself very knowledgeable about these

simple local styles of building and there was clearly a connection between his interest in what small-town carpenters had achieved in the way of evolving a style out of their technique of handling wood and his own fascination with the material's industrial potentialities. His sensitiveness, too, to the surviving vernacular traditions, and his comments on them, reflected a keen awareness of the role architecture had played a generation earlier during Finland's fierce struggle to assert her cultural – and consequently her political – identity. Aalto felt deeply about Finland's political problems and the precarious relationships she had to maintain, but this did not prevent him from being wryly humorous about them – as he was about himself.

In Vyborg Richards was full of admiration for the Library, still in the process of construction. Here he parted from Aalto, and returned via Helsinki to England. He did not visit Finland again until after the war, so never saw the completed Library. On his many post-war visits to Finland he usually spent time with Aalto, who 'showed me most of his own buildings in Helsinki as they were completed', and he saw also the summer house that he had built for himself at Muuratsalo. 'But Viljo Rewell was more usually my guide to how Finnish architecture was developing. He had himself become one of the leaders. Modern Finnish architecture was no longer only one man thick.'

TWO SAILORS AND AN ANGLER

Richards was perhaps the most amateurish sailor to have recorded his experiences in Finnish waters. There were many genuine mariners, who, inspired possibly by Arthur Ransome, wrote about sailing on the Baltic. Sailors, like anglers, usually write for their own fraternity, rather than for a wider readership, but since the Baltic sailors belong to the picture of travel during this period I have caught a couple of them as they come ashore, leaving most of their jargon on board.

K. Adlard Coles

Coles had purchased *Racundra* from Ransome for £220 when the latter returned to live in England; he renamed it and sold it on, so it did not return with him to the Baltic. One of his many sailing books, *In Finnish Waters* (1932), describes a four-week summer cruise from Turku, first through the skerries to Estonia.

As they rounded Hanko Head by the 'outer route', the wind fell off, enabling them to enjoy a leisurely and memorable dinner:

> The evening was particularly beautiful. Grey smoky clouds hung high in the western sky, and on the horizon lay wisps of driven clouds, with veins of gold and copper and blue showing through the gaps. The sea in the distance was steel grey, but near at hand the waves glittered gold and white. Low islands and square beacons stood in silhouette against the setting sun. In the east the sky was cobalt blue, and the rocks were tinged with pink and yellow. The whole scene was inexpressibly representative of the sea. Even the islands were wet and slippery-looking, rising out of the water in every direction like enormous seals.

Later, heading from Turku to Stockholm, they stopped at Finland's last outpost, Utö, needing to buy petrol. Eventually an old fisherman let them have a little of his own meagre supply. To show their gratitude the crew presented him with 'a three-pound pot of English marmalade', clearly feeling that he was the one who should have been grateful:

Marmalade is not easy to get in Finland, and English marmalade of good quality must have been an unexpected joy to a grandfather with numerous grandchildren in this remote part of the world. We parted with much hand-shaking and good wishes.

A second excursion, described in *Mary Anne among 10,000 Islands* (1938), was taken with his wife in a yacht from Helsinki by the 'inner route' to Hanko, across to Tallinn and back to Helsinki. Coles writes modestly in his Preface that the book 'tells the story of such a happy holiday that it may perhaps give some pleasure to other sailing men'. It may well, but non-sailing men will be bemused and baffled by the jargon. His description of a brief episode on shore at Ekenäs (Tammisaari), 'an attractive looking little town', may give some pleasure to landlubbers, though, especially as the town has been largely neglected by British travellers.

We intended to go ashore to buy a few provisions and then sail again in the evening, but before we had finished lunch, and before the sails had been properly stowed, it began to rain, so we waited until the worst was over before going ashore, and decided to stay where we were for the night.

A large and formidable policeman appeared to be waiting our arrival at the quay in the dinghy. I had our passports ready, but to our surprise he moved away when we landed. Although I took the passports with me each time we went ashore we were never in fact asked for them, and at Ekenäs we were subjected to no formalities nor harbour dues, beyond being hailed back on our departure to sign the harbour master's book, giving name of yacht, owner, where from and where bound.

We took the first road into the town. The surface was composed of a kind of dusty gravel or sand, not at all like our English gravel, for it was finer, rounder and rather pinkish in colour, like the Finnish rocks. During the following weeks we grew very accustomed to these roads, and also to the wooden houses, which are the rule everywhere except in the biggest towns.

The distance to the square around which the shops were centred was short. It was quite a large square and the buildings round it were bigger than elsewhere in the town. Then we started shopping. At Helsingfors we had the help of Captain and Mrs. Hjelt of the 'Aallotar', who kindly took us to the shops and helped us with our purchases. Here we had to shift for ourselves, and very good fun it was too. First we went to a general stores and found the things we wanted. We then pointed to them and the assistant wrote down the price. In many cases the English word was sufficient. There is sufficient similarity between English and Swedish to make a common understanding. If you want a bottle you ask for a flask; if you want a batten you ask for a lath; beer is pilsner, öl, or ale repeated frequently; bread is brod, butter is smor (pronounced 'smer'), and so on. But vinegar has some odd name, and the only thing to do is to search until you find it. The triumph of the day was the purchase of an oil lamp. This simple purchase gave me the utmost pleasure, for previously I had to rely on candles in the evening, which are not good to write by. I got the lamp by drawing a picture of it. They gave me an enormous one to start with, but whenever I said littler they produced a smaller one, until eventually they found the right size . . .

Afterwards we visited a book shop, post office, baker's and fruiterer's. There were some rather nice coloured postcards at the book shop which gave a very good idea of the inner and outer skerries. These we sent to our friends at home. Postcards and airmail stamps became quite an item on this cruise, especially as we had to purchase a variety of unused stamps at each country we visited for our small son who was at school.

The banks were shut, but we went to one next morning and cashed some of Mr. Cook's excellent cheques, which seem as good as cash everywhere. The bank manager could speak a little English, as once he had been manager at a works in the interior of Finland where he had business connections with England. He was most obliging and tried to buy some fish for us. Fortunately there were absolutely no fish in Ekenäs that day. I cannot think why the Crew asked him for fish, for this involves cooking and makes a smell in the ship. Anyway, good luck saved us from this on that occasion, and she bought meat instead, which certainly involves cooking but does not smell – so much, anyway.

We liked Ekenäs very well. It was simply a timber and market town of 3,000 or 4,000 inhabitants, without any pretensions or tourist attractions. True, there was a large café on the pier, and good bathing, but the main qualities of the town were entirely natural, due to its position on the fiord. This must be an important timber centre, for westward we passed many big saw mills, and there was every evidence of a busy trade. Until late in the night men were engaged in the odd occupation of heaving logs off the quay into the sea, within a circle composed of a line of logs joined end to end. Next morning we learnt the reason why. A motor boat took the lot in tow and drew them to a tug, where they formed one of a large number of rafts which were taken in tow.

Douglas Dixon

Dixon and his wife sailed to the Baltic from England in a thirteen-ton smack through the Kiel Canal to Denmark and

Stockholm. *A Sail to Lapland* (1938) describes sailing through the Åland Islands, where their yacht sustained a broken boom. They hailed a schooner heading for Stockholm with a load of firewood. 'What the Finn can do with an axe,' claimed one of the crew, 'would take most carpenters a full set of tools, and perhaps a full-scale drawing.' The makeshift repair got them without trouble to Turku, where the proprietor of the boat-yard, Herr Lindblom, 'a most interesting, good-hearted bloke', undertook the repair.

> He also advised supper at the Samppalinna among the trees overlooking the river, where the fisherman come from the sea to sell their fish and the farming folk come down the river to sell their spuds and their onions and their strawberries. Their nondescript open boats lie along-side the cobbles in the stream of the Aurajoki. Under fantastic sails, or an old sheet or a tent construction of ancient petticoats, the boat folk live in the town until all their wares have been disposed of, and the fisherfolk must go again down to the islands and the strawberry grow-ers up-stream to their land. Leisurely contented folk they seemed for all their poverty; old wrinkled faces with skins dried and browned like bark; dirty, some of them terri-bly dirty, but every lass or toothless old crone with a gay handkerchief for a colourful headpiece.

Later they spent longer than they had planned in the archi-pelago south of Uusikaupunki; on the island of Lypertö they waited for the arrival of the steamer bringing supplies and post from Turku.

> As the time approached for the steamer, little boats kept coming from all directions to cluster round a little pier. We joined the jolly little throng. A horse brought a sledge over the rough ground from a little farm. A little bull calf came with it and played rough little games with everyone.

Calf, farm, cow, therefore milk. There was some milk, but none to spare, at least that is what we gathered. I was cross about this milk business because the captain of the *Ontoori* had so particularly rubbed it in that milk in Finland was not only cheap but very good and plentiful. We talked about it, probably rather loudly; anyway we talked loudly enough to attract the attention of a girl who, to our surprise and delight, talked to us in very fair English. She was a real help. She told us of an island shop and introduced a dear old dame who was waiting in her boat for her supplies from the steamer. She told us how the steamer could fetch our letters and save the mate [presumably Mrs Dixon] a tiring trip, and then she asked us questions.

'How long do you think to stay in Lyperto?'

'Oh, we are only waiting for the wind to go round from the north; we want to sail to Tornea.'

The girl passed on the information to the folk around us. Slowly the faces spread till everyone, bull calf included, was giggling with glee. 'Wait for the wind to go round from the north. Ha ha ! Ho ho ho ! Wait for the wind – Oh ha ha he!'

When the girl recovered a bit from the general merriment she explained it. 'They say you may wait till the winter. It often blows here from the north for all the summer round.' So that was it. A sort of minor Trade Wind area . . . Well, well. It must only stiffen our determination. The steamer came and we arranged for our letters. We helped the old dame with her bottles and boxes and went round with her to the shop. The shop was priceless, just a few cupboards in the *stuga* kitchen, but the most priceless thing about it was an ancient, wizened, merry little gnome who turned out to be the proprietor and a man of considerable property. He took charge of us completely. He sent the old dame to dig up fresh potatoes, insisted on my sampling all his brands of cigarettes, ran round the houses, and came back with an armful of wizened beetroot, onions, tiny crumpled carrots, and the saddest bunch of lettuce that ever was seen. He sold us one of the gargantuan beer bottles, full of *drycka*, and several little bottles of *omskakas*. Leastwise I called them *omskakas*, for that was the biggest word on the label. Actually they were bottles of sterilised cream or *gradde*, and *omskakas* the word for 'shake the bottle.'

In the course of the summer they managed to tack as far north as Tornio before settling down for the winter in Luleå, and finally sailing to Lapland.

'Vagrant'

The hospitality of the English Fishing Club at Imatra had been mentioned as early as 1882, and few tourist guides from that time onwards fail to tempt travellers with descriptions of tremendous trout and superlative salmon. 'Verily,' Mrs Tweedie had written in 1897,

> Finland is a paradise for fishermen. A paradise for lines and rods, reels and flies, for masters of the piscatorial art; there are to be found freshwater lakes, and glorious rivers full of fish. Some call it the heaven of anglers, and permission to fish can easily be obtained, and is absurdly inexpensive.

I can surmise only that it was such a paradise that anglers kept it a close secret, since there is virtually no published writing about it, not even by that noted angler Arthur Ransome. Hilkka Aaltonen has only thirteen entries under 'fishing' out of the 4912 items in her exhaustive bibliography, and only a few of these refer to angling. Such descriptions as do exist seem to be lifted from the tourist brochures. 'Finland for the Angler' in *The Field* is a case in point: 'Although good sport is to be met with practically throughout the country,' writes H. Beck, Lapland is preferable as it 'still retains the charm of practically virgin country'. He studiously records the weights of the fish he caught in Lapland. Another angler, identifying himself only as 'Vagrant', recommended Finland in an article in *The Fishing Gazette*. Two hours by bus from Rovaniemi station he had found at his 'first angling headquarters': 'an excellent inn, superior bedroom, and bed fitted with the last word in mattresses, worthy of Mr. Heal'. The first evening he caught a trout, and clearly no angler could have dreamed of greater success:

> Three pounders running from the first place selected on a strange river, in a strange country, seemed too good to be true, and made me forget the mosquitoes raising molehills on the back of my neck.

'Any keen angler,' he concludes, 'with slender purse and a month at his disposal is recommended to give Finland a trial, as he will come into contact with perhaps the wildest and most sporting trout in the world.'

A. D. Scott

The extraordinary achievements of Finnish athletes seem to have roused limited interest in Britain: no delegation set off to Finland to see 'how they do it'. Ten years after MacCallum Scott had seen the triumphant Finnish athletes returning from the Paris Olympics another Scott – probably a Scottish one – did travel to Finland to catch 'Some Glimpses of Finland's Athletic Activity', which he recorded in the *Aberdeen University Review*. His first glimpse is more dramatic than most contemporary images of Helsinki:

It is one of the long evenings of the Northern summer. The scene is an island of greensward separating two streets in Helsingfors. A typical outcrop of rock marks one side; a fringe of birch trees the other. To the onlooker, all looks peaceful and idyllic. Suddenly comes the sharp crack of a pistol. Four men, their arm muscles working in the sunlight, burst into view, slow down walk back, repeat the motion.

At every space he comes to Scott sees some sporting or athletic activity:

Here a dozen boys are shooting at goal. Just over the way is a public park. Within, on an area of sub-baked sand, a group of young men and women are playing Finnish baseball. They are taking it seriously; clad in spiked shoes and training costumes. Further out again, in the suburbs, one glimpses from tram or 'bus, a green fence-enclosed stretch. There are many such. It seems to be a training ground, for men are jumping and practising the discus throw. The black curve of a cinder track marks its verges. Men are running on it, with a tireless, machine-like action.

He observes these activities everywhere he travels in Finland, and not only in towns; he meets runners on country roads and forest paths. It is very different from England:

The Englishman, who has always been wonderfully content that his country dabbles in athletics, may well ask himself what it all means. The answer is this. Finland has taken itself seriously, and during the past decade in nothing has it taken itself more seriously than in the matter of athletics and athletic training. Familiar as indeed most people are with Finland's triumphs on the Olympic stage, few have hazarded a guess at the amount of preparation in the wings. Fewer still have any idea of the intensity which characterizes it.

Scott illustrates this further by describing a visit to the principal stadium in Helsinki, where to his amazement 'the gates are wide open'. He is further amazed by the sight of 'Athletes of renown; stout perspiring senior partners; junior aspirants after school honours – they are all training together'. When all this has been observed, he writes, 'it requires little effort to understand why so relatively small a country holds such a disproportionate number of world records.'

The first athletic meeting which Scott attended gave him a clear picture of the place which athletics occupied in Finland. It was 'a mid-week affair':

> To the average Finn it was quite an ordinary meeting – nothing at all to be excited about. To an outsider the list of international celebrities competing placed it on a semi-Olympic level. Incidentally it was a marvel of expedition and efficient organization. Twelve contests were down for decision. Beginning at 6.30 p.m., the programme was over in two hours. Advance booking done in the usual way through a city sports emporium procured one a stand seat opposite the finishing tape, the cost, 40 Finnish marks, or 3s 10d, seemed frankly ridiculous for a meeting of 'cracks'; but there it was. So having bought a programme (without the faintest hope of understanding it) one sat down to await results. On one's right, quite fortuitously, was the Chief of Police. On the left fluttered a beautiful but very red-lipped Jewess, the cause later of one missing Kotkas clearing his 193cm. But on the whole the stand was quiet and orderly. White-coated vendors of the popular ice-slab, 'Eskimo Brick', found ready sales. The evening sun beat down strongly.

'A Finnish crowd,' Scott writes, 'is perhaps the most singularly undemonstrative entity in existence.' On this occasion, however, this fabled composure was put to the test. Three of the competitors in the 3000 metres were 'the redoubtable Olympians, Nurmi, Isohollo and Lehtinen'. On the fifth lap (of seven) Lehtinen broke away from the pack:

> Had he shaken off everyone? Not a bit of it. Like a terrier the bald-headed Nurmi was close behind. The pace was again normal. The tail made up slightly, but the race was between two only. Came the last lap, and they were left with a fifty-yard burst for the tape. They went for it. Nurmi lost by six yards. It was an amazing race – or else an amazing fiasco, for the time was bad. The Finns accused it of being 'pulled'. To us it seemed like a calculated trick that had come off. But either way its success was this. It succeeded in putting a phlegmatic Finnish audience into something approaching respectable delirium.

V. C. Buckley

Bernard Newman, who cycled across Åland in 1938, reflected that many of the inhabitants 'had never seen such a modernity as a railway train. Yet to all of them the aeroplane is a common sight.' Newman himself might possibly have looked up to see the very plane which was taking our next traveller to Finland: Buckley had boarded at Stockholm a sixteen-seater 'German tri-motor Junker all-metal monoplane' belonging to the Finnish Air-line AERO and named *Sampo*. His first view of Finland was from the air as the plane headed for Turku:

> In our half-hour's flight over the sea, we were continually passing over rocky islets. In one quite large group, called Åland Islands – belonging to the Finnish archipelago – I could plainly see houses, roads, and the tiny harbour of Mariehamn. It seemed as if the islands were stepping-stones from the Swedish to the Finnish coast,

along which there is no more obvious demarcation between land and sea than on the Swedish side. In the southern potion of Finland alone there are no less than twenty
thousand islands, all large enough to have names.

As we neared the coast, we began to sink from the alti-
tude of about four thousand feet at which we had kept all
the way. The waters below were now a vivid green and I
could clearly see the rocky foundations of the pine-covered
islands. Lines of white encircled them as the waves broke
against their dark formation. Sailing amongst the islets
were yachts – dots of white on the transparent green water. Gradually we sank lower towards a small town on
the coast. Air-pockets bumped us up and down until at
last we landed on a diamond-shaped airfield and taxied
towards the white airport buildings.

After refreshments at Turku airport the flight resumed; Buckley's description of approaching Helsinki by air opens a new
chapter in this chronicle of British travellers:

> As we drew nearer Helsinki, the sky to the west was
> a curtain of pink, while in front of us, to the east, thin
> black clouds drifted across an expanse of green and yel-
> low. From the air one can see how this capital, one of
> Europe's newest, is bordered on three sides by the sea, and
> approached through an archipelago of rocky islets.

Buckley is described in a publisher's 'blurb' as 'a well-known
travel writer who frequented country houses and night clubs,
consorted with "high society", drove dashing cars, and travelled the world in great ocean liners'. After arriving in Helsinki
by air he travelled by motor car, and stayed in the best hotels.
The Finnish section of his *Happy Countries* (1939) is less than
a quarter of the book. His writing reminds me intermittently
of Stephen Leacock's parody, in *My Discovery of England*, of
the ability of English writers to produce instantaneous 'impres-

sions' wherever they travel: 'My first impression of Helsinki was its surprising newness,' writes Buckley, and amplifies this insight with 'my impression of Helsinki was of an extremely interesting city'. His impressions apart, though, there are some sections of his book certainly worth preserving.

There was – self-evidently – nothing out of the ordinary about his sight-seeing in Helsinki. He was, like many other visitors, overwhelmed by the Academic Bookshop: 'I felt as if I were walking through the book department at Harrods.' In the streets, though, he thought people not as well-dressed as in Stockholm and Copenhagen, and he 'was surprised at the number of young soldiers'. 'I shall always remember Helsinki,' he writes, 'as the city of lilac trees.' Seurasaari was the place he liked best and admired most: 'Every detail has been thought out in forming this museum.' He admired also the new stadium, captioning his fine photograph 'HELSINKI STADIUM – where the Olympic Games of 1940 will be held':

> The new stadium at Helsinki is an amazing piece of architecture. At one corner of the white oval arena, whose seating capacity is fifty thousand, stands the strangest-looking tower. It is more than two hundred feet high and pure white. In the distance it looks no thicker than a factory chimney. On closer inspection one sees a spiral staircase on the outside, and on each of the twenty-three floors is a tiny round balcony. Against a vivid blue sky, with a bright sun throwing shadows under the balconies, it looks like a row of giant's teeth. On the top is a radio station from which they will broadcast to the world the results of the 1940 Olympic Games.

Helsinki called for superlatives: 'The Parliament House is probably the best equipped in Europe, and Helsinki's railway station is certainly the finest.'

From Helsinki Buckley and three companions – an English

woman, her daughter, and Olav, a guide and interpreter who spoke no Finnish – headed north, stopping at Hämeenlinna:

> It is a sleepy settlement of white wooden houses. No-one seemed in a hurry and most of the inhabitants must have been taking their afternoon naps from the deserted appearance of the place . . . Not even the Union Jack in front of our car seemed to arouse the passers-by from their lethargy.

In Tampere they stayed, naturally, at the Tammer Hotel. After a chaotic cinema visit they set out for a night on the town:

> Then we thought we would try and find a restaurant and have some supper. As we re-crossed the bridge the statues stood silhouetted black against a topaz sky. The factory chimneys were sombre exclamation marks of brick. Hearing the sound of music coming through the windows of a building, we went in and found ourselves in a large room that looked like a conservatory, but was obviously a sort of restaurant. A band on a dais was playing a Sibelius sonata; the musicians were dressed in the oddest clothes, black evening trousers, white silk shirts, and black bow ties. The room otherwise was empty save for three tables occupied by parties of men.
>
> At the top of a menu was the name of the restaurant, the 'Teatterinravintola.' It was, of course, printed in Finnish, so that items such as *Vasikanpaistia ja kurkkua – Kahviaamiainen y. pikkulämmin*, might have been ham and eggs or ice cream sodas for all we knew. Whilst vainly trying to decipher this menu a waitress came to our table. She only spoke Finnish, but produced a menu printed in English – or near-English.
>
> Clem and I astonished the poor girl by laughing uproariously over some of the items as they were printed. I quote a few examples verbatim:
>
> Smoked eel with schrambled eggs.

Sausages with beer and sour coal.

Pure goose lever.

Day Soup.

Fried kidness in sauce.

Mushroom delicates in sauce cream.

We chose day soup, 'delicate' mushrooms and sour coal! What we actually got was chicken broth, fried mushrooms and *Sauerkraut,* all extremely well cooked and for the sum of 3s.

Heading north the next day, they stopped for tea at Lapua:

From the size of lettering on the map we expected to find Lapua was a large town, but in reality it consists of only a few white wooden houses, a church, and half a dozen village shops. It was pouring with rain when we drew up in front of the local inn. Rain dripped gloomily on to its wooden veranda; the lace curtains in the windows were torn, and one or two gaudy advertisements glared at us from the walls. The instant I entered this place I felt as if we were about to take part in a Tchekov play . . .

A few peasant men and boys with healthy sun-tanned faces and vacant expressions sat in a sort of tea-room-cum-bar. They stared at us with open mouths as if we had descended from another planet.

The landlady appeared from a dark passage; of uncertain age, she had a mass of tousled blonde hair, a white shawl was drawn round her shoulders, and from the corner of her mouth drooped a cigarette. I was fascinated to watch this woman moving slowly about the rooms as if in a trance. She spoke a few words of Swedish, so that Olav was able to make her understand that we wanted some tea.

The parlour was clean, but a hideous wall-paper, artificial flowers, and antimacassars were poor substitutes for

the log walls and wooden utensils of the old Finnish cottages I had seen at the folk-museum in Helsinki. When the
tea arrived it was brought in by a girl who made up for her
inability to speak to us by smiles and giggles.

The Finnish teapot certainly needs understanding. There
is a large pot containing the water and pick-a-back on it is
a smaller one holding the tea which had been poured into
it in the kitchen minus the leaves, so when one pours out
a second cup one gets only hot water! Its construction,
I presume, is a sort of miniature replica of the Russian
samovar.

The next stop was the Seurahuone at Kokkola. A 'foreign'
detail which Buckley notes here is one which Mrs Tweedie
had complained of before him: the bedroom windows had no
curtains.

Just as the name Kokkola bore a similarity to that of the
famous American drink (advertised in the United States
as persistently as Bovril is in England) the town itself re-
sembles a lonely prairie town way out in the Middle West.
The few streets of wooden houses, on which white paint
had worn off in places, looked deserted and colourless.
Although it was only nine o'clock when we arrived, there
was a singular hush over the town. The hotel was easy to
find for it was a three-storied building and about the most
conspicuous in the place. It was called the 'Seurahuone,'
and on one side faced an open square and on the other the
main street.

There was no one in the hall when we arrived and only
after shouting 'Oi' several times did a man eventually appear. While Olav and I carried the suit-cases up to lofty
rooms with flowered wall-papers, iron bedsteads, bright-
coloured woollen rugs, huge porcelain stoves and no window curtains, Clem said that she and Elizabeth were going

into the dining-room to order my birthday dinner. Olav offered to help, but they said that with their phrase-book they knew more Finnish than he did.

My birthday dinner consisted of boiled eggs and jam omelet, the outcome of Clem's phrasebook!

After this regal repast, we went out to explore the town. It was half-past ten, and still broad daylight, but the whole place was enveloped in a subdued quality that darkness brings to a city. Once, as we walked arm-in-arm in the middle of the road, the barking of a dog, followed by the sound of a motor car, echoed strangely down the street of wooden houses. Some boys and girls stood at street corners and giggled as we passed, someone threw open a window, but even sounds seemed muffled by the curious 'deadness' of the place.

By the time we had walked a few hundred yards, a mist had blown in from the sea, which lay a mile or so from the town. It was as if a grey veil had been thrown over the expressionless face of a sleeping woman. The street came to an end opposite two small houses and a round brick tower, from the top of which there would certainly be a fine view of the surrounding country-side.

Jokingly I said, 'I am going to ring the bell of that house and ask how one can get up the tower.'

'Really, you can't ring bells at eleven at night – there *are* limits!' Elizabeth said. But she continued in the same breath: 'Go on! I bet you don't.'

I did, and after a long wait a man appeared in shirt-sleeves and carpet slippers. Directly the others saw him they walked away, so I was left to explain why I had rung the bell. I pointed to the tower and went through the motions of walking up steps. The man, who did not appear to resent in the least being knocked up late at night by a foreigner who wanted to go up a tower, smiled and shook his head. I then bowed, and he bowed, and that was that.

We had nearly reached our hotel when a man on a bi-cycle suddenly came around a corner and, on seeing us, stopped and got off. After exchanging a few words in Swedish with Olav, the latter turned to us and said: 'Can you beat it? The man in the carpet slippers had taken the trouble to ring up the local fire brigade who have the key of that tower and told them some foreigners wished to go up it.'

We hated to offend the fireman, but there was really no point now in tramping up a tower as the mist had be-come thicker. Olav told him this and he agreed. Before he rode off I gave him one of the souvenir Coronation medals which I happened to have in my pocket. He beamed from ear to ear, and the next morning while we were driving round to find a petrol pump I saw him standing outside the fire station, the medal pinned on his jacket.

It was market day in Kokkola. Not a bustling affair but one of leisurely tempo with a few peasants gathered in the market-place beside the hotel. Some displayed their pro-duce on wooden benches and others at stalls over which white awnings had been erected. Whilst not a very colour-ful market, it had a distinct charm. The old women wore white handkerchiefs over their heads, making frames for kindly weather-beaten faces. Some were unpacking baskets of eggs and laying them on benches; others had bundles of vegetables in front of them; some were selling flowers. There were buckets filled with mauve and white lilac and enormous bunches of lilies-of-the-valley costing a penny. I saw no other flowers but these.

Some of the women displayed shiny new suit-cases filled with packets of butter, an odd way to carry butter to market. At the stalls sporting white awnings women were selling loaves of dark brown rye bread, rolls baked in the shape of a motor tyre (they felt about as tough) and sticky-looking cakes. Behind one of the benches they had placed baskets of berries. The baskets were made out of birch-bark and contained bilberries and a species of berry I had never seen before. There were also stacks of gaily-coloured rugs similar to those we had found in our bed-rooms at the hotel. They are woven on hand-looms in the cottages and farms during the long winter evenings.

Buckley frequently mentions and describes the soldiers he sees almost everywhere, but he never considers what their presence might signify.

William Richard ('Bill') Mead

1938 provides more British descriptions of Finland travel than any other year; taken together they provide an unmatchable picture of a young country well into its stride, with only the smallest hints of the catastrophes lying just ahead. Bill Mead was one of the few travellers who maintained their interest in Finland after the war: he visited Finland almost every year un-til he was well into his nineties. He was awarded Honorary Doctorates by the Universities of Helsinki, Turku, Uppsala and Lund. When he died in 2014, a week short of his ninety-ninth birthday, he had published seven books about Finland, five about Scandinavia including Finland, and about seventy arti-cles about Finland; in the last days of his life he was putting the final touches to yet another book. He masterminded the revival the Anglo-Finnish Society after the war, and wrote the history of the Society for its centenary in 2011. His academic career led him to University College London, where he was Professor of Geography from 1963 until his retirement in 1971. In the last fifty years there can have been very few Fennophiles who did not know him or know of him.

The account of his first visit in Finland is taken from *The Adoption of Finland*, published on his ninetieth birthday, a book he describes as 'not an autobiography, simply the Finnish constituent in a life history'. For this reason, he explains, 'the narrative avoids the first person singular': his unrelenting third-person narrative and passive verbs, sadly, do his writing no favours. He did allow himself an occasional 'us', the only hints that he was accompanied by a 'not uninterested brother'.

From the upper deck of *Aallotar* it seemed a long way down to the two berth cabin. It was the beginning of the £10 return journey to Helsinki ('including victualling' as the phrase had it). The two and a half day crossing over summer seas could not have been more agreeable; likewise, the modest company. A high point was the appearance of an Ålandic four-master in the Danish Sound. The Travel Bureau brochure advertised passages to Finland on ships from the Australian grain run during the last leg of their journey from Falmouth or Cork to their home port of Mariehamn.

Then, there are patchy, but vivid recollections. Finland was smelled before it was seen. With the coast barely visible, the strong scent of hay was succeeded by that of coniferous woodlands. The profile of Helsinki's white buildings rose above the low shoreline. The sun shone brightly. A taxi to the hotel on Rautatie cost ten Finnmarks. The first night's dinner was at the restaurant Royale on Esplanaden. (Students could afford the extravagance at 223 Finnmarks to the pound). It was decided not to take one of the droshkys back to the hotel, the bony horses of which stood flicking their tails in the sultry heat. There was a strawberry lunch the next day at the Seurasaari open air museum, its old wooden buildings yielding up their tarry scent in the hot sunshine. And, was it true that there was a nude bathing beach along the shore?

The inland journey took off from Eliel Saarinen's already renowned granite railway station. It was a wooden world which was entered. The wooden upright seats in the hot wooden coaches were left with relief after the wood-burning steam engines had laboured up the gentle inclines on the track and rattled excitedly down the slope to the next fretworked railway station. Viipuri, the destination, had a more solid station. A brief stroll around the old city was followed by a local train journey to Imatra where the art nouveau hotel made an appropriate impression, though Imatra falls disappointed. From here to Lappeenranta there was a different prevailing smell heavy on the air. It announced forest fires across the border in Russian Karelia.

A small white steamer on the quayside waited to carry us on the 36 hour journey to Kuopio. Surprisingly, it accommodated a seemingly impossibly large crowd of travellers, a few of whom squeezed into the handful of tiny cabins. In the cramped dining room, seated elbow by elbow, the dishes of the smorgåsbord circulated round and round the horseshoe-shaped table. Chicken wire looped around the narrow deck was barely sufficient to protect children from falling overboard. Hot oily smells from the engine room mingled with those of coffee.

There appeared to be little traffic on Lake Saimaa, but on two occasions immense rafts of logs were passed. They were tugged so slowly that they appeared to be motionless. On the log rafts there were little huts or tents in which the loggers lived during their journey to the mills on the south shore of Lake Saimaa. At intervals, the low wooded shores opened up to reveal comfortable farmsteads. Sometimes, there were small herds of cattle standing up to their udders in the shallow lake waters and half lost among the tall rushes. It was too early for the grain harvest, but tawny patches of barley or oats stretched away from rows of potatoes. Occasionally a rowing boat sat idly in the water at the end of a wooden jetty. There was no visible sign of fish, but we were assured that there were plenty for catching and trapping. It was imparted that, if it had been Saturday evening, the tell-tale smoke of the sauna would accompany every sign of settlement.

Intermittently a little plume of smoke arose from the steamer's funnel and, in anticipation of a landing stage around the next bend or the next-but-one, a modest siren would sound. Usually a handful of women and children, some with baskets of berries for sale, waited to welcome the steamer. Sometimes a rowing boat waited to collect a passenger or sometimes a horse and cart. It was all very leisurely – the whole atmosphere very Scandinavian.

Savonlinna overnight – birch-shaded waterfront, sandy promenade, stern Olavinlinna. An open Victorian carriage with a sleepy horse, several conscripts with sturdy cycles, two old men (with archetypal Finnish faces) smoking distinctive Finnish cigarettes sitting mutely on a wooden seat. A white wooden hotel, a verandah with a white rocking chair, a white bedroom with a feather dun, small yachts with folded white sails. A silent night save for a whining mosquito – the first . . .

Kuopio's busy little quayside seemed to belong to the coast rather than the lakeshore. The customs house seemed out of place until it was realised that Saimaa Canal gave access to foreign trading vessels. Back from the waterfront, a chequerboard of streets pronounced Kuopio to be a planned town, with a busy market square at its centre. There is a memory of lots of summer berries for sale (Kalakukko and the perennial *Rouva Partanen* were only to be recognised as icons for Kuopio in the future).

Gravel and dirt roads were lined with wooden residences of varying styles – old structures of square-cut logs, some with stables behind them, clapboard houses, with would-be classical façades, a few Jugend-style buildings with mushrooming roofs. Most dwellings seemed to be clustered around garden areas – grassy patches (no mown lawns) with occasional fruit trees and bushes, solitary flower beds with geraniums and begonias. Piled logs to feed the wood-burning stoves were a common feature. A scatter of stucco buildings seemed to serve the administrators: brick for schools and for the modest Orthodox church. An austere granite cathedral looked down upon alien Siberian larches. Elsewhere, graceful birch trees lined the streets. There was an unsophisticated park with a wooden bandstand. There was no time to visit Puijo. Overnight was spent at a so-called Co-operative Hotel. (Finns as a nation of co-operators had yet to be appreciated.) All that was to be seen of Kuopio's modest industry were the tops of smoking chimneys above the surrounding pine forests. A store bearing the name Minna Canth was pointed out. And there were purchased as souvenirs a woven wallhanging and a wrought iron candleabra.

Bright and early the next morning, another wood-burning train carried us to Jyväskylä. There seemed no particular reason why we should stay here unless it was the new hotel. It was to be recalled for the beautiful blue ceiling and the chandeliers in the dining room.

Thence, the slow and smoky journey to Turku. No real time to look around. It seemed very much a town proud of its granite – the cathedral with its granite steps, the granite embankments of the Aura river, the formidable granite of the castle, the granite cobblestones and setts of the streets. SS *Arcturus*, of early twentieth-century vintage, was disappointing after *Aalotar*. She proved a seaworthy if not especially well appointed vessel, ignoring thunderstorms in the Baltic and a choppy North Sea. (Tourist passengers had to run the gauntlet of an open deck from the rear hatch to the dining room.)

The summer journey was a satisfying introduction to southern Finland – sufficient to make the adequate statistical material and general reading to be fitted into a geographical background. As for the rest of our travelling companions, the entire experience could best be summed up in a phrase of W. H. Auden – 'a taste of joy in an innocent youth'. Links were maintained with them for a generation.

John Gibbons

Gibbons, another prolific writer who took himself off to the Baltic in 1938, shared none of the predisposed admiration for Finland which marked most British travel writing of this period. Indeed, he admitted in the preface of *Keepers of the Baltic Gates* (1939) that he hated even the prospect of his proposed journey:

> Few travel writers, though, can be choosers. Here was a London publisher wanting so many articles on the New Baltic States, and I could not afford to refuse the commission.

As if this admission were not enough, Gibbons chose to compensate for his lack of interest by writing in a flippant and chatty style. He did not help himself by arriving in November, but he did at least see something of the country: '[a] conscientious travel-author simply must get out of the bus sometimes'. He set off each day in the blithe belief, often justified, that wherever he ended up an English speaker could be located, if only by telephone. His preference was to choose places whose names he could pronounce, and that is why he found himself one day in a town little visited by travellers, Salo.

There was Salo that I went to, and it's a not very big town perhaps sixty kilometres from Abo and ever so many miles inland, only on the tail-end of a very broad creek that winds up through the flats from the Gulf. It has quite a good modern hotel and ever so many cafés with gramophones and electric light, and, of course, the ubiquitous telephone. And yet the place nearly drove me mad. There is a sort of central square with the shops and business offices of the little town all round. Most of them seemed to be banks, and there are more, I think, in Finland than even in America, and I suppose that the amalgamation process has hardly yet started. To find myself in a square entirely surrounded by bank managers was in itself a depressing experience, but it was the outskirts of the place that really did it. Walk any way you like, and you seemed to come to water, ice-cold and cruel. And if you walked a bit farther you came to wood. In the utter silence, unbroken by so much as a single foot-fall, the snow was coming down all the time. An hotel bedroom isn't exactly my idea of gaiety, but I went and locked myself in the place as in a tiny fortress against the unknown powers of an enemy world without.

Rather puzzlingly, Gibbons published another account of this trip six months later. Perhaps he was double-crossing his publisher, but the fact is that despite a great deal of padding he did not have material for even one book. In *My Baltic Journey* (1939) a shorter, smaller and even more relaxed account of the same journey, more light is thrown on Salo, and there is a rare mention of Karis (Karjaa).

But here, inland in Salo, the language was pure Finnish and nothing else, and as I wandered miserably about in the half-darkness of the Northern afternoon I felt rather lost. You can't even drop into an inn, as in most other

175

countries, because there aren't any, and a *café* that only offers coffee and a gramophone doesn't exactly make for sociability.

Eventually he

came to a place called Karjaa, and about the only thing that happened there was that I very nearly went back to Abö [*sic*] again! Karjaa is a railway junction, and – for Finland – quite an important one, with a long station plat-form and about three rows of freight-trucks standing in a deserted-looking siding. All the people got out of my bus, and the conductor came to me, pointed to his watch, and was obviously trying to get it into my head that there was ten minutes' halt; which was exactly the sort of thing that would naturally happen in England.

Gibbons ran into the station, failed to locate the restaurant, then in his haste got on the wrong bus, the one heading back to Turku. The Helsinki bus, with his luggage on board, came in pursuit:

I was transferred, rather like a parcel that had gone astray, 'my' bus turned round again, and off we started once more. But nobody laughed.

'I was a bit frightened of Finland,' Gibbons had written before setting out: 'If this was the far south, the warm part of the country, what was the rest going to be like?' In fact, his exploration never extended beyond 'the southern coastal strip'. All he found worth relating about Helsinki was a visit to a barber.

I didn't know the right thing to say, and all I could do was to sit down in the chair the lady-operator pointed to and rub my hands briskly over my chin and cheeks. Thereupon she produced an enormous towel, rammed the bulk of it into my mouth so as to stifle any protest, and immediately proceeded to cut off most of what hair I've got left.

Next she shampooed me, sprinkled me with all the perfumes of Arabia, and plied every other art of her trade that she could think of. She shaved me, by the way, last of all; and even then she seemed reluctant to let me escape.

Gibbons had begun his visit in 'Abö', and concluded it with equally lazy inattention: 'I spent three days in Helinski,' he wrote, where 'nothing in the world ever happened'. 'Helinski' is his preferred spelling throughout the book.

Lady Diana Cooper

A few months before Gibbons made his listless and lethargic way across southern Finland British visitors of a very different stamp were approaching Helsinki by sea. Alfred Duff Cooper was First Lord of the Admiralty, and relished the opportunities which the post afforded for high living aboard the official yacht *Enchantress,* a sloop with the stern converted to living quarters, and carrying a crew of 150. Cooper was firmly established in the English upper class, a friend of the royal family, and had married Lady Diana Manners, daughter of the Duke of Rutland, and the most illustrious beauty of her generation. Her life had included working as a hospital nurse during the First World War and a brief and very successful career as an actress, but now she and her husband knew and entertained almost every celebrity in a gay and extravagant social world. The were known as 'the golden couple' of their age. After the war Duff Cooper became British Ambassador in Paris, and was raised to the peerage as Viscount Norwich.

Early in August 1938 they set out from Portsmouth for a Baltic cruise, and berthed in Helsinki harbour for a courtesy visit. Lady Diana kept a diary of the cruise, and her observations on their visit were printed in the second volume of her memoirs, *The Light of Common Day* (1959). Her descriptions are lively, alert and intelligent, but her amused condescension towards almost everyone she met, especially members of the Finnish government, will not be to the taste of some readers.

Helsingfors   *13 August*

Everything progresses well. It's a life of extremes – ghastly moments and enchanting ones. The one-and-three-quarter days at sea [from Danzig] came under 'enchanting' – rest after effort, smoothest waters, purest sky, the full moon rising over the starboard side and the sun sinking on the port side. We walked round the rather nice watery town with Russian traces left, and then there was the usual scramble to dress for dinner with the British Minister, Mr Snow. Mrs Snow is everything that is best in British womanhood, long-legged, good, unaffected and serene. He told me that they sit down with Finns at 6 p.m. to a crayfish feast and stay until 2 or 3 a.m. with scarcely a word spoken.

The Air Attaché West, V.C., with a wife and wooden leg, chucked a luncheon party to picnic with us. They told their host that as they could not be back until 4 and as lunch was for 1.30, they'd be too late. 'Not a bit,' said he. We saw them off at 3.45. They told me later that they'd really got down to it at 5 and I saw them come home at 10.30.

Tonight at the Snows' well-run house I sat between the host and the Finnish Foreign Minister, named Holsti, a darling English-speaking *douce-viveur*. The great Field-Marshal Mannerheim was there. He made Finland and is treated half-royal, half-Godhead. He looks fifty and is said to dye his hair (and Brendan swore that he had rouged lips) and he is only seventy-two. He's old Russian Imperialist (that I find irresistible) and says in French '*Pardon*'. I had never heard of him, had you? Field-Marshal Mannerheim.

14 August

We (Snows, West and Holsti, our party, the Sub and the Doc) all went on a picnic. Four motor-cars. It took place on a high flat rock. The day, as always, was perfect and a large lovely lake shimmered at our feet. Some of us scrambled down a long rocky steep to get a bathe, not so successful as it was quite a shallow lake and grounded with very yielding black slime. I said to my sweet old Holsti: 'Do you like picnics?' 'Better than anything else in the world,' he said, with the sincerity of a saint professing his faith. Everything practical is done by the Cabinet in this country. George [Gage] wanted a canoe for the sake of exercise. The Minister for Defence was consulted and the Minister of Agriculture for worms and rods. The Foreign Minister is always opening the car-door, and is ready for any odd jobs.

Finns are like beavers. They work in a violent unceasing way for themselves, cutting and building and quarrying silently, and are delighted with the results. They've done a good job in their Parliament House. It's a modern Versailles with a dash of Solon about it. The Members do their lobby-strolling in a really fairy-like *galerie des glaces* of marble and crystal. I suppose that, with all their achievements and pride of independence, they can be chewed up by one of several countries in a jiffy.

The Prime Minister [Cajander] took us over his Senate and his stadium and then it was aboard again to dress for Mannerheim's blow-out. Wonderful house, marvellous food and wines, all of which he arranges, the right flowers, china objects and the right lighting, and after dinner a first-class budding she-pianist. She played everything I liked best and so beautifully that I gave her a handsome jewel off my person. A man said to me at dinner: 'In England you have very good cow and pig races.' I wish we had!

15 August

Do you know about a Finn-bath? It's world-famous. They steam you up Russian-fashion and then flog you within an inch of your life with birch-rods, and so hurl you into cold water. George and I started the day by walking to the town in quest of this sensation, but when we arrived it was not yet open, so we had to content ourselves with a bit of shopping without words. Trying to get a dish of yoghourt was very funny. I acted milking the cow and cutting a lemon, licking and putting on a wry face. It worked.

Our dinner tonight on board was rock-bottom. I had Field-Marshal Mannerheim and the Prime Minister. I worked my hardest and so did Troubridge, but it was like working stickjaw; and the food tasted to me filthy because of Mannerheim's epicureanism.

Bernard Newman

Newman's hundred or more books comprise travel, politics, spy stories, and popular novels; as a lecturer he could always 'fill a town hall'. Despite his fame he comes over as one of the least pretentious and most engaging of all the British travellers who have written about Finland. His *Baltic Roundabout* (1939) opens, as it continues, modestly:

> When I consulted an atlas, I discovered somewhat to my surprise that I had visited every country in Europe except Finland. Naturally I decided on the spot to go there.

The frontispiece of *Baltic Roundabout* is a photograph of Newman's bicycle, nicknamed George, which had already achieved some literary prominence of its own, most recently in *Ride to Russia* (1938). In *Speaking from Memory* (1960)

Newman wrote that '"George" became a very popular character. His and my "adventures" were featured in the BBC Children's Hour for years.' Although George 'might be classed as an ordinary pedal cycle', it – one should perhaps say 'he' – boasted a three-speed, such a novelty in Finland that he was often stopped on the road by people wanting to try it out.

Exploring by bicycle gave Newman a distinctive experience of Finland: many travellers, Gibbons, for example, rather prided themselves of having occasionally got 'off the beaten track', but Newman managed it much of his time. On Åland a boatman was puzzled by the bicycle, understandably, since although the island they were heading for 'housed a small village it had no road whatsoever'. Even when he found paths, they were often unbeaten:

> For hours I rode through forests. There was no rule of the road, and I chose paths which offered the most shade. There was no need for rules, since traffic is so sparse . . . [I]n my first fifty kilometres from Mikkeli I did not meet a solitary human being.

Those he did meet were what he terms 'ordinary people'; this was assured by his contract: the publisher limited his expenses to five shillings a day. Repeatedly he records the 'profound, indeed, overwhelming' hospitality which he experienced in 'peasant cottages' where 'it was only with the exercise of much tact that I succeeded in paying for my night's lodging'. He spells out his intentions in the Introduction: 'I would not have ridden fifty miles to see a waterfall, but more than that distance to meet interesting people.' In other words, *Baltic Roundabout* was not a sightseeing tour.

Starting his roundabout journey in Copenhagen, Newman remarks that 'Denmark must rank with Holland as the cyclist's paradise.' Not so Sweden: he arrived in Stockholm covered in mud, 'the result of the unequal contest between a cyclist and heavy vehicles'. Åland he thought primitive, even 'compared with the out-of-the-way districts in Sweden', but for Newman that was an attraction. His unusual and often entertaining experiences began as soon as he landed, with a very bizarre incident:

I had arrived at Saltvik, where two or three men were working in desultory fashion repairing the little church. Two of them were hacking stones into shape – rather clumsily, for they were probably far more at home with the shaping of timber than stone. Eventually they got a great stone raised on to the primitive but ingenious arrangement of timber and rope which served as a hoist. As I stood watching, however, the hoist slipped and the stone descended from a height of two or three feet on to the toes of one of the men.

In a way, of course, he was lucky, for had the stone ascended another few feet before it dropped it might have squashed him flat. In any case, his toes were very badly damaged; yet he sat sedately while his companion and I cut off his boot, and surveyed the damage.

'Is there a doctor here?' I asked.

'Not to-day – he's away: we shall have to take him into Mariehamn.'

'Is there a car?'

'Not to-day; he'll have to go by cart.'

'Is it necessary?' asked the injured man. 'Can't we deal with it ourselves?'

'But look, man,' I said; I had been swabbing at the broken toes to get a better estimate of the damage. 'Look at your little toe in particular – it's simply squashed to pulp.'

'Then cut it off,' he cried. 'It's no use like that! I have a knife in my pocket.'

And when I looked again, it seemed the obvious thing to do. I know little about surgical operations, but summoned a plentiful supply of boiling water from a neighbouring cottage, and sterilized the enormous hack-knife which the wounded man passed to me.

By this time, naturally, a full company had gathered. It was almost pathetic to see the confidence in me, a stranger. The injured man was quite unconcerned, and I was glad that he had no inkling of my own inward tremors. Quite calmly he sat on a grassy bank and watched me cut off his toe – naturally, without any anaesthetic. Actually the operation was quite easy, for the bone was completely smashed.

After landing at Turku, Newman pedalled towards Helsinki:

It was Saturday evening in the little town of Lohja. The people took their amusement in rural fashion. The grown-up girls in their best frocks promenaded up and down the village streets – closely followed, I need hardly say, by the youths of the town. Mother gossiped under the eaves with the lady next door, and the kids splashed happily in the lake in their birthday suits.

The only surprise in Lohja was the church: 'One does not suspect these plain-living countrymen of perpetrating atrocities in colourful designs,' he remarks.

In Helsinki, among other unscheduled experiences, he unaccountably found himself at the zoo on Korkeasaari, 'accompanied by two children speaking only Finnish'. Like many of his compatriots, he was astonished by the Academic Bookshop, where he was so captivated by a young lady assistant that he bought one of his own books to present to her.

From Helsinki he set off for Heinola, but he never got there:

Halting at a peasant cottage for final refreshment before tackling the last hour's ride, I found myself greeted heartily in English.

The peasant, a man in the thirties, insisted that I should be his guest. We settled down to conversation, and I was amazed at his culture – his knowledge of philosophy was infinitely deeper than mine. And when I saw his library of books I cried out aloud.

'Yes, I am taking a degree,' he explained. 'I take my finals this year. I have been a long time getting so far, for I have my farm work to do as well, of course.'

'And what are you making for? The law?' I asked.

'No – my degree.'

'Yes – but afterwards?'

'How do you mean, afterwards?'

'I mean, what are you going to get out of it?'

He looked at me in gentle reproof: he was getting nothing out of education but education. A Scotsman would have understood his mentality better than I did. Yet he did me good, and when I am tempted to think of culture and finance in the same moment I always recall that Finnish peasant as a corrective.

His cottage was typical of a thousand others I entered in Finland. Central feature of the living-room was the great stove, superfluous in summer but essential in winter, when even the mattresses would be laid on its broad expanses. The bedroom carpet was of cow-hide, woven locally, and most of the furniture was made by native craftsmen. On the floor of the living-room were scattered fragrant leaves, which raised an invigorating scent every time they were trodden below foot.

One incident was intriguing. Over supper I commented on the excellence of the butter.

'Maybe you have tasted it before,' my host suggested. 'Our village sends quite a lot of butter to England.'

'I don't ever remember seeing Finnish butter on sale,' I said.

'No. We have been told that there is an ancient preju-
dice against Finnish butter. So it is shipped to a firm in
Copenhagen – who sell it to England as *Danish* butter. So
everybody is satisfied.'

In this way Newman got to know, and within a short time
deeply to respect, the Finnish people and their country.

Another incident occurred between Lahti and Mikkeli:

> One afternoon I halted to chat with a peasant. His hay
> harvest was gathered, and he was already ploughing. I ad-
> mired the depth and straightness of his furrows, long lines
> of rich earth.
>
> 'Yes, this is fine land,' he agreed. 'It is glebe land. In
> the old days men gave a share of their best land to the
> church.'
>
> 'I see. So this is not your own?' I said.
>
> 'Yes, it is.'
>
> 'But if it is glebe land, surely you have to rent it from
> the local pastor?'
>
> 'My dear sir, I *am* the local pastor.'

Heading north, he 'went to church in a Finnish village', a very
long and solemn service. He noticed that many of the farmers
had brought their dogs with them, and that some of the congregation returned home in 'the great communal boats maintained
for the purpose'. He 'was amused to see some of the the girls
removing their best frocks before entering the boat, and sitting
solemnly in their petticoats'.

Heading now for Mikkeli, he was introduced to the sauna
('one of my biggest ordeals'), before getting a second roasting:
spotting a forest fire, he heroically tried to beat it out before
discovering two men who were actually in charge of the burning. He said to one that it looked like a long-term project:

> 'Yes,' he agreed. 'It will not carry crops in my day.'

'Then why do you work so hard?'

'It will carry crops for my son!'

Here was the spirit of peasant Europe, unbreakable and unconquerable.

From Mikkeli 'it was a wonderful day's ride':

The country was perhaps even more pleasant than before, and I was never far away from trees and water. So often as I was hot and dusty, so often I was able to take a cooling plunge.

This ride took him all the way through Savonlinna to Punkaharju, and it was shortly after this that his most unusual adventure occurred:

The evening after Punkaharju I descended upon a little village near Lahdenpohja. The little inn was scrupulously clean, and fed me royally – for a matter of three shillings, covering dinner, bed and breakfast. After dinner the locals gathered, and the company was lively, for four or five men spoke some language which I knew . . .

This evening in this Finnish village inn, a small, grey-faced spectacled gentleman came up to me and addressed me in very halting German.

'I wonder if you would be good enough to do me a favour?' he said.

'Of course,' I replied. 'What is it?'

'May I borrow your trousers?'

I suppose I looked alarmed. 'Borrow my trousers?' I echoed.

'Yes.'

'What, here and now? What am I to do without any trousers?'

'Oh, I will lend you some, if you wish – unless you have no spares of your own.'

'I have some shorts,' I said. 'But tell me, what is the idea? Why this sudden passion for my trousers?'

'Well,' he explained. 'You see, I am the local tailor: several young men of the village have been admiring the cut of your trousers, and have asked me if I could possibly make them trousers of the same pattern. So if I could borrow your trousers to study them in detail and to make myself a pattern, you would indeed be conferring a favour upon me.'

Naturally I could not resist a plea like that. I changed back into shorts and went round with him to his shop while a dozen husky Finns watched in admiration as he cut a paper pattern to the shape of my trouser legs.

Even where Newman is describing the most popular of all tourist expeditions, to the island monastery of Valamo, he takes an original and practical view: 'There was a stiff breeze blowing,' he writes, '. . . and soon men and women were being unashamedly sick over the rails.' Returning to Sortavala he wanted, like Ingram before him, to see more of the primitive Karelia. He stayed in a village (which he does not name) where the schoolmaster was very interested in folklore and old customs, and also spoke French. He took Newman to hear one of the very last of the *runo* singers; this description is the last of many given over the years by British travellers.

We found the old man in his cottage: although the morning was warm, he was crouched by the enormous stove. But then, he was nearly ninety, and the blood was running thin in his veins. Beside him hung two sides of bacon, lean and of a hard brownness. Above were rye loaves, a hole through the middle of each, so that they could be threaded on a string. I had tried to eat this rye bread, but failed – army biscuits are comparatively soft. But one man complained that when he went to the town he was glad to get home, for they insisted on feeding him on white bread!

The old man was willing, but weak. He was not a real *runo* singer, he confessed, but his father had been. Yet at least he could show how it was done: a girl was despatched to summon a crony from a neighbouring cottage.

The two old men sat by the stove, facing each other, and holding each other's hands.

'Brother, do you know this song?' one asked: then began to croon, in his halting ancient voice, some traditional air. Soon its spirit seized him, and he cast off his years.

The moment he finished, the other man struck up a song: his voice was surprisingly powerful for so old a man: it was a song of love he sang, and I might have been listening to an ardent lover of twenty.

('Of course, you understand that this is not quite the real thing,' my host whispered. 'These men are singing traditional songs – the old *runo* singers used to improvise them. The art is now lost – these men are just showing you *how* it was done.')

The faces of the two old men were alight with a new youth as they chanted the songs of long ago. Sometimes the group about them would join in a chorus: the heat of the stove brought strange but not objectionable odours from the foods stored about it: through the window I heard a merry tinkle of bells, for it was Sunday morning.

With a final jangle the bells halted. The two men released hands, breaking off in the middle of a verse.

'They can sing no more,' my host explained. 'It is the hour of the church service.'

Newman kept within his budget of five shillings a day, to cover everything. A good hotel room could be had for four shillings a night, though, so he was clearly not 'roughing it' in the way that Ingram had been. His economical way of living and travelling ensured importantly that the people he came across usually belonged 'to the peasant class or its equivalent'. His is the only bicyclist's view of Finland in this volume; most of his wanderings were off the main roads, and he was able to visit places which even the bus did not serve. He cycled on through Karelia, recording only one meeting, with a shepherd playing a pipe.

'You like it?' he asked.
'It is very musical,' I lied.
'It is not intended to be musical. It scares off the bears.'

On he rode, through Imatra to Vyborg. There he failed to obtain the visa which he required to continue into Russia, so he set off by train for Helsinki, spoiling himself by taking a sleeper. At the Russian office 'I hung about for two hours, and then was abruptly and with unnecessary rudeness informed that I could not be granted a visa to Russia.' In *Ride to Russia* (1938), entering from Romania, he had never 'known such a searching customs examination as that at the Russian frontier', but had eventually been allowed in; here '[t]here was no explanation – I just could not go', so the next morning he caught the boat for Tallinn.

As we steamed across the smooth Baltic, I looked back at Finland in affectionate fashion. In my journey through the country I had encountered nothing but friendliness.

Newman returned to the region after the war, recording it in *Baltic Background* (1948). This is a very different sort of book, containing astute political history and analysis, but on the Finland pages he recycles several of the episodes from his earlier book, beginning the section with a page devoted to admiring comments about the Finns, 'physically and mentally one of the finest races in the world'.

The dust jacket of *Baltic Roundabout* promotes it as 'A TRAVEL BOOK of the GREATEST TOPICAL INTEREST', but there is nothing topical in the Finland chapters; not a cloud in the sky. From the viewpoint of the twenty-first century Newman's book has a poignancy much more moving than anything found elsewhere in the cluster of books from the late 1930s. He discovered Finland during the last full year of peace, and reading today his accounts of the seemingly unchanging patterns of country life, and of the timeless world of Karelia, one is struck by a sense of its innocence and vulnerability. Newman speculated in his Introduction that British people have no interest in the Baltic states because 'most of them are unlikely to disturb the peace of Europe'. Everything was about to change. The next wave of British visitors would have neither the leisure nor the interest to listen to singers, nor the opportunity of visiting Vyborg and Ladoga. *Baltic Roundabout* marks the end of an era.

THE WINTER WAR

Lady Diana Cooper's casual supposition that Finland 'can be chewed up by one of several countries in a jiffy' was soon to be put to the test. Fifteen months after the *Enchantress* left the Baltic Russian bombs fell on Helsinki, and the Winter War had begun.

Harry Bell was in Helsinki on the morning of 30 November 1939 'when Russian bombers swooped':

> I was starting on my round of business when I heard the air-raid warning. Almost at the same moment came the sound of guns. Then the Russian planes were overhead and the bombs were dropping.

During this period of the 'Phoney War', a term used to describe the first nine months of the Second World War, Finland became briefly the centre of the world stage, and, as Evelyn Waugh wrote, 'Mannerheim held the place in English hearts won in 1914 by King Albert of the Belgians.'

The British involvement is, of course, only a small strand in the complex history of the Winter War, a war which concluded a period of fruitless negotiations during which the Soviet Union had demanded military agreements and boundary changes which would protect its territory from any invasion through Finland by a foreign power. Finally running out of patience, it fabricated a border incident and renounced the non-aggression pact of 1932. It commenced hostilities, with no declaration of war, and simultaneously set up a puppet government in Terijoki, which acceded to all its demands.

The war was a David and Goliath struggle in which Finland, as Harold Macmillan wrote, 'caught the imagination of the world', and it certainly caught the imagination of the British public. For three months, in one of the coldest recorded Finnish winters, the Finns, although vastly outnumbered, repelled the Red Army, inflicting many defeats. In the Battle of Suomussalmi meagre Finnish forces destroyed two entire Soviet divisions: 'In the annals of warfare,' writes one military historian, 'one must look to classical times for parallels to the annihilation of such a large number by so few.' The League of Nations Assembly used Article 16 of the Covenant to expel the Soviet Union, and urged 'every member of the League to provide Finland with . . . material and humanitarian assistance'.

In Britain responses to the Soviet attack on Finland were personal, public, and political. The Finland Fund was set up, raising money from contributions, collections, and concerts: Bell records that '[t]he ordinary man in the street sent in his shillings and half-crowns; a ploughman's wife sent her mite; and half-a-crown was sent in by "Three Messenger Girls"'; the King and Queen also contributed. Students 'solicited funds in Cambridge market place using as receptacle a Russian trench boot and "tin hat"'. The courage of the Finns and the romance of the perceived situation inspired contributions of more than £300,000. This was used for medical and military supplies, flown out during February. Winston Churchill, now First Lord of the Admiralty, broadcasting on 20 January, 'could not let the opportunity pass once again to stoke the fires of moral indignation against communism':

> Only Finland – superb, nay, sublime – in the jaws of peril –
> Finland shows what free men can do. The service rendered
> by Finland to mankind is magnificent. They have exposed,
> for all the world to see, the military incapacity of the Red
> Army and of the Red Air Force. Many illusions about So-
> viet Russia have been dispelled in these few fierce weeks of
> fighting in the Arctic Circle. Everyone can see how Com-
> munism rots the soul of a nation; how it makes it abject

and hungry in peace, and proves it base and abominable in war. We cannot tell what the fate of Finland may be, but no more mournful spectacle could be presented to what is left to civilized mankind than that this splendid Northern race should be at last worn down and reduced to servitude worse than death by the dull brutish force of overwhelming numbers. If the light of freedom which still burns so brightly in the frozen North should be finally quenched, it might well herald a return to the Dark Ages, when every vestige of human progress during two thousand years would be engulfed.

The heroism of the Finns gained their cause widespread support; a correspondent in *The Times* pointed out that St Henry, Finland's patron saint, was an Englishman, so 'this early bond gives an added reason – were it needed – for us English to do our utmost, both by our prayers and by our "alms", to help this heroic nation'. There was less sympathy for Finland from the political far left: a curious situation was described on the front page of *The Sunday Dispatch* on 31 December:

> An extraordinary position will arise in Canterbury Cathedral this morning. Dr. Lang, Archbishop and Primate of all England, will be present at a service at which special prayers will be said for Finland.
>
> In attendance on Dr. Lang will Dr. Hewlett Johnson, the Pro-Soviet Dean of Canterbury, whose latest book, *The Socialist Sixth of the World*, is a eulogy of Russia and all things Red.

The newspaper was assured by Canon Crum, the officiating cleric, that 'Canterbury will go on praying for Finland and for confusion to Russia.'

Churchill's responses were mixed: on one hand the moral arguments for helping Finland against Soviet Russia were powerful, but as a minister of the Crown he 'could not take

a central role in the popular movement'; his personal involvement went no further than donating his own pair of skis to
the Finnish army. The official compromise could be described
as 'notional neutrality': the government encouraged unofficial
aid to Finland, but publicly kept other options open. Churchill
realised that Finland was not a key element in the war against
Nazi Germany: as Markku Ruotsila has written, he placed the
Winter War 'within a broader geostrategic constellation' which
'included dimensions that were more important to Churchill
than the mere fate of Finland'.

A recruitment agency, the Finnish Aid Bureau, unofficially
sanctioned by the government, was set up in January, and attracted many thousands of military volunteers. Following what
has been termed 'The Spanish Precedent', a British Volunteer
Contingent was formed: it was Finland now that became the
symbol of democracy in peril. While the British volunteers in
1936 had been largely communist sympathisers joining the fight
against fascism, in 1940 it was communist Russia which was
the enemy. Eventually four contingents of volunteers, totalling
227 men, left for Finland; they were idealistic, but not always
suitable (one of them had a wooden leg, another was crippled
with spinal meningitis). When the Winter War ended some of
them were already at Lapua in western Finland, the mustering
point for international volunteers, but most were still on their
way through or from Sweden. For the Finnish authorities they
became first an embarrassment and then a headache; it was
some two years before they all finally dispersed. Most of them
made it back to England, by diverse and devious routes, but
some 'ended up in German prisoner-of-war camps; others simply disappeared'. They were never, in any case, going to make
any military impact.

While the volunteers were mustering, the Cabinet, despite
Churchill's convictions, was developing a plan for Allied intervention, combining military support for Finland with a plan

to deprive Germany of Swedish iron from the ore fields at Gällivare. Despite the categorical refusal of Sweden and Norway even to consider transit permission, the forces were ready to sail – indeed, the stores convoy was already at sea – when the Peace of Moscow on 11 March ended the Winter War. This was a punitive settlement in which Finland ceded 10 per cent of its territory and 30 per cent of its economy. The losses included most of Karelia with the historic city of Vyborg, and the southernmost port of Hanko (leased for thirty years). Twelve per cent of the population had to be evacuated. The Baltic states, which had been forced to accede to demands similar to those made of Finland during the previous autumn, were incorporated into the Soviet Union in August. The Peace of Moscow lasted little more than a year. In July 1941 Finland, 'reasonably assured of the Führer's protection', and with the Red Army occupied in stemming the German advance, opened a new offensive and by the end of August the pre-1940 frontier had been regained. The 'Continuation War' lasted for three years rather than three months, and ended with arn armistice even harsher than that of 1940.

Several of the British subjects who, in different capacities, were in Finland during the Winter War, were still there during the short period which was allowed to evacuate the territories which had been ceded. Their accounts are, in their own way, as painful and harrowing as the descriptions of the actual war.

At no other time, except perhaps during the Olympic Games in 1952, have there been as many British visitors – writers, reporters and special correspondents as well as volunteers – in Finland. 'Most correspondents,' reads one account, 'fought Finland's Winter War at the Hotel Kämp's bar, which had been reinforced and turned into a bomb shelter.' One of the exceptions was George Steer, who for six consecutive days had a front-page story from Finland in the *Daily Telegraph*. Steer had famously reported for the London *Times* from Guernica during the Spanish Civil War; he wrote from Porvoo that the Soviets 'had studied well the Nazis' tactics in Spain, hitting symbolic targets hard to cause psychological distress'. He was comforted by the undamaged cathedral, and by noting that '[t]he population preserved "an almost fantastic calm" as planks fell from their falling houses and only the stone chimneys remained standing'. From Vyborg he reported that 'its black shell of desolation was like the broken towns of Flanders and Northern France after 1914'.

John Langdon-Davies

Like Steer, John Langdon-Davies had been a war correspondent during the Spanish Civil War. He was one of many socialists who at the end of 1939 repudiated the Soviet Union as a betrayer of the socialist cause; his concerns took him to Finland to see for himself and to report what he saw. His *Finland: The First Total War* (1940) contains caustic and contemptuous reflections on Soviet apologists who continued to justify the attempted subjugation of Finland. He is often reminded of his experiences in Spain, most strikingly when he describes the evacuation of Hanko, where 'curiously similar piles had been waiting beneath the scorching sun to be removed to safety from Franco's bombs'. Langdon-Davies was a man of very many parts; the author of more than forty books on diverse subjects, one of his special interests was warfare, especially its technical aspects. His book, based on two months spent in Finland in 1940, is partly an account of strategy and weaponry, but reveals a very acute understanding of Finland, especially when he examines the social and political structure of the country.

He arrived in Turku by air in January:

Hundreds of red, yellow and green specks illuminate the snow beneath us like an iced birthday cake. Everybody watches with intense excitement; and I believe everyone felt as I did, 'Hurry up and get down, so they can put those lights out.'

In less than a minute we had made a perfect landing in the centre of the circle of coloured lights, and a second later we were once more surrounded by unmitigated night . . .

A separate anthology might be made of British accounts of Soviet bombing, especially of observers' experiences of bombing raids on roads and railways, and of their descriptions of scrambling for safety into the snow, and hiding in the forests. Those written by Langdon-Davies are among the most vivid, beginning in Turku:

There was an hour or so before my train to Helsinki. I stumbled through an invisible town, guided only by the pallid snow beneath my feet; but against the brilliant stars I saw in every direction the architectural fantasies of modern war, brick chimneys cutting off the light of the Milky Way, all that was left of a row of wooden houses burned by Molotov; the jarred edges of splintered timber, and the functionless shapes of shattered stone.

In the train, up and down the corridor there walked men in white fur caps and white coats with yellow armlets on their left arm with V.S.S. printed on them. V.S.S. is Finnish for A.R.P. [Air Raid Precautions]. These were the wardens watching the lights and prepared against emergency.

At midnight emergency came. The warden opened the door of our carriage, and muttered the Finnish word for air alarm, which most foreign journalists called 'halitosis' to the end. Down the line they had signalled the presence of Russian planes. The train had stopped, and out of the carriages there jumped men, women, and a few children.

As always in Finland, the forest grew to the very edge

of the permanent way. Those of us who had white hoods and capes put them on, and we stumbled through the soft snow of the embankment, and stood beneath the trees.

My first air alarm in Finland is printed for ever in my memory for the utter beauty of the experience. I had never before seen the brilliance of the frozen northern stars, which, with snow as their reflector, filled the world with as much light as the full moon.

As we listened for the planes even the wind held its breath. The trees, covered with ice and snow, were utterly motionless. Beneath them the imperturbable Finns stood at attention saying nothing and moving no limb. Only the two children standing in our group moved to get inside their mother's coat, not because they were frightened but because it was cold.

I leaned against a wood pile, carefully choosing the side away from the direction in which a low whine could be heard somewhere amid the stars. Planes were nosing around for the railway track and our train. The whine came nearer, lost its way, faded out, and came again, and finally wandered away towards the great bridge near Ekenäs. Not a word had been said; not a sign that either the passengers or the trees above their heads were alive.

Thus for one hour the frozen world stood still. Then came the 'All Clear' signal from up the line. We walked back to the train.

Later air-raids were equally memorable, but their 'utter beauty' was short-lived.

I saw thirty-two Russian bombers in perfect formation, fourteen-eight-eight, and then two stragglers, all coming directly towards me.

The first reaction was one of incredulity. This could not be happening to *me*. And at the same time the sheer beauty of the shining wings, like kingfishers in the sun, held back for a split second the realisation of danger; but, as I looked, something totally unexpected happened, a thing which I had never imagined nor bargained for. As the roar increased till it sounded as if the blue sky was piece of calico forcibly rent in two, I saw with my own eyes red objects, somewhat like a ship's buoy at sea, released from the foremost planes, steady themselves after a moment of swaying, and fall until the speed of their approach made them invisible.

I fell full length in the snow, as close to a tree trunk as I could, and stared up. I had often been in danger before; but this was the first time that I had been thus exposed, utterly unprotected, to the malevolent cold beauty of visible planes in action.

My eyes had astonished me with what they had revealed; but within a second the contribution of my ears brought sheer terror. There can be no sound so ruthless as that of a shower of bombs, and this was no question of half a dozen, or a dozen, or twenty bombs dropping as they did in Barcelona, where the likelihood of your being hit was so small that it scarcely occurred to you: this was quite literally a shower of bombs.

Riihimäki provided a different experience:

We all ran for the trees, and crouched deep down in the snow. But the bombers were not interested in us. Their mark was the town a little further on. We heard their bombs drop, and waited.

When a little less than an hour later we pulled into the station we found a desolate scene. Five raids in twelve hours had wrecked most of the buildings in Riihimäki and blackened the snow all around. The track had been torn up ahead, and we were told when the time came we should all have to walk half a mile along the twisted rails to another train waiting on the other side of the obstructions.

There was nothing to do in the station itself. Even the restaurant had ceased to function. It looked as if it had been swept by an earthquake. There were great holes in the platforms. In the station square a wooden hotel had lost half its front. Two or three fires were still burning in the station yards, and everywhere that pock-marked blackness on the face of the snow.

Repeatedly in Langdon-Davies's accounts the blackening of the virgin snow acts as a sort of metaphor for the violation of Finland's innocence. The passengers survived a second wave of incendiary bombing 'squatted low against the ground' in a trench; 'I had often been in danger before,' he wrote, 'but this was the first time that I had been thus exposed, utterly unprotected.' When the all clear finally sounded

We walked down the road together. It had not been immaculate on the way up; but now it was like a suppurating skin disease, the yellow and black pock-marks running into each other; and littered with every kind of broken thing.

On 11 March the Alko shops suddenly closed. 'People began to realise,' wrote Langdon-Davies, 'that something very grim might be coming.' The population was 'totally unprepared psychologically for what was coming,' but the foreign correspondents already knew. 'I cast about in my mind for a suitable spot in which to listen to the news.' The Hotel Kämp bar was impossible: the company of journalists 'who had proved themselves incapable of realising that they were paid spectators of a national tragedy, would at such a moment be beyond bearing'. He went instead to the crowded but ominously silent Elanto Co-operative restaurant. Over the radio came Luther's hymn, followed by Foreign Minister Tanner:

It had been the same hymn that the otherwise silent crowd had sung spontaneously at Helsinki railway station when last year the negotiators had gone to meet Molotov in Moscow . . .

Every now and then as the true tragedy unfolded itself my eye was caught by a quick short movement first from one table and then another. It was the movement of a man or a woman suddenly brushing away tears, which could never be allowed to reach their cheeks.

Twice there was another movement. Of course I could not understand anything that was being said, except the proper names. It was the words Viipuri and Hanko, that produced this movement. A spasmodic stifled cry, which seemed to come from almost everyone in the room, as if in response to a physical blow from an unseen weapon.

The mother and sister at my own table were now sitting with closed eyes. The girl at the next table was staring at the young man in uniform, as if something incomprehensible had frightened her. It was quite clear that it had never occurred to her to think, 'Peace means that he will not be killed', although it was quite possible that mother and sister were thinking 'Why was he killed?' . . .

The restaurant emptied in almost absolute silence, and out in the streets in the weak sunshine, which scarcely gathered enough strength to melt the soiled city snow, people walked to their work, their eyes fixed immediately in front of them on the ground.

John Sykes

Among the unit of Quaker volunteers who went to Finland was an ambulance driver, John Sykes, aged just twenty-one. In 'An Encounter during the Winter War', the opening chapter of his

1967 memoir, *Direction North: A View of Finland,* he recalls vividly his experiences in early 1940. The opening paragraph sets the scene:

> It was still winter, and mostly night. Dusk filled the afternoons. Some days it snowed, on others the sun that splashed and sparkled through the forest till midday was swallowed in haze, and then before dark a dim red orb shone through. A clear sky brought out the planes, so the dull hours suited us best; we could sleep and eat and service the ambulances before the evening round began. That was our busy time.

He had, of course, never experienced the cold before:

> For a climate that was reaching minus forty centigrade, and regularly hung around minus twenty, we wore felt boots and sheepskin coats, with layers of khaki woollens beneath, and white fur hats, and around our arms Red Cross flashes were pinned, and over all, even over the flashes, we wore white smocks that if the gong sounded would enable us as we grovelled in the snow to look no different from it.

Against this Arctic world are set occasional moments of welcome warmth:

> . . . as it was Thursday the communal stock-pot steamed with pea soup and pork, our weekly change from potato stew and beans, and maybe it was horse meat but never enough that we could be sure about that. The pork tasted good on Thursdays. Thursday was also a milk-drinking day; so after the pork and the milk and the soup, and the rye-bread brought in from the snow that was a convenient unfailing larder, and plenty of butter, and sugared coffee, and some of the jam that we had brought from England, and cheese and Quaker chocolate, and anti-scurvy pills,

we were especially ready, Thursday fit, for the work that would take us through the night to some hour of the following morning.

The detailed descriptions of servicing and driving the ambulances are enlivened by descriptions of the Finnish soldiers he encounters, especially his 'companion', a lugubrious character known only as Kanada:

> He knew the way, whatever the night, familiar it seemed with every tree, and he gave the password to the succession of sentries. He watched my driving without comment, except, as we hit ice or were adrift in snow or entered the deep ruts of the lorries, to make demonic steering movements, that were wilder and faster than those I was making, that were calculated to nerve me through but which afterwards he had difficult in stopping. He blazed momentarily; but then he was back as dour as ever . . .

> Driving by starlight was a different experience from driving in a snowfall. Even without lights one could see the vicinity, ghostly lit with its battle junk. Macabre objects that in the mist loomed up with poetic horror, like a single stack of bodies, or a single tank, still with the timber that had crippled it thrust between its wheels, or a pillbox or the contortions of wire or a single grim white-clad figure that for marooned seconds one feared to be a Russian, now reproduced themselves in quantity. There were lines of such tanks, rusting, rotting, cemeteries of wire, of abandoned defences, and multitudes of soldiers dead and alive quartered in the unending glades. The whole operation weighed more on one, its range along the frontiers, the place names involved, the rivers, the lakes, the destroyed villages, and to our rear the chain of blacked-out cities with their grieving but tireless populations – all this was suddenly apparent, drawn into one's driving perspective.

Of course, even now, when one could see the road, could see the frantic convoys of sleighs and brace oneself for a flurry of lorries, it didn't help much to know that this was Syskyjärvi, then Pyörittäjä, then Leppäsyrjä, then Suistamo, and so down the line: for still, as in a treasure hunt, what mattered was the turn following the bridge, the sharp fork right, the manor house, after which one had to count a kilometre then turn left then be ready for the sentry. But, this attended to, this working script, one was forced by the starlight to broaden one's horizon, to realise Finland pitted against Russia and, beyond, the whole of tortured Europe feeling its way into the abyss. It was the beginning of March 1940.

In a later chapter Sykes recalls his role during the immediate aftermath of the Peace of Moscow:

They had nine days to vacate Karelia to the new imposed frontier. First came the soldiers streaming past our billets, an unending stream and straggle of skis and sleighs and horses and heavy lorries, all cut to the same speed, the speed of worn-out infantrymen, heavy-faced, resentful that foreigners should be witnessing this private misfortune.

Next began the departure of civilians. The sleighs returned seventy to a convoy, aided by buses, lorries, trains, and odd vehicles such as our ambulances, in what was by now a seven-day effort to get the people and their movable goods back behind the safety line. Outside every house still in use, in farms, villages, market towns, there were piles of furniture and trunks and tools to be taken first to the nearest railhead, then by train to a series of depots. As always the organisation was meticulous – and remarkable in that it was improvised, coolly and correctly perceived in a flash and carried through with a hunter's flair. Finns, pushed to the last extremity, were able to keep a grip on reality . . .

One of the wounded soldiers Sykes had transported through the barrages from the battlefront to the field hospital for some reason caught his imagination: this was a 'stocky bulldog man, still, it could be, wrestling with the affront of his first major physical indignity'. His name was Pekka Suusanen, 'a socialist from Tampere', he learned. Sykes never forgot him, and a quarter of a century later returned to Finland to visit this 'rough uncompromising fighter, a moralist out of the arctic dark'. *Direction North,* based on a visit lasting many months, is one of the finest and most insightful of all British books about Finland. Sykes also renewed his acquaintance with the Swedish-speaking (and English-speaking) doctor, the man who, in the course of their conversations at the field hospital, had alerted him to Suusanen's existence:

> 'He hates our [i.e., Swedish speakers'] guts. He sticks to his principles. I see him as a man of the deepest morality. I admire him. He is a contemporary hero.'
> 'A war hero?'
> 'Oh more than that. In ten, twenty years from now he is the sort who must speak for Finland.'

This was the Finland which Sykes was to discover and explore twenty-five years later.

Sir Walter Citrine

Walter Citrine was another disillusioned socialist. The self-educated son of a seaman, he left school at the age of twelve to be apprenticed to an electrician. Working himself up through the Trade Union movement, he became General Secretary of the Trades Union Congress in 1926, and presided over the World Trade Union Conference in 1945. He published a number of books on social and Socialist issues, the most significant of which at this time was *I Search for Truth in Russia* (1936), which he was pleased to find on sale in the Academic Bookshop in Helsinki.

Like many socialists, he shared 'the dismay and horror of the civilised world' at the Soviet invasion of Finland. 'Comment in the Labour Movement was bitter,' he wrote. Against the background of reports about 'Soviet aeroplanes . . . bombing open towns just as Germany did in Poland, without a declaration of war of any kind' the leader of the Labour Party, Clement Attlee, received a telegram from Finland, from the Secretary of the Social Democratic Party, Aleksi Aaltonen, and the Secretary of the Trades Union Congress, Eero Vuori, asking for a delegation from Britain to examine the situation at first hand. The three who went were Citrine, John Downie of the Co-operative Union, and Philip Noel-Baker, a Labour MP who had run against Kolehmainen in the Olympic Games in Stockholm in 1912. In 1959 he was awarded the Nobel Peace Prize. Citrine's *My Finnish Diary* came out as a 'Penguin Special' in March, within a few weeks of his return to England.

The party flew to Copenhagen via Amsterdam, took the train to Stockholm, and flew to Turku, arriving on 24 January. There they examined the ruins of shops and houses, 'crawling over piles of bricks, twisted ironwork, and the charred remains of wooden walls, and found the process both exhausting and depressing'. Throughout his account, Citrine describes his bewilderment and dismay at the evidence of a Socialist state's 'destruction of the homes of these poor people under the hypocritical guise of liberating them'.

In the evening they set off on the first leg of their journey:

> We departed in bright moonlight, the snow gleaming so white that it was really unnecessary to switch on the headlights, although it appeared that we had special permission to do so if this was necessary. I noticed that other

vehicles which we occasionally passed on the road were driving without lights.

We came across quite a number of peasants on the roadway. They were on foot, but sometimes we would see a man and his wife sitting side by side on a narrow sledge with a sturdy horse trotting along at a steady pace. So far as I could judge the people were neatly and evidently very warmly clad. Many of them had fur hats, and the women usually wore heavy coats with fur collars, and both men and women wore snowboots.

The snow lying on the surface of the road was not very deep, and I was just congratulating myself on the way in which the car was holding the road, when suddenly we rounded a sharp corner, and before I knew what was happening the car was lying almost on its side in a snowdrift . . .

After a time we found a rope from somewhere or other and just at that moment we heard a lorry mounting the hill behind us. As it drew near we called to the driver, who readily undertook to help us, and manoeuvred his car into a position from which it could pull on the rope in a somewhat sideways direction. Then we all got our shoulders to the car, generally obstructing one another in the process, but finally we succeeded in lifting the lower side, until the car was once more back on the road.

Now our driver felt it incumbent upon to make up for lost time, and we sped along at an increased pace. The country was rather hilly and pine forests were frequent. We passed a number of villages, some of them containing ancient churches, one of which we were told was over six hundred years old. It had a long slated roof rising steeply to the apex. In fact, the longest I have seen.

As we approached Ekenäs [Tammisaari], which we reached at eleven o'clock, after roughly three hours of driving, Vuori told me that the Russian 'planes made a habit of bombing this little town practically every day. I asked what provision there was for the people in the way of air-raid shelters, but Vuori shrugged his shoulders and said that unfortunately they had not been able to provide proper shelters as yet, and so the people had to take to the forests. Practically every day now brought its regular routine of the women and children trooping into the forests, taking their food with them and staying until darkness fell, despite the bitterly cold weather. I said I hoped that Comrades Stalin and Molotov would be a little more considerate towards us, and allow us at least to have a decent night's rest. We were assured that we need have no concern on this account as the Soviet aeroplanes never flew by night.

We stayed at the Hotel Societetshuset, which we found to be constructed of wood. It was comfortable, clean and well heated. Unfortunately there were not enough rooms to go round, and several of us had to share. As we were thoroughly tired, that proved no inconvenience. Our room had running water, central heating and other modern conveniences. I spent a long time writing up my diary, and it was well after midnight when I was able to get to bed.

In his diary he notes that Ekenäs is 'a small pleasure resort, and it was difficult to understand why it had been so mercilessly bombed'.

After breakfast at the hotel they drove to Hanko, which 'seemed utterly deserted'. Here, as everywhere they went, they were scrupulous about establishing the truth of the reports of the bombing of civilian targets, the dropping of incendiary bombs, and the machine-gunning of civilians from the air. Citrine always insisted on first-hand evidence. After a couple of hours spent carefully recording the evidence of the bombing they set off for Helsinki, returning through Ekenäs:

as we recrossed the two bridges into the town I noticed a fine schooner and a small coastal steamer jammed close to one another in the frozen harbour.

In Helsinki they had lunch with Väinö Tanner, the Foreign Minister, and later were interviewed by foreign journalists at Hotel Kämp. Among many interviews which he records was one with Alex Matson, well known as a translator from Finnish, who had witnessed the shooting of civilians from the air.

It was extremely late when I got to bed and on going to open the curtains to allow some fresh air into my room, I read a notice which rather dissuaded me. It was to the effect that it was absolutely forbidden to open the windows during darkness, together with a friendly intimation that the sentry on guard had 'orders to shoot to enforce this.' I didn't feel it necessary to put his watchfulness to the test.

The next destination was Vyborg, where once again he logged details of the devastation. Over breakfast they were briefed by General Öhquist before setting out to visit Mannerheim at General Staff Headquarters:

As we approached the front line there was a strange stillness for a time. We hadn't sighted a single aeroplane since we arrived in Finland, and now that we were near the scene of the fighting, the guns seemed to have quietened down as well. I commented upon this, and the Swiss, M. Vallotton [President of the Swiss Parliament, travelling with them], retorted:

'My concierge told me this morning, "Things are very quiet now because there is a British Labour Delegation here. That is, of course, known to the Russian army and so they hold their fire now. We hope the Delegation will stay a long time."'

They were at this time about three kilometres from the front line, but were 'extremely disappointed to be told that it was undesirable to go further'. When Citrine replied that they were prepared to take the risk, an officer replied drily, 'We think you are of more service to Finland alive than dead.'

Every day Citrine seems to have enjoyed a good breakfast. At GHQ he excelled himself:

> There we had a splendid meal, simple but very adequate. Porridge made as well as any Scottish housewife could make, boiled eggs, ham, butter, potatoes baked in their jackets, excellent coffee with an abundance of butter and milk.
>
> We waited upon ourselves although there were several red-cheeked girls bringing up the supplies and enjoying the way in which everyone tucked in. Generals, staff officers and everyone else queued up in their turn, although they tried to insist upon helping us. I liked the porridge so well that I had two big platefuls.

They visited the injured – horses as well as soldiers – and seemed satisfied with the conditions of the Russian prisoners they interviewed.

The novel experience of the sub-arctic temperatures is, unsurprisingly, a recurrent topic; for the Finnish soldiers, he learned, it was not a problem:

> We were told many stories about the phlegmatic character of the Finns. During a very cold spell, one of the officers had inquired from his soldiers whether they felt the cold very much.
>
> 'It is cold,' answered one soldier.
>
> 'But why don't you run about and take some exercise?' said the officer.
>
> The man pondered this for a few seconds, and after balancing up the relative discomforts, replied deprecatingly,

'Oh, but it's not so cold as all that.'

An overnight train took them to Mannerheim's headquarters near Mikkeli, though Citrine does not name it. After breakfast (another 'excellent meal') they set off by car to General Staff Headquarters. Their conversation with Mannerheim was practical and military, but Citrine's first impressions are worth recording:

> In the course of this conversation an orderly brought an intimation that the 'Marshal' was ready to receive us. We passed along a corridor into a small room whose walls were occupied by maps and diagrams. In the centre was a table containing books and more diagrams, and behind this stood Field-Marshal Mannerheim. I had read a good deal about Mannerheim, and had been told many anecdotes of him since our arrival in Finland. His name is almost a legend amongst the people, and everywhere I went I found the most implicit confidence expressed in him.
>
> As we entered the room he drew himself up, and after we had ranged ourselves on the opposite side of the table and shaken hands with him, he read to us in English a short address of welcome. He spoke good English but with a noticeable accent.
>
> I looked closely at him during the time that he was addressing us. He had a decidedly strong face, with great powers of concentration visible in his brows, and a determined square jaw. I should think he would stand well over six feet and had very dignified carriage. Unlike some of his officers, he wore only very few ribbons, a single large white cross with gold borders being his only decoration.

He gave the delegation a wry summary of the military situation: 'Smiling rather sadly, Mannerheim said: "We have butter but not guns."'

The party returned to Helsinki by train, for a meeting with

the Prime Minister and Tanner, stopping en route to visit a large paper-making factory, where Citrine lectured the manager on the rights of workers. It was here that he had his first experience of a Finnish sauna, and found it, on the whole, a pleasant experience:

> I was afterwards massaged in an adjoining room by an elderly woman, rather to my embarrassment, but she took it all as a matter of course, and scrubbed and soaped me with as much indifference as though she were laying out a corpse.

In the evening they took a train for Tampere:

> The train was crowded with soldiers, but there were a considerable number of civilians including women and children on board. We all surged in together as soon as the train arrived, and we were so tightly packed that there was little comfort on the journey. Some people had to stand, but we all accommodated ourselves one way or another so as to make things not too irksome.
>
> The train was supposed to take four hours but in fact it took over five, and we did not reach Tampere until after one o'clock in the morning.
>
> It was impossible to read, of course, as the train lighting was even dimmer than in England during the worst period of our black-out. I sat wedged between two young soldiers, while opposite me was a woman nursing a young child, her other little girl of about four years of age resting on the knee of another soldier. The luggage racks were jammed with military equipment and the atmosphere was stifling. Fortunately I had a few sweets in my pocket, and the children were glad of them.
>
> I wondered to myself whether the apologists for Stalin and Molotov would have felt very happy in this company.

The soldier next to me said something which I did not understand, but a man sitting near explained that he was apologising for crushing me. I laughed at this, and explained that I knew very well that any inconvenience I had to go through was nothing compared to what the soldiers had to withstand.

This gentleman then asked whether I was a member of the British delegation, and on my confirming this he very soon spread the news round the coach. That broke down any little reserve there might be, and the soldiers soon began to pour out their experiences.

Two young infantrymen mentioned that they were going home on leave to see their parents, and remarked in the most casual fashion in the world that they had been posted as having been killed.

'But haven't you telegraphed to your parents?' I asked. 'Just think of the shock it will be to them when you walk in the house!'

They treated this as a good joke, and it was evident that they were determined to give their parents what they thought would be a pleasant surprise.

In Tampere Citrine did his usual grim sightseeing in the bombed areas, then visited a cotton mill. Here, as in every workplace that he visited, he went very thoroughly into the working conditions; a good trade unionist, he quizzed the employers on worker representation and wages. It is truly astonishing that these industrialists, in the middle of the Winter War, could find the patience to listen to lectures from a foreigner on industrial democracy. Citrine displayed a similar sort of insensitivity at hotels. He thought it a real sacrifice to have to share a room, and when bombing had interrupted the water supply at another hotel he repeatedly rang for the maid; he describes at tedious length how he managed to wash in such difficult conditions. Nonetheless, he was indefatigable, spending all the time he was not interviewing and observing in writing up his diary. His admiration for the Finnish soldiers – and for the girls as well – was unstinting: 'what fine intelligent fellows they looked!'; 'I was greatly impressed by the bearing of both officers and men, and particularly their attitude towards each other.'

The party returned to Helsinki, visiting a succession of schools, hospitals, and workers' institutes. They left for Turku on 2 February, and had an unscheduled stop near Salo when they dived out of the car into the snow to avoid the attentions of two Soviet planes. After a meeting with the Provincial Governor in Turku they left for Stockholm by air.

The conclusion of Citrine's diary is dated 9 March, only a week or two before its publication:

> I shall always treasure a vivid memory of my visit to a gallant people, striving valiantly to preserve their freedom and independence against tremendous odds.

There is no reason at all to doubt his sentiments but, nonetheless, Citrine never seemed to comprehend properly that he was in a country which was in the throes of fighting for its very existence. He was followed to Finland less than a week later by another Englishman, one who understood Finland's plight much more clearly.

Harold Macmillan

Harold Macmillan, patrician, Old Etonian and Oxford scholar, had little more in common with Citrine than a sense of outrage at the Soviet attack on Finland, and an admiration for Finnish soldiers. He was a politician whose public career spanned most of the twentieth century. Enrolled in the Grenadier Guards, he fought in the First World War, and was severely injured at the Battle of the Somme. Entering Parliament in 1924, he held Cabinet posts in the 1950s, and succeeded Sir Anthony Eden as Prime Minister in 1957, retiring in 1963. In his nineties, as Lord Stockton, he made a political comeback, denouncing in the House of Lords some of the policies of Margaret Thatcher.

His journey to Finland is recorded in *The Blast of War*, the second volume of his memoirs, published in 1967. Like Citrine, he kept a diary, and quotes from it extensively (these quotations are italicized in the following text). The background to his visit was partly political and partly personal, as he himself concedes:

> the gallant resistance of the small Finnish people, whose armies could not be destroyed even by superior numbers and whose spirit could not be broken by cruel and persistent bombing against which they had no defence, won the admiration of the world. As a first and largely symbolic step, the British Cabinet, at the beginning of January 1940, approved the formation of a movement to organise aid to Finland, including the recruitment of a small volunteer international force. I heard of this through Leo Amery, under whose aegis a working committee was set up. Although the Government gave full support to our efforts, it was thought wiser to preserve at least the appearance of a private venture. M. Gripenberg, the Finnish Minister in London, acted as chairman . . . I accepted with alacrity the invitation to join this body. In the first place, I shared in the general admiration of the valour of the Finns. Secondly, I was distressed, after so many months of war, to find myself without any job connected with war in any form. Before I agreed to serve, I consulted Churchill. He encouraged me, and I gathered from what he said that there might some greater advantages to Britain than the succouring of the Finns, however desirable and honourable that purpose might be.

The 'Finland Committee' decided to send a delegation to

Finland, consisting of Macmillan and Lord Davies, accompanied by Colonel Serlachius from the Finnish Legation in London. They left England on 10 February 1940, and reached Stockholm on the morning of the 12th, after a delay because Lord Davies had left his false teeth on the overnight train. At 4 p.m., in intense cold, they left for Finland by air. Macmillan was well-equipped with a tall white fur hat which, in his words, 'obtained a certain notoriety when I wore it as Prime Minister on my visit to Russia in 1959'. On the 13th Macmillan and Davies met the Finnish Prime Minister, Risto Ryti, and were briefed by Colonel Godden. Later they dined with Thomas Snow, the British Minister; Macmillan was 'impressed by his knowledge and the objectivity of his approach'.

The next day, 15th February, we left early by car for Borgå, or Porvoo, a flourishing town with various timber industries. It had suffered a heavy attack from the air two days before:

About 70 to 100 houses of all kinds had been utterly burnt out. They were still smoking, covered with icicles formed by the water from the fire hoses. The work of the fire-brigades must have been very efficient. They made a hole in the ice in the river and pumped up the water. There seemed to be no lack of fire appliances. I should imagine that fire is always a danger in their towns and that therefore the fire precautions in peace are normally on a generous scale.

The people were all going about their business as usual. There were few children about, as these – according to plan – have been largely evacuated to farmhouses.

We then returned to Helsinki where we lunched at the officers' mess in the Industrie-Savoy building.

As a result of discussions with Finnish and British officials in Helsinki he sent the following telegram:

To Prime Minister
>Foreign Secretary   Secret
Respectfully urge on you following considerations stop In
spite of heroic resistance Finnish army and unbroken spirit
of confidence Finnish Command expert military opinion
here admits situation very grave stop Unless further material aid can arrive rapidly position will become critical stop
Urgent need artillery all calibres and appropriate ammuni-
tion and aeroplanes both bombers and fighters stop If these
made available at once believe position can be held till thaw
gives short respite stop After that our volunteers or troops
could operate here and preparation should be hastened on
for this stop Please forgive my intrusion which only after
consultation with Finnish and English opinion here.
>   Harold Macmillan

Another telegram went to Churchill: 'Please ask to see my
telegram Prime Minister today stop Situation here demands urgent action stop Do your best'.

On the morning of 17 February, he writes, 'we were taken by
Colonel Serlachius to his home Joenniemi, in Mänttä, a house
of great beauty and considerable size':

> During the day, Lord Davies had been very unwell. It
> was decided that he should stay in Colonel Serlachius's
> comfortable house and that I should go on without him.
> Accordingly, at 8pm, Magill and I, accompanied by Fore-
> lius, a Finnish lieutenant from Headquarters, set out for
> Kajaani. Forelius was normally employed in the textile
> trade in Lancashire, where he had married an English
> wife and settled down. He had returned for the war, as a
> reservist. He spoke excellent English and was a splendid
> companion and guide. The news was grim, the Marshal
> having issued an appeal to the troops reminiscent of Haig's
> 'back[s] to the wall' message. The train was continually

stopped by air-raid warnings and the procedure on these occasions followed a fixed routine:

All passengers . . . ordered to get out and take cover in the forest. This we did, presenting a ludicrous appearance, with one of the Company's sheets each to cover our dark overcoats. To drop off the train (a drop of several feet) into deep snowdrift, to stumble along for twenty yards in snow up to one's waist, to climb up an embankment and over a fence of pointed stakes, and finally to sit in a forest of fir trees, wearing a fur hat, a smart London fur coat, a sheet, and carrying a dispatch case – all this represented an absurd and fatiguing manoeuvre which we resolved not to repeat. After about ten minutes, the 'all clear' was given, the passengers climbed painfully back into the train, and we proceeded on our journey.

This happened at 10 a.m. and again at 11. On each occasion, when the 'all clear' was given, the Druid-like figures returned from the forest and re-embarked. We changed into another train at Iisalmi and in the evening were again bombed, although no actual damage was done. The weather was wonderful, cold – 10 or 15 degrees below zero – but little wind. The air was crisp and clear. Nobody liked this weather, for the Russians could attack better, both on land and in the air. Everyone was praying for blizzards and heavy falls of snow. Finally, we arrived at Kajaani at about 7.30 p.m. on 18 February, without further incident.

Kajaani was the HQ of General Toompo, the commander of a front of about 200 kilometres, running from Pielisjärvi, near Lake Pielinen, in the south to north of Lake Kianta, near Juntusranta, in the north. For this task he had forces amounting to less than one division's strength. General Toompo sent Lieutenant Vihma, of his staff, to meet us and bring us to his headquarters for a meal. After supper, the General gave us an enthralling description of the course of the war in this sector. Major Magill trans-lated. There were plenty of maps to illustrate the story.

After sleeping the night in Kajaani, Macmillan and his party drove to Major Kari's Headquarters, 160 kilometres away, passing through Suomussalmi, which presented 'a strange and melancholy scene' in the aftermath of the great battle. They then 'went on by car to Captain Harola's position'. 'Harola was a very attractive man with a charming smile, fearless, sin-cere, and with a great sense of humour'. Macmillan brought his own military experience to bear on his understanding of what the Finnish troops had achieved:

> Seldom have I seen troops with such a high morale as these splendid Finnish soldiers.
>
> *The discipline among these troops stuck me as excel-lent, and in many ways rather like that of the Brigade of Guards. The drill, saluting, standing to attention while addressing a superior – all was perfect. When the Major passed, men who were some yards away would stand to attention. When a tent was entered, all at once stood up. I noticed one small point of custom, which was rather pleasing. When a man gives a message to an officer, both remain at the salute while the message is being given. Combined with this high discipline, there seems to be (as in the Brigade) great familiarity and good fellowship be-tween officers and men.*

We got back to Kajaani deeply impressed. On arrival, we found a telegram from Colonel Serlachius, saying that owing to the almost desperate situation on the Isthmus it was impossible for me to go there, or for the Field-Marshal to see me. It was suggested that I should try to rejoin Lord Davies, who was now better. He had collected all the necessary information and was on his way to Vaasa. He would wait for me there.

The next two days were taken up in long and rather wearisome journeys. The Russians were making a continuous series of attacks on the trains, hoping to dislocate the entire system. Nevertheless, in spite of long halts and continuous air raids, there was no confusion or panic. In the first six hours we travelled only about sixty kilometres. Sometimes we would find a station on fire and sometimes we were bundled out of the train by recurrent air-raid warnings. Fortunately, on Wednesday the 21st there was a raging wind and a snow blizzard which, it was hoped, would reduced the air attacks.

Air raids were soon to become familiar to us all at home. Meanwhile, the procedure adopted by the Finns gave us a foretaste of what we should be called upon to endure:

This has been a day of waiting, always enlivened by a number of air raids and all that this involves. All day . . . the Russians have been attacking the junctions and even the small stations on this line. The Finns have at present nothing to oppose to it other than sheer courage. The ordinary procedure is this. When the 'air-raid warning' (halytys) is given, if you are in a town of any size, this is done by sirens like ours (giving a 'warbling' note) or by the factory hooters. In some of these small towns there have been eleven or twelve such warnings in the course of a day. Your procedure is (a) to stay in your home and go on with your work or pleasure, or (b) to go to the cellar, or (c) to go to any dug-out that may be in the square or other public place. (These dug-outs, incidentally, are only splinter-proof. Some of the worst casualties have been caused by direct hits upon them.) Or (d) you may retire to a neighbouring piece of wood and stand under a tree. When the air raid is over or the 'all clear' given, usually the church bells are rung.

By 6.30 p.m. on 21 February we had reached Riihimäki, where we had to stay until after midnight.

We found, nevertheless, a restaurant open, full of troops on leave or returning from leave, where an excellent meal of sausages and potatoes, [with] either beer or coffee, was served. [An] incident which . . . amused me here was that on asking for the lavatory, I was informed by the porter (Lieutenant Forelius translating) that I must do my business outside, as there was unfortunately a dud bomb in the gentlemen's cloakroom, as yet unexploded.

At 1 a.m. on Thursday morning we got into another train and finally arrived at Vaasa at 2.30 in the afternoon. I said goodbye to my guide, Forelius, with some emotion. He was a fine man. At the Consul's house I found Lord Davies and a number of other officers and civilians interested in organising the volunteer forces.

This was the end of our visit to Finland. Although I knew in my heart that the Finnish resistance could scarcely be prolonged, I still hoped for a miracle. I have retained for the rest of my life a vivid memory of those gallant and fearless people.

They flew from Vaasa to Stockholm, and Macmillan felt the contrast painfully:

After my experiences in Finland, it was strange indeed to come to Sweden. We left a country struggling for its very life. We seemed to pass into a very different world.

He had harrowing interviews with Eljas Erkko, the Finnish Minister in Stockholm, about the desperate military situation and the uncertainty of British help to Finland. He heard much the same story in Oslo, and found nothing to cheer him when he returned to England.

The first days of my homecoming were melancholy. I was

obsessed with the Finnish tragedy. Yet there was nothing which our committee could do now but wait upon events.

The events are now matters of history. Back at Westminster Macmillan took part in a two-day Commons debate 'largely centred upon events in Finland'. He spoke effectively, condemning the British government's inaction, and describing Finnish resistance in moving terms, but it was too late. Finland was already becoming a sideshow in the gathering pace of the war.

It was not Macmillan's last sight of Finland. In August 1963, as Prime Minister, he made a three-day official visit. This is not described in his memoirs, and the only record of it which I have is a booklet with many photographs recording his visit to Valkeakoski on 7 August. It describes how he, Lady Dorothy, and their suite were enthusiastically welcomed to the town with a colourful display of pairs of Finnish and British flags; giant arches, bearing the words 'Welcome Mac', spanned the road.

AFTER THE WAR

James Bramwell (James Byrom)

One of the oddest schemes to have got off the ground during the 'phoney war' was that eight of the volunteer firemen from the London Auxiliary Fire Service should take a fire engine to Finland. Once the idea had been born it thrived, and the fire engine, sponsored by the Finland Fund, had a champagne 'christening' by Madame Gripenberg, the Finnish Ambassador's wife, in Berkeley Square. If all this seems remote from the realities of the desperate situation in Finland, one can say only that it was. It was a fanciful enterprise, and trivial in comparison to Sykes's Quaker unit, which comprised fifty-five men and nineteen cars.

Bramwell, educated at Charterhouse School and Oxford, lived a life of leisure before the war, publishing six slim volumes of verse. Around 1939, he wrote, 'I began for the first time to have misgivings about my career as a writer with enough private means to travel the world.' Rather like George Orwell, he made a deliberate choice to engage with working-class life, and, as he put it, 'to look through the window that opened on to the backstreets'. When war broke out he found employment with the London Auxiliary Fire Service, one of the avenues by which non-combatants could help the war effort yet avoid conscription. Bramwell was one of the eight volunteer firemen chosen to go with the Finland Fund engine, beginning for him an association with Finland which lasted many years, and which changed his life.

It was by this time rather the custom than the exception for British visitors to Finland to take a sauna, but Bramwell is the only one to have published a poem about it; *Sauna* (1959) is, in fact, a sequence of thirty-eight poems.

Bramwell's memoir *The Unfinished Man* (1957), published under the pseudonym James Byrom, is an autobiographical account of a young pacifist's war experiences in Finland, Normandy, the Ardennes, Germany and Palestine, and the way in which these shaped him and developed his views. About one third of the book describes his fifteen months in Finland immediately after the Winter War. He returned after the war to teach, first at Åbo Akademi, and then at Helsinki University, but although he has left no account of these years *The Unfinished Man* shows an understanding of Finland and the Finns obviously attained during this later and longer residence.

The firemen arrived in Stockholm only to find that the war in Finland was over, but they nonetheless embarked on an overcrowded ship, the *Oihonna*, to Turku. Bramwell's account of crossing the Gulf of Bothnia in winter is the first published British description of this experience since the early nineteenth century, long before the advent of ice-breakers.

It was good to come up from this atmosphere[in the saloon] into the pure world of ice and snow the ship was now ploughing into. The ice was so thick that every yard had to be fought for. Icefloes banged against the hull, and the whole ship quivered with the travail of the screws. It was exhilarating to stand in the bows and watch the stem butting its way through the ice-field. Instead of the swish of water and the feathery clot of the bow-wave, a black seam went hissing ahead of the ship and great blocks of ice disappeared beneath the stem, to leap suddenly from the oily blackness of free water as the pressure of the hull relaxed. Sometimes the bows mounted right on top of the ice before their weight succeeded in crushing a channel.

Towards evening the ice became thicker. Several times we were brought to a standstill. The ship went astern to gather momentum for the next assault. As the sun sank into the Gulf of Finland the ice kindled with fantastic colour. Each time the snowy ice was crushed under water, the broken fragment reared up from the blackness, rolling over like some sea monster on whose glistening back the acid green and crimson of the sunset was reflected for a moment with eerie brilliance. All night the old ship groaned and trembled, driven on by pistons that seemed to gasp for steam, battered by the floes which packed and jostled round her stern.

During the night the ship became stuck fast, and the dawn revealed 'another ship, with spars and ropes of hoar frost, but a ship that might have been stuck there for years – the tomb of some lost Arctic enterprise'.

About midday a gaunt ice-breaker carved its way through to us and started to make a passage. We steamed in the wake for several hours, until the ice-breaker itself stuck fast. With its huge whale-like counters, eyed with anchor holes, and with its powerful screws thrashing up the water, I seemed to be witnessing the last struggles of some mechanical monster which ploughed backwards and forwards to the sound of clanging bells and whirring machinery, gradually losing way as the inexorable ice packed round it. Some hours later it was set free by another ice-breaker, and at last we were under way again. It took three days to reach Turku – a twelve-hour journey in normal weather.

Arriving in Finland without their engine, the firemen were given three days' sightseeing in Helsinki:

Black figures walking in the snow, white cars with bullet-starred windscreens, the blackened anatomy of fire-gutted buildings: my first impressions were all in black and white.

They were found work in Ekenäs (Tammisaari), helping with the desolating task of evacuating the nine thousand inhabitants of the Hanko peninsula (leased to Russia as part of the Peace of Moscow). They then settled into a routine of duties in the Ekenäs area:

> By this time we had moved from the woodland lunatic asylum where we had been lodged hitherto to the local fire brigade station in the centre of the town. The demand for transport was still considerable. Since we had only one real lorry at our disposal, we got permission to strip the three period fire-engines which were the pride of the Ekenäs volunteer brigade. For several days in succession I found myself driving a Tin Lizzie round the countryside . . .
>
> Now that winter had simultaneously lost its grip on me and the countryside I began to enjoy being in Finland. Little brown pine-clad hills were beginning to emerge from the white waste, and though the landscape was still somewhat colourless and practically scentless, the sound of trickling could be heard on every side. I had a feeling of *attendrissement*, of secret activity beyond sense-perception. I noticed the delicate skin of the silver birches, peeling like slivers of mother-of-pearl, and the sticky blobs of snow which the pine-needles now pierced, as if sending out new green shoots. The woods, which had seemed so hostile in their birdless and freezing silence, now seemed to draw closer to the red cabins of the peasants: the shades were more intimate and the light that filtered into them lay in patches of moist gold.
>
> Often our errands took us far afield. In a country of so many lakes and forests we were frequently lost, sometimes delayed for hours by skids and snowdrifts; but we always managed to get back with labourers' appetites and a story to tell. Even then the day's work was not necessarily finished. The fire station was also the ambulance post, and

since we were its only residents at the time, we had to deal with any calls that came in during the night. We had several cases of appendicitis, and one suicide – a dispossessed farmer who had drunk a whole bottle of carbolic acid. We were often conscious of the improbable nature of the work we were called upon to do. We could easily imagine ourselves doing the ambulance work: even delivering a suicide to the mortuary seemed connected with the war. But undertakers? The dice of nations seemed strangely shaken on the day when it fell to an English solicitor and an English advertising agent to scour the frozen Finnish archipelago in a dismantled fire-engine, searching for the body of a defunct islander.

On their return to Helsinki they expected to be sent home, but got no further than Stockholm before the Finnish Home Office 'decided that they needed us to get our machines in order and show the Finnish firemen how to use them'. As the year wore on, and the Russian visas which would have allowed them to return to England (Denmark and Norway were now occupied) did not materialise, they felt increasingly unwelcome. England was no longer viewed as the friend and ally it had seemed to be during the Winter War. 'Meanwhile we had work to do,' Bramwell wrote, 'and that more than anything kept us from making a desperate bid for freedom.' In contrast to the leisurely routine around Ekenäs, his work as a fireman in Helsinki was serious and could be dangerous; he describes vividly a nightmare experience fire-fighting on the seventh storey of a blazing warehouse. It also had moments when their behaviour must have appeared a strange contrast to the sombre mood of a nation still suffering and smarting from defeat and annexation:

I remember how fresh the summer air felt, with dawn or sunset colouring the sky, or headlights boring the unfamiliar emptiness of familiar streets. With the sirens screaming in our ears and the wind in our faces as the leading machines raced each other to the destination, excitement was whipped up to such a pitch that we often found ourselves shouting and singing like schoolboys out on a charabanc trip.

Although there now seemed to be no legitimate way out of Finland, the post was still getting through:

It was the arrival of my clothes from England that first made me conscious of pining to get back into 'civilian life'. When I walked out of the gates of Helsinki fire station in my old tweeds I had a feeling that I was beginning to live again. It was delicious to go and browse in the biggest bookshop in the town, and then sit in the sun drinking iced beer, reading some familiar book whose smell and form often excited me more than its contents.

Though the act of buying books reminded me of Oxford days before I knew enough about my ignorance to feel the nightmarish quality of big bookshops, I was not buying just for the pleasure of feeling like a ghost. I had already been approached by the universities of Helsinki and Turku about taking a lecturing job for the coming academic year. After many luncheons and much correspondence between the British Legation and the British Council, I decided to accept the job in Turku, where I knew the professor of English, an Oxford D.Litt. and a scholar of distinction. [This was H. W. (Henry) Donner, Professor at Åbo Akademi, and later at Uppsala University.] The prospect of going home had once more faded into the uncertain future. For a time I had had hopes of returning via America, but the American ship these hopes were built on turned out to be a phantom, like all the other ships that were supposed to repatriate us. And though it was agreed that I should be free to go, should any opportunity present itself, the virtual encirclement of Finland by the Germans encouraged me to start reading seriously.

The British firemen were still at liberty, unlike the military volunteers, now confined in a camp in central Finland. Bramwell went to Turku to teach at the two universities (Åbo Akademi and Turun Yliopisto). Here his life was so dominated, indeed so overwhelmed, by a love affair with a Finnish woman that little else seemed to register. Consequently his account of his time as a 'lektor' makes sombre reading. He high-mindedly turned down an invitation from the British Legation to spy for them in Turku, although the 'codes and secret ink' which they promised him might in fact have made his life more interesting. It certainly needed enlivening:

> That winter in a provincial Finnish university town was a period of exile. Tramping through frozen streets, from the Swedish to the Finnish university, then back again to my hotel bedroom, I was hardly aware of the town of Turku, which sprawled between one activity and another like periods of mental vacancy. In the huge inevitable square, which I crossed and recrossed a thousand times, the droshky drivers sat inanimate behind their ancient, half-frozen horses, each apparently waiting for the head of the line to come to life. The shabby yellow trams, converging on the centre of the town, queued patiently outside the shops, as though waiting to transport the dead to a graveyard.
>
> Yet there were surprising passages of beauty – perspectives I remember as direct paintings on my mind when its canvas was almost entirely blank. All these paintings include the River Aura – in winter a broad, white highway for pedestrians and skiers, which swept into view below the cathedral and continued straight down to the port, its

last half mile a sunken avenue between the rimy spars of hibernating ships. If one stood on the central bridge joining the two halves of the town the 13th century seemed to follow the river down to the 20th. As the frosty sun sank into the archipelago beyond the smoking silhouette of factory chimneys near the port, the cathedral rose from the opposite direction, mellow with a red that glowed in the mind long after the lights along the river bank had announced the hour of municipal darkness. On the rare occasions when I was not in a hurry to get from my hotel to the Swedish university I used to make a long detour and walk up the river. I could never quite believe I was walking on the wide brown stream of summer, which buoyed up yachts in the shade of lime trees, and brought the flagged and painted traffic of the archipelago right into the heart of Turku.

Something of Bramwell's aesthetic sense remained, but for him Turku was an eternal winter:

> As the academic year wore on I had less time for personal writing in the private glow of my bedroom lamp. The telephone became insistent; and on my table there was a growing pile of neglected correspondence, exercise books, and works of reference. There were lectures to prepare, minutes of meetings to write, and outside my window it was winter, interminable winter, with rooks circling the black and white trees and smoke rising from a nondescript building whose occupants I never saw. The wood pile in the yard grew smaller, and its tarpaulin of snow was renewed many times, while the smoke went on rising and the rooks circling. For all the kindness of the Finns who entertained me and the warm friendship of Henry, my professor, I cannot imagine a provincial town in which a foreigner would be likely to feel more lonely.

Bramwell writes very little about his teaching, his colleagues, or his students, but there is one telling episode:

One morning in December my Swedish students were translating a passage about Spring in the north. When we came to a sentence about Spring roaring like an unchained beast I stopped the girl who was translating.

'But surely it can't mean that? Spring doesn't roar.'

I had a mental picture of the typically English Spring – woods full of violets, and banks of primroses . . .

My remark was greeted by a subdued titter. 'But in the North the Spring does roar,' the girl insisted. 'You'll hear for yourself.'

The student was right: it took the dramatic arrival of spring to awaken Bramwell as the city itself came to life:

Where the Aura stood fast the ice, already bluish, began fissuring into seams of ebony. Patches of yellow water lay on the surface, and gradually the force of the current, exploiting the flaws wherever they opened, started gliding slowly down to the sea. Within a week this smooth gliding had become a furious spate. Gathering momentum from thousands of tributaries, the flood rose boiling up the banks of the river, and hurled huge blocks of mud-coloured ice jostling and crackling through the town. Out in the archipelago the islands were now cut off from the mainland: from the rocky sounds came the echoing explosions of the ice splitting, like some gigantic blasting operation.

The violence of the natural change was quickly reflected in the people. They crowded into the streets laughing and talking, and only the old were dressed in black now. I did not know that there were so many people in Turku, such animation of voice and gesture. They were set free spiritually and physically. In back gardens there was a hammering and painting of boats; gangs of cyclists set out in the morning to rediscover their lost countryside; and in the port of Turku there was frantic activity as the ice-bound ships lying in the estuary were warped into their berths for unloading.

When term ended Bramwell moved to Helsinki. As the Continuation War got under way in 1941 the British volunteers still remaining in Finland were rounded up. He and the other English teachers from Turku were interrogated by the police on spying charges, but were saved by the intervention of Professor Donner.

I joined the rest of the firemen and all the military volunteers at a station in central Finland, and after a week's travelling in locked coaches we found ourselves not far from the Norwegian frontier, at Malung in Swedish Dalarna.

Eventually they arrived in Kalmar, in south-east Sweden, boarding the ship which had brought the Legation party from Helsinki. It was to be a long journey back to England, by way of Portugal. 'The familiar name *Oihonna* stared back at me from a lifebelt as I went up the gangway,' he wrote – it was the same ship that he had taken to Turku fifteen months earlier. 'For a long time I remained on deck, lost in my cloud of misery. Then at last I felt the stinging of the rain.'

Constance Malleson

Born Lady Constance Annesley, Malleson was the daughter of the Fifth Earl of Annesley. She grew up at Castle Wellan, the ancestral home in Ireland, received a liberal and cosmopolitan education in Dresden and Paris, and then trained at the Royal Academy of Dramatic Art (RADA) in London. As 'Colette O'Niel' she had a successful acting career from about

1914 until she left the stage in 1930. She was an ardent pacifist, and during the First World War become deeply involved with Bertrand Russell, who was her lover for many years; she was still in contact with him during the 1940s. He has left a vivid account of her and of their relationship in his *Autobiography*. The obituarist in *The Times* wrote that 'she was as intense on the stage as she could be in life'; her writings show the intensity which she brought, at different times, to causes such as the Anti-Slavery Society and the Howard League for Penal Reform. In 1940 it was Finland which aroused these powerful feelings, seen in highly articulate letters to *The Times*. 'Finland,' she wrote in retrospect, 'was left to bleed to death, deserted by every country in Europe.' She volunteered for work with the Friends' Ambulance Unit in Finland but, finding that it did not accept women, she went to Finland of her own accord.

It is evident in her autobiographical volume *In the North* (1946) that she had a long familiarity with Sweden, had made several visits to Lapland, and had previously stayed in Finland. The book is in three sections: a Lapland expedition; a year living in Sweden with a friend distinguished only as Lavinia; and – more than half the book – living mainly by herself in Finland. Finland is her subject, seen principally through her experiences in one small village, but she mixes in autobiography in a way which leaves some loose ends. She does not give her reasons for going to Finland, but they can be inferred. She had a close friend, Vasti, whom she had met in Muonio a few years earlier, the wife of the Rector of Vehmersalmi. One of several letters to *The Times* during the Winter War quotes part of a letter from Vasti, Malleson adding, 'In a short while I hope to visit this brave woman in Vehmersalmi – and take to her and her people all the help I can'. She identified closely and passionately with Finland's plight: 'it was Finland's lot I'd come to share,' she wrote; she had given 'what gold trinkets I had to the National Gold Collection'.

Few British writers have immersed themselves as deeply in Finnish life as she did; it is difficult to imagine, as she chronicles the hard life in the Savo countryside, that she was the daughter of an earl, had been a guest at Buckingham Palace, and had arrived in Finland with a letter of introduction to Mannerheim.

She landed in Turku from Stockholm after five days battling through the ice on the *Polaris,* soon after the Winter War had ended:

> There wasn't a room to be had in Turku. There wasn't a taxi. The local fire engine obligingly transported my bags to the flat of a total stranger. This cheerful Swedo-Finnish housewife gave me her sofa to sleep on, her rations to share, her whole flat to make myself at home in. Her husband was away in the army; she hadn't seen him since the war began.
>
> Next morning we went out together to take a look at Turku: at what was left of Turku . . . Turku, of course, looked exactly like any other bombed town: eyeless, toothless, blistered, charred, ruined, barricaded.

Malleson was one of a small party which drove out through central Finland, where they were able to 'understand something of Finland's loss'. They passed through Lahti, drove on to Mikkeli, badly bombed, where the homeless were 'living, eating, sleeping in the church'. They spent the night at Savonlinna, where a seemingly endless train of refugees was coming in from Karelia.

> The biggest factory in Savonlinna had been taken over as a sorting centre for the refugees as they passed through. When we went out next morning, they were still straggling into the town. It was a long, slow, heartrending procession. In sledges they came; in little carts; on foot. They had come all the long way from Karelia. Those with horse and cart had to go on after resting only one night. Those on foot

were allowed to stay longer. Night after night, thousands of refugees slept in that factory: thousands of that quarter of a million human beings who had lost everything: sons, homes, lands, province. The yard was full of kerchiefed women attending to old, roughly fashioned sledges and carts. All were piled high with every imaginable thing: bedding, pots and pans, garments, implements, anything and everything that could be rescued from calamity.

The next day her companions left her at Kuopio, 25 kilometres from her destination, Vehmersalmi, on the shore of Lake Kallavesi. Everywhere, it seemed, the war lived on:

Standing at my hotel window that afternoon, waiting for Vasti's sledge, I saw that the street was gradually filling with people. They were thronging from the beautiful old white church and were lining up, quietly, all along the pavements. Suddenly, all movement stopped – and a profound silence fell. Then, slowly, slowly, at foot's pace, Finnish soldiers came past in their hooded white battle dress. Upon their shoulders rested the coffins of fallen comrades. Each white coffin was shrouded in the white and blue Finnish flag. Upon each, a handful of earth was thrown. Upon each lay a small bunch of pink tulips. Upon the air wailed the Dead March. There was no movement, no sound amongst all that mourning crowd, until the last funeral music had faded and the last white-clad figure had passed. Then a sob that was almost a moan broke the silence. I think it will dwell forever in my mind, muffled by the tramp of Finnish soldiers burying their dead . . .

I shut my window and at down on my bed. A profound despair took hold of me. All Finland's history marched before my eyes.

Finally she set off.

It was almost evening before Vasti drove up in a rough, low, country sledge – drawn by one of those sandy Finnish horses with whitish mane. The driver, Lassi Koponen (he rented the rectory fields and farmed them) took my ruck-sack and bundled it in on top of us. With Vasti's red Lapp dog lying on our stomachs to keep us warm, we sledged for two hours across snow lakes in the sunset – until it grew dark and the stars came out, blinking peacefully above the spruce forests which surround Vehmersalmi. At the last crossing of Kallavesi Lake, the old horse charged a steep snow bank and jolted us up to the door of the rec-tory – a long, low, grey wooden building looming dark against the snow.

The Rector was still with the army, so Vasti and a curate were coping with the problems of the parish. Malleson's first weeks in Vehmersalmi found her in the thick of the chaos, deprivation and misery involved in the aftermath of war. The burial of the soldiers, the grief of the widows and orphans, and the resettlement of Karelian refugees were chief elements of life at the Rectory.

Malleson spent more than a year at Vehmersalmi, slowly adopting the rhythm and pattern of Finnish country life. In May she set up house for herself, and as the wounds of the war began to heal a timeless way of life seemed to pick up again:

> In those first weeks of June, I often went in to Kuopio to market. The white lake steamer picked me up at five o'clock in the morning from the little jetty below my cot-tage. Two hours of crystal waters, silver clouds, clear sky, endless lake, endless forests – on the way to market. It was like steaming through a silence of crystal and pearl, with-out blemish, without smirch. At the tiny landing stages, we picked up old countrywomen with clear eyes and gnarled, deeply lined faces; with baskets over their arms and ker-

chiefs over their heads. They were often accompanied by little, sunburnt, barefoot, blue-eyed boys. Lake and forests; forests and lake; everything idyllic; nothing anywhere to hurt the eye. This was beauty. This was Finland.

The countryside itself, returning to vivid life after the harshness of winter, seemed to be signalling a return to tradition:

Summer had come – a crescendo of berries. First, the little pine-scented, wild strawberries – everywhere in the grass and amongst the bracken fringing the forest; more fragrant by far than the *fraises des bois* of Paris restaurants. Then, the whortleberries, misted with bloom like grapes; turning all the country children into juice-stained, grinning little devils. Then, the wild raspberries. And before they are gone, the earth is scattered with round ruby cranberries. Upon the market stalls golden cloudberries appear . . .

Toadstools of astonishing size and colour leap up on every side. And then the mushrooms begin: yellow, gold, orange, coral, fawn, purple, white . . .

In my cottage garden a clump of purple iris blazed. It was the most magnificent weather: hot, too hot. Three and four times a day I plunged into the lake. In the long, white nights, Puijo Hill shone an amethyst jewel in a molten sky. If I went to draw water from the lake at midnight, I stood transfixed with wonder at the beauty of it: lake and sky; sky and lake; and always the encircling benediction of the forests: endless, endless. It was at first a wonder and a delight; and then an ache –

In July, Kirkkoherra [the Rector] held a number of services in distant, outlying farms. We would go by the white lake steamer – or by a little motor boat which delivered milk to the town – and travel for hours and hours over the lake which broadened, twisted, turned, narrowed, so that you lost all bearings and didn't know where you were. At some tiny wooden jetty beneath silver birch tress, we'd put in – and walk up slowly through the sunset to an old wooden farmstead. Barefoot, our host would come to meet us. In a huge, raftered kitchen, or out in the bake-house, all the country folk from miles around would be gathered. In the sitting-room our hosts would offer coffee and homemade bread. Then Kirkkoherra would go out to the people – and with the dying sun slanting in at open, geranium-filled windows, he would lead the singing of a hymn. Without any accompaniment, the people lifted up their voices and sang the well-known verses. They lifted up their hearts too, you felt. There were howling infants and yapping dogs. There were refugee servant girls. Shoulder to shoulder we all sat upon the hard wooden benches. And then Kirkkoherra would preach a short sermon out of his head.

Later, we'd have supper with the farm people at a long, heavy table in the great kitchen. Above our heads, sledge shafts hung in the rafters; huge copper cake-shapes gleamed upon the walls. All around the kitchen, suspended from hand-fashioned pegs, hung the implements of forest and farm. Then, under a full moon shining burnished bronze through the silvery trees, we'd put out once more across the lake and reach home towards midnight.

Despite the colossal disruptions of the war, the traditional way of life which Malleson chronicles hardly seems to belong to the new republic so lauded by the progressive travellers of the 1930s. Yet her account has a double perspective: these details of her daily life are punctuated with summaries of the course of the war in the rest of Europe, and of the relentless demands made as Russia tightened the screws on Finland after the March armistice.

The daily routine at the farm was enlivened by accompanying the Rector on his visits to the outlying hamlets and farms in his huge parish; on one occasion he 'administered Holy Communion out of a medicine bottle on the kitchen table'. One memorable day was a farm party:

It was on the first Sunday in September that we were bidden to a party at Rautaharju Farm. The Master of Rautaharju was celebrating his sixty-fifth birthday. The question was how we were to get there. Rautaharju (the place-name means Iron Ridge) is almost the last stop the lake steamer makes on her run from Vehmersalmi to Kuopio. The lake steamer, therefore, was no answer at all: since she disdained any hour later than five o'clock in the morning. Vasti's bike was no answer – since it was rather too long a way. And though everybody in Vehmersalmi owned a sledge, they didn't seem to own any other kind of vehicle. It seemed likely we should have to give up the idea of Rautaharju. Then, at the eleventh hour, one of the villagers came forward with a dog cart.

It was already late in the afternoon when he came jogging along in a very old, very high, very angular-looking dog cart. He pulled up at the signpost which points the way to Varkaus – and we got in. We were presently driving along as typical a Savo country road as you could wish. It meandered, narrow and rough, through a tangle of forest. It had a few small, switchback hills; and it ran for a while along the spine of high ridge with Kallavesi lying below us in the west.

'We shall pass two villages on the way,' Vasti said.

A little later, as we jogged past a few red cottages, Vasti said: 'This is Kirnumäki village.'

A little further, as we came to few scattered farms, Vasti said: 'This is Litmajärvi village.'

I swallowed my surprise and realized that it is because such tiny collections of scattered cottages or farms are called villages, that the Scandinavian term, 'church village', has arisen – to define that one of them which contains the church which serves all of them. Vehmersalmi parish is about thirty-five kilometres long by about twenty-five broad. Its total population is about four thousand. But it contains no less than twelve villages; and the population of the actual church village numbers only about four hundred souls.

When the Vehmersalmi Poor House came into sight, we pulled up on the opposite side of the road, in front of a tiny cottage: a cabin, really. In it lived a very old couple. The husband had a wooden leg. He and his wife subsisted upon whatever their only son could spare them from his wages. He worked aboard one of the lake steamers. To this old couple, even a very little extra money would seem a miracle – and we had it in our pockets. I'd asked Vasti and Kirkkoherra to decide how much they should have, but I was a little horrified at the smallness of the sum. Vasti, though, would do the giving – and I supposed that she and Kirkkoherra knew best.

These two old people were probably the poorest in the whole parish. Their cabin didn't differ very much from any small cabin in Northern Ireland – except that it was clean, was built of wood, and had a stove instead of an open fire. There were two wooden trestles against the wall and there was a table in the middle of the room. The trestles were the beds. On one of them, the old husband was lying, smoking his pipe and philosophically contemplating his wooden leg which hung, at the moment, upon a peg on the wall. On the other trestle, the old wife sat grinding some substitute-coffee. She looked up at Vasti with good-humoured delight and crooned her pleasure at the small gift – very much as Irish cottagers do when you bring them some extra tit-bit . . .

The Master of Rautaharju came out to meet us: tall, thin, vigorous looking – with a long, narrow head on him. 'Iron Ridge' was an excellent description of him. He had sat in parliament as a member of the Right. A good looker he certainly was: you'd have said he was at least ten years younger than his age. Around him on every side sprouted sons and daughters and masses of grandchildren. The guests, with plates of food in their hands, seemed to be streaming hither and thither in every direction as we came into the hall. Soon we were doing the same ourselves – for the meal (dinner) was laid out upon a huge dining table around which there were no chairs and no places laid. Plates and knives and forks were in piles. You helped yourself to them and to food; and then departed, feeling rather like a dog with a bone, to find a chair and a table at which to eat. In this fashion, four courses were consumed. Word went round from the hostess when a new course appeared – and back you went and helped yourself. All the coming and going did not seem to make for sustained conversation: you were apt to lose the person you were talking to. But the food was so delicious that nobody but a pedant (or an Irishman) would have hankered after 'good conversation'. *Maksalaatikko* it was which most took my fancy: rice, liver, currants, syrup, butter – cooked all together and served in big copper dishes straight out of the oven. You couldn't wish for anything more delicious. I made up my mind that I would give Vasti no peace until she taught me to make *Maksalaatikko* . . .

In the darkness we climbed into our dog cart and settled down to the long drive home. Our driver, who had also taken part in the feast, regaled us with sidelights upon the past history of some of the non-local guests; decorating his story (which was of lovers' trysts and midnight escapades) with quips and quirks – a flourish here, a pirouette there – in true Savo fashion. Savo province is called 'the merry Savo' – and you must have a ready tongue in your head if you don't want to lose face up there.

When in October her cottage was needed for the new organist Malleson took lodgings at Antto Koponen's farm, and here she fell in with the pattern of traditional farm life, little changed from that recorded by Mrs Tweedie in Savo nearly half a century earlier. She often sees parallels between Finland and Ireland, nowhere more convincingly than a little cameo which anticipates Seamus Heaney:

> all day long, up and down, to and fro, [Koponen] drove his plough across the stony field; while his chubby small son paced by his side, never leaving him for a moment.

For Malleson every season had its enchantments:

> These early days of October were the most brilliant I could ever remember living through. The pattern of the world seemed beaten on an anvil of copper and gold; everything sharp and clear in the cold air; everything on the ground white with frost in the early morning. The sun shone so strong and the lake blazed so blue that you could hardly look at it with the naked eye.

At Christmas she was invited for the traditional dinner at the Rectory, but now food supplies were dwindling. Rationing became tighter in the new year and – worst of all for a writer in Finland in winter – the oil ration was reduced until, in March, there was none at all. So after ten months at Vehmersalmi she and her typewriter took the overnight train to Vaasa, to a Finland very different from Mrs Tweedie's:

> Though everything was still in the grip of winter, it all looked wonderful to my country eyes. The Vaasa bookshops were a feast; the Vaasa flower shops a paradise of

colour. My eyes dwelt upon the roses, tulips, narcissi, lily of the valley – and all the primulas of early spring – filling the shop windows. Even more astonishing to Savo eyes were the foodstuffs, of a kind not to be found in Kuopio or in Helsinki. I spent much time posting off food parcels to friends in town. But if I imagined I'd come to Finland's riviera, I'd made a very great mistake. It was bitterly cold in Vaasa.

The hotel, though, was everything a hotel should be. A lift wafted you from your bedroom down to a pine-smelling *sauna* in the basement. Opposite, was an up-to-date air raid shelter. Each bedroom had its own spacious hall with letter box and large built-in cupboards. Two shades of white and leaf green were the colours against which the blonde birch furniture of my room was set. The telephone on my writing table was white too. In the shaded light of an electric lamp I sat working in peace, perfect peace. The cost of perfect peace was about five shillings and sixpence a day.

Then, one early evening, spring swept over Finland. Impossible to describe how that first glitter of strong sunshine goes to your head after the long, dark, northern winter. Even though there isn't one speck of green on any tree. Even though the icicles show no sign of beginning to drip. But the sun is blazing. And you know that soon – in all this land of lakes – spring waters will be breaking free. I lifted my face to the sun's light and I almost forgot that Bulgaria had just joined the Nazis.

After many days of sitting riveted to my typewriter, I walked out one morning to take a look at Vaasa. Where, I wondered, did its thirty thousand inhabitants hide themselves? The road winding along the shore of the Gulf was as deserted as the West End of London on a day in August. *That* is one of the delights of all small northern towns;

you aren't pressed and hemmed in; you aren't pushed and jostled by swarming crowds; there is room to breathe and move freely.

After long visits to Oulu and Kaajani Malleson returned to Vehmersalmi, but the Continuation War was now under way and she could no longer get money from England. She foresaw, but tactfully skates over in her account, other difficulties which anyone with a British passport would soon be experiencing in Finland, and with a very heavy heart she said her farewells in Vehmersalmi, and left for Sweden. Even in the peace of her Ramsnäs cottage she could think only of Finland.

Epilogue

During the spring and early summer of 1941, with their army larger and much better equipped than it had been eighteen months earlier and with the Red Army deployed to halt the German advance, Finland saw the opportunity to regain its lost territory. The Continuation War began in late June, and by September Karelia had been regained, with most of the pre-war borders re-established (they were lost again in 1944). The Anglo-Soviet Agreement of July inevitably made the position of the British nationals in Finland increasingly uncomfortable. Bell was still working tirelessly for British Relief for Finland (presumably the successor of the Finland Fund) in increasingly difficult conditions. He continued to administer the Fund, working from his bedroom, Room 216 of the Hotel Societetshuset, where, he wrote, he operated 'an ever-open bar'.

> That room was an exciting place in those breathless days. It was, one might almost say, a little piece of Britain. The Finns were extraordinarily tolerant of my activities there. At a time when my countrymen were clamouring for the means of flight, I had to put the notice on my door: 'Swedish Visas Sold Out!' There were two other notices on that door: 'Change Here for Petsamo!' and 'Conscientious Objectors Prohibited!'

There was also in Finland a group of British women volunteers, ambulance drivers and nurses, led by Mary Runciman. Bell records how he managed to get them to Petsamo 'in time to catch the last steamer to leave Finland during the Finnish-Russian War Number Two'. Bell himself, surely the most established Briton in Finland, decided in the late summer that he too would have to leave. There was nothing common or mean about his departure:

> Government officials provided me with petrol for my car, procured exit permits and visas, allowed me to take with me all the foreign currency I wished, and gave me full diplomatic privileges. I left Helsinki with my faithful Finnish chauffeur who insisted on flying the Union Jack on the bonnet of my car; and every respect was accorded to the flag, the car and its occupants during our ten hours' journey to the airport at Rauma.

Bell could not get from Sweden to England for many months, and became one of a sad group of 'Distressed British Subjects' in prolonged transit:

> We were a mixed bag, and, altogether, a sorry looking lot, including crying children and tired English spinsters who had been making a precarious living teaching their native language in Finland.

By the autumn of 1941 there were very few British nationals left in Finland; those who did remain were either rounded up, or made their own way out. At the end of the year, on the twenty-fourth anniversary of independence, Britain declared war on Finland – 'out of loyalty to our ally Russia', as Churchill explained in a personal message to Mannerheim. By now, for the first time in centuries, probably, there was no British presence in the country.

W. H. Auden dismissed the 1930s as 'a low dishonest decade', but for Finland it had been little short of triumphant. Even as war loomed in 1939 preparations for the 1940 Olympic Games were still going ahead. The stadium was complete, and the Finnish athletes who had been astonishing the world for twenty years were preparing to be seen on their home turf. As Robert Edwards has written:

Finland was working, it paid its debts, it was clean, bright, new, and – most important to the economic environment of the 1930s – solvent. The nation looked forward to giving the world a guided tour.

There were, indeed, guided tours in 1940, but they were of bombed and burnt-out cities, and of Arctic battlefields. These more or less mark the end of the British discovery of modern Finland; it would be many years before the next generation of travellers arrived to rediscover the new republic.

Postscript

It was not until 1948 that Harry Bell returned to Finland, this time for a holiday, travelling from Copenhagen on the *Ariadne*, and negotiating his case of Scotch whisky through various customs controls with consummate diplomatic skill. The welcome which he received as the ship docked in Helsinki made him feel 'that even a lifetime's service could not have earned such warmth of affection and regard':

> So, eight years later, I returned to the Hotel Societetshuset for a peep into Room 216. I found that historic chamber bedecked with flowers in my honour. Finland had not forgotten even Room 216! I shall never forget those flowers.

Notes and References

Epigraph

Cooper, 194.

Prologue

Bell, 120.

Preface

Lurcock (2013), 240.

Introduction

North, 213; Bramwell, 81; Malleson, 141; Gibbons, *I Wanted to Travel*, 107; North, 53; Clark, 50.

The background of independence: Clive-Bayley, 8; Newmarch [1904], [2]; Kirby, 25; Lyytinen, 29; Mannerheim: Clements, 213; Kirby, 55, 55, 58; Nevinson, 161; Agar, 111; Bell, 88, 153.

The British discover modern Finland: Hjelt [1]; Halmesvirta, 27; Gilmour, 28–9, 134; Lurcock (2013), 163; North, 186; Lurcock (2013); Fox, 121; Sutherland, 16 (the story is related also by Scott, 138); Stamp, 295; Söderhjelm: Malleson 98; Westermarck: Sutherland, 16 ; Gray, 26–7.

A new breed of traveller: North, viii–ix; Bell, 11; Fox, 121; Gilmour, viii; Clark, 21–2; Tweedie, 163; Clark, 17; *Spectator*, 24 March 1939, 36; Frankland: see Lurcock (2010), 182; Bunbury: see Lurcock (2013), 100; Atchley, 6–7; Stamp, 295; Gilmour, 81; Fox, 29, 31; Scott, 51; Scott (1925), 240; Jones, 201; Tickell, *The British Soroptomist* (1930), 250 ; Sutherland, 23; Clarke: see Lurcock (2010), 96; Gibbons, 66; Aalto: *The Times*, 13 May 1976; Langdon-Davies, 195; Powell, 172–4; Cook's *Handbook* (1939), 436; Atchley, 19; North, 198; Sutherland, 24; Malleson, 179–80;

Citrine, 151; Langdon-Davies, 195; Rothery, 133–4; Gilmour, 65; Atchley, 22; Rothery, 197; Sutherland, 17; Gilmour, 64.

Finland on £10: Clark, 9; Laughlin, 389; Sutherland, 278; Ingram, 55; Franck, 7; Gilmour, 11; MacDougall: see Lurcock (2013), 15; Buckley, 185; North, 108, 132.

Prohibition: Agar: Ferguson, 43; Fox, 139, 143.

Transport: Franck, 77–8; Clark, 24; Ingram, 55; Gilmour, 4–5; North, 104, 179; Russell: *The Field,* 16 June 1927; Rothery, 55; Atchley, 71–2; Colville: *The Field*, 2 October 1937; North, 120, 121; Gilmour, 6, 8; Ingram, 78; North, 175, 167, 175; Scott, 37; Fox, 33; Gilmour, 94; Ingram, 100; Malleson, 130; de Windt, see Lurcock (2013), 186; Newman, 83; Cotton, 1092

Lapland: Sutherland, 15; Ingram, 93, 53; Gilmour, 138.

Henry McGrady Bell

Bell, 68, 74–5, 81, 89, 104, 108; Mannerheim: 116, 117; Agar, MS diary, Imperial War Museum, London.

Arthur Ransome (i)

Ransome (1976), 159–60; Vyborg: Ransome (1997), 86; Ransome (1919), 59, 60–1; Wraxall: see Lurcock (2010), 40; Ransome (1919), 1, 2–4.

Paul Henry Dukes

Chambers, 114; Ferguson, 52; Dukes, 5; Cromie: Ferguson [1]; Dukes, 12, 13, 19, 18–22, 23–7; St Petersburg to Helsinki: 111, 115; Bell, 90; Dukes, 166–8; Bell, 90–1; Dukes, 173–7; Maria, Merritt's former housekeeper, who provided a 'safe house' for Dukes in Petrograd, and 'was the only person I took into my confidence as to all my movements': 98; Bell, 15.

Augustus Agar

Agar, 28, 30–1; Finland: Agar MS diary; Agar, 40, 51, 61; 'refugees': 124; 68, 78, 74; the *Oleg*: 87, 104; As it turned out, the sinking was just a few hours too late to affect the final assault on Krasnaya Gorka. Sanatorium: MS diary; train 116–17; 148, 190; Mannerheim, 205–6; in fact Mannerheim had failed to be elected as the first President of Finland (25 July); 207, 215. The surviving CMB is now on display at the Imperial War Museum at Duxford, Cambridgeshire.

Arthur Ransome (ii)

The name *Racundra* is awkwardly contrived: ra = Ransome; c = Carl (mate); und = and; ra = Evgenia Ransome (as she was to be). 'precursor': Chambers, 314; Ransome (1923), 84, 87–90.

Alexander MacCallum Scott

Scott, 30–1; 'Arcadian': see Lurcock (2010), e.g. 98; 35–6, 42–4, 44–5; 'to every man . . .': Biblical (Judges 5:30).

Kay Gilmour

Gilmour, 71–3, 56, 35–6; Lapland: 144–5, 146, 147, 162.

Jim Ingram

Ingram, 54, 37, 44, 49, 51, 52; Clive-Bayley, 222–44; Ingram, 65, 79, 81–4; Lapland: 89, 92, 92–3, 95–6, 115–16, 119–20; Oulu: 123–5.

F. J. North

North, viii, 2, 89, 30; Suursaari: 30, 48, 53, 228, 123, 97; Renwick: see Lurcock (2010), 270; 167–9, 175–7; Rovaniemi: 196, 197, 209, 224.

Halliday Sutherland

For example, *Pulmonary Tuberculosis in General Practice* (1916) and *The Tuberculin Handbook* (1936). Biographer: *DNB*; Sutherland, 92, 23, 24, 17–19, 32–3, 35; Lapland: 71, 81, 93–4, 151–2; orphanage: 174–5, 205, 213, 242, 277–81, 284, [295].

Young Pioneers

Levick, 26, 42ff.

Norah Gourlie

Tweedie: 312, 225; Gourlie 101–2, 117, 115–17.

Joan and Peggy Webster

Webster, 11, 46, 49, 51–2, 57, 61–3, 67–8; further north: 79, 81–2; Clark, see Lurcock (2010), 71–7, 105, 161; Enontekiö website.

Visits to Sibelius

Newmarch (1939), 47–8; (1906) 19; Stevens, xi; **Gray** (1931), 53; Legge: Sanders, 70; *The Musical Times*, March 1935, 218; 'The Table-Talk of a Great Composer', Sanders, 71–4; Bell, 131, 135. Legge anecdote told me by Terry Curran. There are variant versions. Gray (1931), 26–7; (1985), 255–9. **Cohen**, 65; 'daughter': Scott-Sutherland, 159–60; Cohen, 206, 207. **Coward**, 36, 37, 38; Coward had visited Prince Radziwell in Poland (p.10); Sibelius, 39–41. Sir Malcolm Sargent: Aldous, 187; Reid, 386; Tawaststjerna III, 330–1.

J. M. Richards

Richards (1966), 8; (1980), 107, 107–8, 108–9, 110, 116.

Two Sailors and an Angler

Coles (1932), 89–90, 108; (1938) 42–6. Dixon, 138, 154, 166–8. 'Vagrant': English Fishing Club: Gallenga, see Lurcock (2013), 18; Tweedie, 152; *The Field*, 17 June 1933; *The Fishing Gazette*, Vol.112, 18 April 1936, 445–6.

A. D. Scott

Scott [108], [108]–109, 110–11. 'Kotkas': Kalevi Kotkas, Olympic high-jumper.

Vivian Charles Buckley

Newman (1939), 64; Buckley, 150, 151–2; 'blurb' (1979); (1939), 161, 167, 160, 173, 166–7, 175; Hämeenlinna: 178, 181–2,184–5, Mrs Tweedie: Lurcock (2013), 164; Kokkola: 187–8, 189–90.

William Richard ('Bill') Mead

The Adoption of Finland is unpaginated. Puijo: hill and tower near the city centre of Kuopio.

John Gibbons

Gibbons, *KBG*, 83, 91–2; *MBJ*, 33–4, 35, 48, 50; *KBG*, 82, 56.

Lady Diana Cooper

Cooper, 194–5; 'cow and pig races': he evidently means 'breeds'.

Bernard Newman

Newman (1939), [11]; (1960), 76; Gibbons, *KBG*, 85; (1939), 65, 91, 11, 42, 64–5; Lohja: 71, 83–4, 85–6, 86, 89–90, 90–1, 93–4, 95; *runo* singers: 110–11, 113, 119; (1938), 94, 253; (1939), 120–1.

The Winter War

Bell, 181; Waugh, *Men at Arms* II, 2; Macmillan, 24; Condon, 94; Bell, 185; Cambridge: Whittaker, 178; Churchill: Ruotsila, 82; broadcast 20 January 1940; *The War Situation: House of Many Mansions. The Times* quoted by Clark (1966), 126; Canterbury: Johnson, 157; Ruotsila: 89, 92, 88; Clark (1966), 209; 'reasonably assured', Kirby, 133; Kämp: Alternative Finland website; Rankin, 168–9.

John Langdon-Davies

Langdon-Davies, 124, 132–3, 138–9, 140–1, 142–3; announcement of peace: 113–18.

John Sykes

Sykes, [13], 15, 16, 25–6, 38–9; Suusanen: 30, 21.

Sir Walter Citrine

Citrine, 5, 43, 46–9, 50, 53,57, 63; near the front: 84, 90, 91, 84; Mannerheim visit: 104, 106; 127, 136–7; Tampere: 92, 90; 192.

Harold MacMillan

Macmillan, 24–5; 'Finland Committee': 25; 32, 33, 35; to Kajaani: 38–9, 41, 43, 44–6, 53.

James Bramwell

Bramwell 17; 'The Unfinished Man' is a phrase taken from W. B. Yeats's poem 'A Dialogue of Self and Soul'; Bramwell probably intended a pun. Bramwell 35, 36, 41–3; 'solicitor' etc.: the firemen were drawn from various professions.; 47, 51, 52, 65, 79–80, 81–2, 89, 97.

Constance Malleson

Malleson 99; Russell's *Autobiography*, Vol. 2 (1968); her most striking letter is dated 11 February 1941. Vasti's letter dated 23 February. Finland's fate, 37; Turku: 103, 107, 110–11; Vehmersalmi: 121, 123–4, 122; Tweedie, see Lurcock (2013), 150ff; 134–7, 145 (see Heaney's poem 'Follower'), 141, 171–2.

Epilogue

Bell, 230, 199, 202, 203; Edwards, 18. W. H. Auden 'September 1, 1939'.

Postscript

Bell, 231.

Bibliography

Primary sources

Agar, Augustus, MS diary. Imperial War Museum.
— Baltic Episode: A Classic of Secret Service in Russian Waters.
   1963.
Atchley. T. W., Finland. 1931.
Bell, Henry McGrady, Land of Lakes: Memories Keep Me Company.
   1950.
Bramwell, James ('Byrom, James'), The Unfinished Man. 1957.
Buckley, V. C., Happy Countries, 1939.
Chapman, Olive Murray, Across Lapland with Sledge and Reindeer.
   1932.
Citrine, Sir Walter, My Finnish Diary. 1940.
Clark, Sydney A., Finland on £10. 1938.
Coles, K. Adlard, In Finnish Waters. 1932.
— Mary Anne among 10,000 Islands. 1938.
Cooper, Lady Diana, The Light of Common Day. 1959 (Penguin
   edn, 1963).
Coward, Noël, Future Indefinite. 1954.
Dixon, Douglas, A Sail to Lapland. 1938.
Dukes, Paul, Red Dusk and the Morrow: Adventures and
   Investigations in Soviet Russia. 1922.
Franck, Harry A., A Scandinavian Summer. [1930].
Gibbons, John, Keepers of the Baltic Gates. 1938.
— My Baltic Journey. 1938.
Gilmour, Kay, Finland. 1931.
Gourlie, Norah, A Winter with Finnish Lapps. 1939.
Gray, Cecil, Musical Chairs. 1985 (1948).
Ingram, Jim, I Found Adventure. 1951.
Langdon-Davies, John, Finland: The First Total War. 1940.
Levick, George Murray, Young Pioneers in Northern Finland: A
   Record of the Second Expedition of the Public Schools Exploring
   Society, 1933 [1934?].

Macmillan, Harold, *The Blast of War*. 1967.

Malleson, Constance, *In the North: Autobiographical Fragments in Norway, Sweden, Finland: 1936–1946*. 1946.

Mead, William Richard, *The Adoption of Finland*. 2005. [University College London].

Newman, Bernard, *Baltic Roundabout*. 1939.

North, Frederick John, *Finland in Summer*. [1938]

Powell, Anthony, *Infants of the Spring*. 1976.

Rankin, Nicholas, *Telegram from Guernica: The Extraordinary Life of George Steer, War Correspondent*. 2004.

Ransome, Arthur, *Six Weeks in Russia in 1919*. 1919 (1992).

— *Racundra's First Cruise*. 1923.

— *The Autobiography of Arthur Ransome*. 1976.

— *Signalling from Mars: The Letters of Arthur Ransome*. Edited by Hugh Brogan. 1997.

Richards, J. M., *Memoirs of an Unjust Fella*. 1980.

Scott, A. D., *Aberdeen University Review*, 21, 1934.

Scott, Alexander MacCallum, *Suomi: The Land of the Finns*. 1926.

Sutherland, Halliday, *Lapland Journey*. 1938.

Sykes, John, *Direction North: A View of Finland*. 1967.

Webster, Joan and Peggy, *Footprints in Finland*. 1940.

Secondary sources

Aaltonen, Hilkka, *Books in English on Finland*. Turku, 1963.

Aldous, Richard, *Tunes of Glory: The Life of Malcolm Sargent*. 2001.

Buckley, V. C., *Good Times*. 1979.

Chambers, Roland, *The Last Englishman: The Double Life of Arthur Ransome*. 2009.

Clark, Douglas, *Three Days to Catastrophe*. 1966.

Clements, Jonathan, *Mannerheim: President, Soldier, Spy*. 2009.

Clive-Bayley, Annie Margaret, *Vignettes from Finland*. 1895.

Condon, Richard W., *The Winter War: Russia against Finland*. New York, 1972.

Cotton, Barbara, 'On Bicycles to the Arctic'. *The Listener*, 25 May 1939.

Edwards, Robert, *White Death: Russia's War with Finland*. 2007.

Ferguson, Harry, *Operation Kronstadt*. 2008.

Gibbons, John, *I Wanted to Travel*. 1938.

Gray, Cecil, *Sibelius*. 1931.

Halmesvirta, Anssi, *The British Conception of the Finnish 'Race', Nation and Culture, 1760–1918*. Helsinki, 1990.

Hjelt, Edvard, Preface to FINLAND: *The Country, its People and Institutions*. Helsinki, 1926.

Johnson, Hewlett, *Searching for Light*. 1968.

Jones, S., 'What about Finland?'. *Blackies Girls' Annual*. [1928].

Kirby, D. G., *Finland in the Twentieth Century*. 1979.

Laughlin, Clara E., *So You're Going to Scandinavia!* 1938.

Lurcock, Tony, *Not so Barren or Uncultivated: British Travellers in Finland 1760–1830*. 2010.

— *No Particular Hurry: British Travellers in Finland 1830–1917*. 2013.

Nevinson, H. W., *Fire of Life*. 1935.

Newman, Bernard, *Speaking from Memory*. 1960.

— *Ride to Russia*. 1938.

Newmarch, Rosa, *Jean Sibelius: A Finnish Composer*. Leipzig [1906].

— *Jean Sibelius*. 1939.

Reid, Charles, *Malcolm Sargent: A Biography*. 1968.

Richards, J. M., *A Guide to Finnish Architecture*. 1966.

Rothery, Agnes, *Finland the New Nation*. 1936.

Ruotsila, Markku, *Churchill and Finland: A Study in Anticommunism and Geopolitics*. 2012.

Sanders, Alan, *Walter Legge: Words and Music*. 1998.

Scott, Alexander MacCallum, *Beyond the Baltic*. 1925.

Scott-Sutherland, Colin, *Arnold Bax*. 1973.

Stamp, L. Dudley, 'Suomi (Finland)'. *Geography*, 16, 1931, pp.284–97.

Stevens, Lewis, *An Unforgettable Woman: The Life and Times of Rosa Newmarch*. 2011.

Tawaststjerna, Erik, *Sibelius*. Translated by Robert Layton. 1997.

Tweedie, Mrs Alec, *Through Finland in Carts*. 1897.

Waugh, Evelyn, *Men at Arms*. 1952 (Penguin edn, 1964).

Whittaker, D. J., *Fighter for Peace: Philip Noel-Baker, 1889–1982*. 1989.

Index of Places

This list gives only the principal accounts and descriptions.